GREUZE

The rise and fall of an eighteenth-century phenomenon

ANITA BROOKNER

Courtauld Institute of Art, University of London

NEW YORK GRAPHIC SOCIETY LTD.
GREENWICH, CONNECTICUT

Standard Book Number 8212-0483-1
Library of Congress Catalog Card Number 72-80422

Published in Great Britain in 1972
by Paul Elek Limited, London

Published in the United States of America in 1972
by New York Graphic Society Ltd, Greenwich, Connecticut

PRINTED IN GREAT BRITAIN

Contents

List of Plates

27. *Portrait of Babuty*. Canvas, 60 × 48cm. (Paris, Pierre David-Weill Collection.)

28. *Portrait of Wille*. Canvas, 59 × 48.9cm. (Paris, Musée Jacquemart-André Collection.)

29. *L'Accordée de Village*. Canvas, 92 × 118cm. (Paris, Louvre.)

30. Study for *L'Accordée de Village*. Drawing, black and white chalk, 51.5 × 32.5cm. (Chalon-sur-Saône, Musée Denon.)

31. *Portrait of the Comte d'Angivillers*. Canvas, 63 × 53cm. (Metz, Musée. Photograph by permission of the Musée de Metz.)

32. *Portrait of Monseigneur de Valras*. 146 × 114cm. (Macon, Musée des Ursulines. Photograph by permission of the Musée des Ursulines.)

33. *Jeune fille vue de dos*. Canvas, 44 × 37cm. (Montpellier, Musée Fabre.)

34. *Tête de jeune fille*. Canvas, 44.5 × 37cm. (London, Wallace Collection. Reproduced by permission of the Trustees of the Wallace Collection.)

35. *Le Paralytique*. Canvas, 115.5 × 146cm. (Leningrad, Hermitage.)

36. *La Charité Romaine*. Drawing, pen and Indian ink, 32.3 × 41.8cm. (Paris, Louvre.)

37. *The Rest on the Flight into Egypt*. Drawing, pen and Indian ink, 17.4 × 37.2cm. (Tournus, Musée Greuze. Reproduced by kind permission of the Musée Greuze, Tournus.)

38. Study for *La Malédiction Paternelle*. Drawing, pen and ink and wash heightened with body colour, 32 × 42cm. (Lille, Musée Wicar.)

39. Study for *Le Fils Puni*. Drawing, pen and ink and wash heightened with body colour, 32 × 42cm. (Lille, Musée Wicar.)

40. Study for *Sévère et Caracalla*. Drawing, red chalk, 36.8 × 30.4 cm. (Paris, Louvre.)

41. *Sévère et Caracalla*. Canvas, 124 × 160cm. (Paris, Louvre.)

42. Poussin: *Death of Germanicus*. Canvas, 137.5 × 198cm. (Minneapolis Institute of Arts.)

43. *La Mère Bien-aimée*. Canvas, 99 × 131cm. (Paris, Laborde Collection.)

44. Study for *La Mère Bien-aimée*. Drawing, red chalk, 37.8 × 28.9cm. (Paris, Louvre.)

45. Study for *La Bénédiction Paternelle*. Drawing, pen and ink and wash, 37 × 50.5cm. (Chicago, Art Institute, Gift of Mr and Mrs Leigh B. Block.)

46. *Girl with dog*. Canvas, 62.5 × 52.5cm. (England, private collection.)

47. *Jeune fille qui fait sa prière à l'Amour*. Canvas, 144.3 × 111cm. (London, Wallace Collection. Reproduced by permission of the Trustees of the Wallace Collection.)

48. *La Poupée Dansante*. Drawing, pen and ink and wash heightened with body colour. (Vienna, Albertina.)

49. *La Cruche Cassée*. Canvas, 108 × 86cm. (Paris, Louvre.)

50. *La Vertu Chancelante*. Canvas 79.3 × 61cm. (Munich, Alte Pinakothek, Sammlung der Bayerischen Hypotheken- und Wechsel-Bank.)

51. *Boy with dog*. Canvas, 59.7 × 50cm. (London, Wallace Collection. Reproduced by permission of the Trustees of the Wallace Collection.)

52. *Girl with gauze scarf*. Canvas, 56.5 × 46.3cm. (London, Wallace Collection. Reproduced by permission of the Trustees of the Wallace Collection.)

53. *Portrait of Mme de Porcin*. Canvas, 71 × 57cm. (Angers, Musée des Beaux-Arts.)

54. *Portrait of Paul Stroganov*. (Leningrad, Hermitage.)

55. *Portrait of Countess Schuvalov*. (Leningrad, Hermitage.)

56. *Portrait of the Comte de Saint-Morys*. Panel, 65 × 54cm. (Nantes, Musée des Beaux-Arts.)

57. *Le Gâteau des Rois*. Canvas, 72 × 91cm. (Montpellier, Musée Fabre.)

58. Study for *La Dame de Charité*. Canvas, 64 × 54cm. (Montpellier, Musée Fabre.)

59. *La Dame de Charité*. Canvas, 112 × 146cm. (Lyon, Musée des Beaux-Arts.)

60. David: *Antiochus and Stratonice*. Canvas, 120 × 155cm. (Paris, Ecole des Beaux-Arts.)

61. *La Malédiction Paternelle*. Canvas, 130 × 162cm. (Paris, Louvre.)

62. *Le Fils Puni*. Canvas, 130 × 163cm. (Paris, Louvre.)

63. Study for *Le Fils Puni*. Drawing, red chalk, 30.3 × 45.4cm. (Paris, Louvre.)

64. *Le Donneur de Chapelets*. Canvas, 111 × 147cm. (Montclair, New Jersey, Art Museum.)

65. *Le Retour de l'Ivrogne*. Canvas, 75 × 92cm. (Portland Art Museum, Oregon.)

66. David: *Belisarius*. Canvas, 288 × 312cm. (Lille, Musée Wicar.)

67. *La Belle-Mère*. (Engraving, Paris, Bibliothèque Nationale.)

68. *Innocence, entraînée par les Amours et suivie du Repentir*. Canvas, 144 × 195cm. (Paris, Louvre.)

69. *L'Admiration et le Désir*. Canvas, 41 × 31cm. (Montpellier, Musée Fabre.)

70. *La Prière du Matin*. Canvas, 66 × 55cm. (Montpellier, Musée Fabre.)

71. *La Laitière*. Canvas, 109 × 87cm. (Paris, Louvre.)

72. *Le Petit Mathématicien*. Canvas, 45 × 37cm. (Montpellier, Musée Fabre.)

73. *Portrait of Sophie Arnould*. Canvas, 61 × 51cm. (London, Wallace Collection. Reproduced by permission of the Trustees of the Wallace Collection.)

74. *La Veuve et son Curé*. Canvas, 126 × 160cm. (Leningrad, Hermitage.)

75. *Psyche*. Panel, 45 × 37cm. (London, Wallace Collection. Reproduced by permission of the Trustees of the Wallace Collection.)

76. *La Colombe Retrouvée*. Panel, 46 × 37cm. (Moscow, Pushkin Museum.)

77. *Innocence*. Panel, 62 × 51.5cm. (London, Wallace Collection. Reproduced by permission of the Trustees of the Wallace Collection.)

78. *Girl with Doves*. Panel, 70 × 58cm. (London, Wallace Collection. Reproduced by permission of the Trustees of the Wallace Collection.)

79. *Jeune fille qui pleure la mort de son oiseau*. Panel, 68 × 55cm. (Paris, Louvre.)

80. *Portrait of Comtesse Mollien*. Canvas, 62.5 × 49.5cm. (Baltimore Museum of Art.)

81. *The Letter Writer*. Canvas, 40 × 32cm. (London, Wallace Collection. Reproduced by permission of the Trustees of the Wallace Collection.)

82. *L'Espagnole*. Panel, 40.5 × 32.5cm. (London, Wallace Collection. Reproduced by permission of the Trustees of the Wallace Collection.)

83. *Lamentation over the dead Christ*. Drawing, pen and brush with bistre, 36.1 × 25.4cm. (Lord Clark Collection.)

84. *L'Amour parmi les jeunes filles*. Drawing, black chalk and wash, heightened with body colour, 11 × 35cm. (Dijon, Musée des Beaux-Arts.)

85. *Psyche crowning Love*. Canvas, 147 × 180cm. (Lille, Musée Wicar.)

86. David: *Paris and Helen*. Canvas, 146 × 181cm. (Paris, Louvre.)

87. *Portrait of Napoleon*. Canvas, 242 × 177cm. (Versailles, Musée National de Versailles.)

88. *Portrait of Gensonné*. Panel, 54 × 45cm. (Paris, Louvre.)

89. *Portrait of Cambacérès*. Panel, 27 × 21cm. (Chartres, Musée de l'ancien Evêché.)

90. Ingres: *Portrait of M. Rivière*. Canvas, 115 × 89cm. (Paris, Louvre.)

91. *Portrait of 'Talleyrand'*. Canvas, 145 × 112cm. (Saint-Omer, Musée des Beaux-Arts.)

92. *Portrait of Citizen Dubard*. Canvas, 66 × 53.5cm. (San Francisco, M. H. de Young Memorial Museum, California Palace of the Legion of Honour.)

93. *L'Effroi*. Canvas, 54 × 45cm. (Paris, Louvre.)

94. *Le Départ pour la Chasse*. Drawing, pen and wash, 39 × 35cm. (Paris, Louvre.)

95. *Le Premier Sillon*. Canvas, 118 × 148cm. (Moscow, Pushkin Museum.)

96. *Self-portrait*. Panel, 52.5 × 45cm. (Marseilles, Musée des Beaux-Arts.)

97. Lépicié: *L'Elève Curieux*. Canvas, 117 × 91.5cm. (New York, Pierre David-Weill Collection.)

98. Lépicié: *Le Lever de Fanchon*. Canvas, 73 × 66cm. (Saint-Omer, Musée des Beaux-Arts.)

99. Lépicié: *La Réponse Désirée*. Canvas, 64 × 80cm. (Paris, private collection.)

100. Aubry: *La Bergère des Alpes*. Canvas. (Detroit Institute of Arts.)

101. Aubry: *L'Amour Paternel*. Canvas, 78.7 × 101.6cm. (Barber Institute of Fine Arts, University of Birmingham.)

102. Aubry: *Première Leçon d'Amitié Fraternelle*. Canvas, 76.2 × 95.3cm. (Kansas City, Missouri, Nelson Gallery-Atkins Museum Nelson Fund.)

103. Schenau: *L'Aventure Fréquente*. (Engraving, Paris, Bibliothèque Nationale.)

104. Schenau: *Le Miroir Cassé*. (Engraving, Paris, Bibliothèque Nationale.)

105. P. A. Wille: *La Double Récompense du Mérite*. (Engraving, Paris, Bibliothèque Nationale.)

106. Boilly: *La Bienfaitrice*. Canvas. (Oslo, private collection.)

107. Boilly: *'Je te donne ma malédiction'*. (Engraving, Paris, Bibliothèque Nationale.)

108. John Russell: *Portrait of Anne Russell*. Canvas. (Present whereabouts unknown.)

109. John Hoppner: *The Broken Pitcher*. (Engraving, London, British Museum.)

110. Geneviève Brossard de Beaulieu: *La Muse de la Poésie livrée aux regrets que lui laisse la mort de Voltaire*. Canvas, 93 × 73cm. (Poitiers, Musée des Beaux-Arts.)

111. Romney: *Lady Hamilton at Prayer*. Canvas, 83.8 × 63.5cm. (London, Kenwood, Iveagh Bequest.)

112. Wheatley: *John Howard relieving prisoners*. Canvas, 104 × 132cm. (Earl of Harrowby Collection. Reproduced by gracious permission of the Earl of Harrowby.)

113. Wheatley: *Maidenhood*. Canvas, 79.5 × 67.3cm. (England, private collection.)

Introduction

There seems little reason to write another biography of Jean-Baptiste Greuze while that of Louis Hautecoeur (Paris, 1913) is still so adequate for the study of this not very lovable painter and that of Camille Mauclair (Paris, n.d.) so full. To weaken the case further, important Greuze research, in the form of a *catalogue raisonné*, is being done in America by Edgar Munhall, whose work will supersede that of Jean Martin, published in 1908. Nevertheless it is fifty-seven years since Hautecoeur's book appeared; many pictures have changed hands; some that were lost have come to light; and although M. Hautecoeur's thesis still holds good, it now appears that certain aspects of Greuze's work mark him out as an historically more important figure than was hitherto accepted. To be sure, very few people like or admire Greuze. His moral homilies no longer move us, his *'têtes d'expression'* seem in equal measure profane and ridiculous, and we have at last tired of pointing out the contrast between the innocence of the girl in *La Cruche Cassée* and the significance of her attribute. Yet visitors to the Wallace Collection may have exclaimed with pleasure at the melting portrait of Sopie Arnould, in the same way that visitors to the Musée Jacquemart-André may have considered the portrait of Wille one of the best produced in the entire eighteenth century, and visitors to the Albertina in Vienna have been dazzled by the brilliance of his drawings. Moreover, there has grown up in recent years an awareness of the close connection between Greuze and a much more important painter, Jacques-Louis David. Indeed, anyone working on David is obliged to take Greuze's peculiar combination of homely moral lesson and progressively Poussinesque composition into account. Although he belonged firmly in an age which placed a high value on Dutch genre paintings and the emotive quality of English novels, Greuze had his own quarrel with the Academy of Painting and was not satisfied with the rank he was assigned. He tried, by a combination of calculation and genuine endeavour, to paint pictures midway between genre and history and thus to erase the distinction between the two categories. In this, his aim was not only to elevate his own style of painting but to humiliate a number of unworthy painters who, by virtue of their subject matter, were awarded the higher dignity. He did not succeed, but David, who must have known his work, gradually extracted from it the valid lesson that a desire to chastise the conscience, allied to a severe planimetric and Poussinesque type of composition, could, if properly applied, teach a moral lesson far greater than that ever dreamed of by Greuze. Greuze's morality is in fact that of a weak man, combining a desire to preach with a need to titillate. He is less like his one-time friend, Diderot, who had genuine passions of the soul, than like so many contemporary dramatists—he was indeed frequently compared with Nivelle de la Chaussée. Nevertheless, his own life was a genuine tragedy, beginning in provincial isolation, progressing to European fame, and ending in unpopularity and financial ruin. Greuze, therefore, has much to tell us, both about himself and about the eighteenth century as a whole, and his progress charts the evolution of painting from the moment when bourgeois taste was in full command to the triumph of the puritan revolution. It is hoped that the present biography will go some way to explaining these various phenomena.

Anita Brookner
Paris, 1971

Sensibilité

It is almost impossible to introduce Jean-Baptiste Greuze to the general reader of the twentieth century. His paintings, with certain exceptions, appear to us tawdry, if not obscene, and it takes a considerable mental effort to remember that in his own time, or rather in the years of his success, from 1755 to about 1785, he was viewed as one of the most important and illustrious artists of the French school. Clearly he appealed to a vein of feeling that has now become extinct. But this vein of feeling was once of considerable strength and influence and it should be examined seriously so that we may understand a phenomenon that today receives little attention, wedged as it is between the more important and recognizable styles of Rococo and Neoclassicism—the phenomenon of *sensibilité*. In order to do this, it is necessary to go beyond painting and to explore the hinterland of literature, philosophy, and even religion, for *sensibilité* is a manner of experiencing the world which has its origins in the religious dilemmas of the late seventeenth and early eighteenth centuries, and of which the pictures of Greuze are only a tardy and tangible outcome.

The eighteenth century in France was both an age of reason and an age of emotion. It began with a period of strenuous and far-reaching intellectual exercise, and although the effort slackened it remained fairly constant until the end of the century. *Sensibilité*, the complement of the age of reason, grew up largely as an instinctive and multiform protest against an increasingly material conception of the universe, in a country exhausted by war and its attendant evils, poverty and religious dispute. Yet once formulated, it led a curiously independent existence, and between 1750 and 1780, it went beyond its success as a fashion and assumed the status of a cult. Like Romanticism, it is a problem difficult to define, not simply because it takes so many forms, but because it has so many roots. On the surface frivolous, charming or merely ridiculous, it is nevertheless worthy of serious consideration, for it is as important to a study of the eighteenth century as the rules of the

Académie are to the seventeenth or the influence of Byron and Walter Scott are to the nineteenth.

Before going on to discuss its origins, it may be helpful to outline some of the more obvious characteristics of mature *sensibilité*. Firstly, it is a luxurious pastime, the prerogative of those with wealth and, more important, leisure. It is a movement which progresses logically down the social scale. For example, the ideal of the country and the Arcadian way of life which at the beginning of the century is supremely expressed by Watteau receives quite another interpretation at the hands of Rousseau. It is a movement which receives impetus from literary salons in which the spirit of preciosity still lingers; for example, that of Mme de Lambert, who, in her *Réflexions nouvelles sur les femmes* of 1727, pleads for more time to be devoted to the education and cultivation of matters of the heart and the affections. It is the chosen field of men of letters and a reading public and in its later stages it is predominantly literary. And lastly, as a movement, it exists on two levels. One must be careful to distinguish between *sensibilité* as a moral and metaphysical movement and *sensibilité* as a fashion in social behaviour. All in all, violent and unnatural as many of its manifestations were, *sensibilité* runs a healthier and more open course than Romanticism. The greater of the *âmes sensibles*—Diderot, Rousseau, Julie de Lespinasse, and to a certain extent Greuze—who exist on a very intense level of emotional activity, create a sort of adolescent enthusiasm in their public. But the bulk of this public, the readers of Saint-Lambert and Baculard d'Arnaud, the models of Aubry and Moreau le Jeune, who absorb *sensibilité* at second hand, do little more than indulge happily in a harmless form of exhibitionism.

It has often been pointed out that a movement whose roots are to be sought in the emotional rather than in the intellectual nature must necessarily take the form of a reaction. The primary source of *sensibilité* lies in a changed conception of religion and a replacement of one set of values by another, due partly to social circumstances, partly to the emancipation of a philosophy latent in the seventeenth century, and most decisively to the theories of John Locke.

The basis of seventeenth-century morality and philosophy was religion. It was a heroic era of Christianity, governed by a sense of duty and a universal recognition of a controlling principle. But the seventeenth century had not been a peaceful period for the church in France which had known the Jansenist struggle and the apparently revolutionary teaching of Descartes, who introduced a sort of provisional rationalism into the domain where religion and philosophy overlap. In these disputes Louis XIV's policy had triumphed, but not without creating a certain opposition. At the end of the century, the existing hostility to the despotism of the French church, typified in the eyes of many by the severe piety of the court of Mme de Maintenon, was brought to a head by the Revocation of the Edict of Nantes. This was an inevitable consequence of Louis XIV's Gallican policy which, as supported by Bossuet, broadened into the right of the sovereign to control the religion of his subjects. The terms of the Revocation were bitter. All edicts of toleration to Protestants were repealed, all meetings for public worship forbidden. Protestant ministers were exiled and schools closed. This had two effects: it suppressed transitions, eradicating the possibility of a rational and recognized Deism such as existed in England in the eighteenth century, and in a spirit savouring of the wars of religion, debarred a large section of the population from practising its faith and taking part in the social life of the country.

Despite the penalty which accompanied the act of desertion, many French Protestants managed to escape to England, a country which had been occupied by more conspicuously awkward religious problems for the best part of a century. The Glorious Revolution of 1688 had, in appearance at least, resolved the conflicts into a business-like medium of broad toleration, and the concessions won by Parliament in the constitutional field had encouraged a certain boldness of speculation in other matters, including religion. The sharp contrast between this state of affairs and the one which they had just left did not fail to impress the immigrants, and the first wave of pro-England propaganda is a direct consequence of this.

In 1715, when Louis XIV died, the result was not a burst of vitality but a deepening of scepticism. The later acts of Louis' reign had been almost frighteningly reactionary, the country was exhausted, yet at the same time aware of the oppressions suffered by its own people. The Catholic clergy, who had upheld the Revocation of the Edict of Nantes, were discredited, and their teaching received with cynicism or indifference.

It is in this set of circumstances that one must consider the effect of the writings of John Locke, all of which were translated into French before 1700. The *Essay concerning Human Understanding*, in particular, ran into several editions and had a decisive influence. Now the moral of the *Essay* may be summed up under several headings. First and foremost, there are no innate ideas. As a corollary to this, it follows that all knowledge is the outcome of a dual process of sensation and reflection. The origin of our knowledge is to be sought in our senses. Knowledge thus acquired is eventually translated into judgement or reason. Reason is our only instrument for finding the truth and we must apply it constantly: 'Reason must be our last judge and guide in everything.' It is important that those moral truths which govern our conduct be submitted to the test for reason, unless they have been made known to us by a direct *personal* revelation from God. (The revelation to another person is not valid.) Reason and faith, or revelation, are therefore entirely different processes. This should be acknowledged. As we cannot, within the limits of our reason, know God, we should use our faculties for what they seem best fitted, a knowledge of the world and of ourselves ('the direction of nature where it seems to point out the way'). Our knowledge of good and evil, and of what is good or bad for us, is determined by our reaction of pleasure or pain. Our interest and our duty lies in a 'careful and constant pursuit of true and solid happiness', i.e. a greater proportion of pleasure than pain.

This is in fact a very reasonable and practical doctrine. But when it reached France it was interpreted in such a way that it was regarded as a teaching of revolutionary implications. Paul Hazard[1] speaks of the new direction given to French thought by the philosophy of Locke. The peculiar circumstances operating in France served to make certain points stand out in high relief, and contemporary writings show how they were construed. Thus to eighteenth-century France, Locke's doctrine appeared as follows. The source of our knowledge lies in our senses which we must use in order to acquire material on which to reflect and construct judgements. (Descartes, who had intimated that material fact and individual reasoning were not to be despised, was now regarded as a pioneer by the cautious or as an academic stick-in-the-mud by those impatient to go further.) Our body will tell us what is good or bad by setting up feelings of pleasure or pain, but with such an instrument at our disposal it is only necessary for our body to transmit the message. If good equals happiness, we must therefore multiply the occasions of pleasure. Knowledge of God must be left to those who deny the force of reason, i.e. the mystics. One must opt for either faith or reason. And, by inference, the doctrines of original sin, grace and redemption are not valid since we have no personal proof of them, and sacraments and priests useless since our instinctive call to good or happiness serves the purpose equally well. The distinction between reason and faith, to which Locke devotes a whole chapter, became one of the basic tenets of eighteenth-century French thought.

The immediate effect of this apparent destruction of Christian first principles is, by and large, the removal of pessimism. After the initial cynicism the eighteenth century becomes incredibly optimistic. Secondly, there is a new emphasis on this world, a positive material approach to man and his place in society. Thirdly, and inevitably with the adoption of the sensualist theory, there emerges a conception of man as the sole guardian of his powers and moral instinct, and of his faculties as instruments for experiment. Virtue, which in the seventeenth century meant conformity to one's duty, now came to mean conformity to one's natural impulses. Hence *'la religion naturelle'*, a theoretically God-given urge to acquire knowledge through one's instincts, or as Bernardin de Saint-Pierre later put it, *'Heureux ceux qui, forts de leur conscience première, ne cherchent l'auteur de la nature que dans la nature même, avec les simples organes qu'elle leur a donnés'*[2]†. And fourthly and lastly, there grew up an interest in England, spiritual home of free-thinkers on every level.

On the debit side, the discredit into which traditional piety had been thrown created a gap, and the attempts to fill this gap constitute the moral history of the eighteenth century in France and provide the ultimate explanation for the feelings of delight and relief which greeted Greuze's moral homilies. Greuze, however, was preceded by men who were only indirectly concerned with family morality, although in constructing a form of religion without priests and sacraments their attention was inevitably drawn to such matters. The men who undertook this task were not all as famous as Voltaire and Rousseau; some, such as Soret or Saint-Hyacinthe, remain obscure, but all played their part in the construction of a moral climate which placed the supreme emphasis on personal experience of violent but self-congratulatory emotion, consciousness of evil being tempered and if possible overcome by the observation of a few principles, accessible to all, and finally a belief in the power of natural goodness. This doctrine is not wholly ridiculous. For some it created the mirage of a better world to be made by men; for others it existed only as a nostalgia for a better world that had once been. But to all who were concerned with defining or illustrating the phenomenon, from Voltaire to Greuze, the matter was a serious one, as any matter concerned with human feelings inevitably is.

The phenomenon of *sensibilité* started, in an almost academic way, with the destruction of the old religion. In the first three decades of the century, a mutilated form of Deism was upheld with enthusiasm by men like Voltaire, Thémiseul de Saint-Hyacinthe, the Marquis d'Argens and the Marquis de Lassay. Perhaps Voltaire was the only man who accepted Deism on its most serious level and with all the responsibilities which it implied.

---

† Happy are those people who, strong in their fundamental awareness, do not search for the author of Nature other than in Nature herself, with the simple instruments which she has given them.

Saint-Hyacinthe[3] takes infinitely more pleasure in demonstrating the fallacies of Catholicism than in clarifying the implications of Deism. Thus, while he asserts that 'Pure Deism is the only real religion ... the only religion common to all men', his main energies are devoted to destroying ideas of grace and faith and what he considers the pagan character of the sacraments. His arguments, which are over-simplified, seem to have been popular for that reason. He makes, for example, the purely utilitarian point that as religion should possess the ability to convince everyone, the fool as well as the wise man, the truest religion is that which takes the form of the duties prescribed by the natural law. We shall hear a great deal more of this natural law upheld by the early Deists in their protest against an authoritarian and purely metaphysical conception of religion. Indeed, the natural law or instinct is the only form of religion to which the majority of middle-class Frenchmen of the middle of the century will conform.

There is more positive content in the Marquis d'Argens whose major philosophical work, however, *La Philosophie du Bon Sens*[4] is devoted to the same iconoclastic ends as the *Pensées Secrètes* of Saint-Hyacinthe. The Marquis d'Argens has an interesting chapter in which he acknowledges both Descartes and Locke, fitting them both logically into the new pattern. He states, in fact, as a first principle, that as God has given us the ability to reason, that faculty cannot lead us astray, but on the other hand we are entitled to reject any teaching or example which comes into collision with our '*Lumière Naturelle*'. This is a significant proposition. Not only does it identify the power of reason with a vaguer, more subjective faculty, but it brings Descartes forward into the eighteenth century and presents him in a somewhat new light. Descartes had considered the gift of reason as yet another pointer to spiritual truth; thus the arguments with which he defended his critical powers had no subversive action in his own mind as they were fundamentally connected with the idea of God. When, however, the idea of God became temporarily obscured, as it did at the beginning of the eighteenth century, the more positive side of Descartes' teaching stood out for the new generation with a new significance. To the Deists of the early eighteenth century, Descartes appeared to be preaching the *independence* of man's critical faculties and the obligation to use them experimentally in order to acquire knowledge or experience. Thus the Marquis d'Argens is pursuing a perfectly logical argument when he goes on to allege 'The Uncertainty of History in a Great Number of Facts', 'The Uncertainty of Tradition ...', 'The Uncertainty of Metaphysics', winding

6

up triumphantly, 'All our ideas have their origin in our senses ... You see ... that man, having no innate idea which does not come directly or indirectly from his senses, cannot begin to think until he experiences sensations'.

The reaction of the Marquis de Lassay[5] is more human. His opposition is directed against the doctrine of innate ideas on the one hand and religious wars and persecution on the other, and he outlines a position that must have been adopted by many. 'I believe in a Supreme Being, Creator and Master of all things, and that religions were made by men, and I have doubts about the immortality of the soul, because for one thing this immortality that we attribute to our soul and refuse to that of other animals is unconvincing: there are too many likenesses between us in this life for there to be so much difference after we are dead.' He then retires from the argument altogether, expressing a mixture of cynicism and distaste for those indefatigable spirits who continue to make philosophical enquiries into the nature of God. This indifference after the initial wave of curiosity must have been the reaction of the great majority to the new problem.

Voltaire is perhaps the only man who considered Deism as a faith, that is to say, he envisages it as a living thing, with responsibilities and rewards. Yet Voltaire's brand of Deism has little to do with the cosier, less stringent thinkers who had merely tired of the religious impasse. It was these men who scaled down traditional piety to concentrate on more comfortable objects. Their strength and their weakness was their diversity of opinion. As Soret put it, *'Que les Déistes ne disent pas que la Loi Naturelle suffit, j'en ai cherché deux qui eussent le même système de religion; je les cherche encore'*.[6]† The major advantage of this was the freedom it entailed, freedom of the individual to accept, deny or modify. Its major disadvantage was that although as body of theory it might satisfy man's reason, it was too unexacting to satisfy his religious spirit and the great love which he had been taught in the seventeenth century to devote to the service of his God. On the one hand it could only be given sincere expression by men of enlightenment and high principle, for it depended much on the honour and good sense of the individual. On the other hand, it denied comfort to the great number whose conception of God had been one of love and trust and who had expended a good deal of emotion in their religious life. Thus the

† Let not the Deists claim that natural law alone suffices; I have been looking for two of them who possess the same system of religion and I am still looking.

modifications made in order to meet the requirements of those who had chosen faith were radical and gave rise to a number of widely diverse beliefs.

The immediate outcome of the inauguration of '*la religion naturelle*', soon to become '*la religion du coeur*' or simply '*le cri de la nature*', was a good deal of licence. Contemporary writers, taking their age into review, all seem to agree on its cynicism, immorality and decadence. This is but an extreme interpretation of Locke's theory that knowledge is to be gained through the senses, and the man who gave doctrinal form to this interpretation was Helvétius, whose works, *De l'Esprit* (1758) and *De l'Homme* (1772), caused a scandal even at the time. More relevant to the present purpose are men who tried to get out of the impasse by admitting that religion and philosophy were fundamentally opposed but that the virtues taught by both could be reconciled. Toussaint, in *Les Moeurs* (1748), successor in style to the *Caractères* of La Bruyère, reveals himself as a complete materialist, placing his faith in social virtues and the power of reason. Yet he is more than a little touched by the religion of pure love and the power of sentiment which is at the basis of Quietism. According to Toussaint, the union between man and God is only explicable and justifiable on a basis of reciprocal sentiment. He admits the existence of God but only as the constitutional monarch of the English Deists, who cannot enforce allegiance. 'All the perfections of God which contribute nothing to our advantage may inspire us with admiration and respect; but they cannot inspire us with love. It is not precisely because he is all-powerful, because he is great, because he is wise that I love him, but because he is good, because he loves me. If he did not love me, what use to me would be his power, his greatness and his wisdom?' Toussaint has the confidence of a man who has found his adversary vulnerable; he also has something of the confidence of the Quietists. This speech, for example, sounds like a lay version of Quietist dogma: '*Qu'on aime véritablement et l'amour ne fera jamais commettre de fautes qui blessent la conscience ou l'honneur; car quiconque est capable d'aimer est vertueux*'.† Greuze's public would agree whole-heartedly with this latter sentiment.

The attitude of d'Holbach is more athletic. He explicitly and deliberately makes the distinction between religion and morality. 'Despite the uselessness and perversity of the morality which Christianity teaches men, its adherents dare to tell us that without religion no man can have morals. But what do

---

† One should truly love and love will never make those mistakes which harm conscience or honour; for whoever is capable of loving is virtuous.

the Christians mean by having morals? They mean incessant prayer, churchgoing, penitence, abstention from pleasures, and living in withdrawal and retreat. What good results from these practices which one can observe without having a scrap of virtue? If morals of this kind lead to heaven, they are useless on earth. If they are virtues, one must agree that without religion there are no virtues. But on the other hand, one may observe faithfully all that Christianity requires without having any of the virtues that reason shows us are necessary for the upkeep of political societies.'[7] Discussing with himself the classic question, 'If God is good, why is the world in such a bad state?', he deduces that something has gone wrong somewhere and that man, instead of accepting the paradox must for the honour of his own reason, modify and improve for himself the only conditions over which he has any control, the conditions of earthly life. '*Il faut donc à l'homme une philosophie humaine, qui l'attire, qui le console, qui le soutienne. C'est pour la nature, c'est pour la terre, c'est pour lui-même, c'est pour la société que l'homme est fait, c'est ici-bas qu'il doit chercher sa félicité.*'[8]†

However drastic their respective theories, Toussaint and d'Holbach are not men lacking in morality. In fact the significance of their teaching lies in their attempt to create a code of morality which stems from both religion and philosophy but is responsible to neither, to create, in fact, a code of lay virtues. Toussaint not only gives rules for behaviour in society and the control of one's appetites but devotes whole chapters to marital happiness and filial duty and is probably the first man of his century to plead the cause of maternal breast-feeding under the twin banners of reason and love. He also conceives of a method of moral teaching which was to have an outstanding posterity and lead to such institutions as the '*rosière de Salency*' and the '*fête des bonnes gens*'—the method of good examples. In the same way, d'Holbach, in *his Morale Universelle*, has extensive chapters entitled '*Devoirs des Epoux*', '*Devoirs des Pères et Mères et des Enfants*' etc., in which he plainly expresses a good deal of serious feeling. It is tempting to suppose that such a work was known to Greuze as it must have been to many members of his public.

But it seems that men were too self-conscious in exercising this spirit of righteousness for it ever to become innate and truly genuine. Once a vague idealism had been admitted, it became difficult to control. It was sufficient to feel the impulse of the heart in order to consider oneself in a state of virtue.

† Man therefore needs a human philosophy which attracts, consoles and uplifts him. It is for nature, for the earth, for himself, for society that man is created and it is here that he must look for his happiness.

Yet as the objects of enthusiasm were so dissimilar, it was taken for granted that the merit should attach itself to the enthusiasm or even to the person feeling it. The original idea became gradually obscured by the penumbra of sensations which it aroused. The next process was to exteriorize the emotion in order for other people to recognize it. This presupposes a great deal of complacency which did in fact emerge very rapidly and can be determined at various stages of development. Levesque de Pouilly published a *Théorie des sentiments agréables, où après avoir indiqué les règles que la nature suit dans la distribution du plaisir, on établit les principes de la Théologie Naturelle et ceux de la Philosophie Morale* in 1747. The theme of the book is that virtue can be pleasant and flattering business. '*Tout mouvement de tendresse, d'amitié, de reconnaissance, de générosité, de bienveillance, est un sentiment de plaisir.*'† It is this imperceptible but whole-hearted replacement of one set of values by another that gives *sensibilité* its equivocal amoral quality. Mme de Lambert, when speaking of friendship, celebrated an ideal because it conferred a sort of painless distinction, Levesque de Pouilly because one got from it a self-congratulatory pleasure. Hennebert endorses this: 'The pleasure of the heart is the interior satisfaction one feels when loving that which is useful and honest.'⁹ Charpentier is one step further advanced in this process of inversion. In his book *La Décence* (1767) he upholds this sentiment for its charm. 'Decency . . . is the most charming characteristic of virtue. The decent man is both virtuous and likeable.' Here he has created a purely synthetic quality simply in order to strike a balance between virtue and the enjoyment of being virtuous. Thus the counsels of perfection that the above authors invoke matter less for themselves than for the distinction they confer on those who espouse their cause. Toussaint's maxim, '*Quiconque est capable d'aimer est vertueux*', broadened into a state whereby it was necessary only to feel and to show that one felt in order to have accomplished a worthy action.

The most extreme outcome of the religious controversy, and one which goes a long way to explain the most complete and excessive expression of *sensibilité*, is the problem of Quietism. Quietism was more than a mystical flowering; it was to have profound social implications as well. It had been latent in the seventeenth century and seems to have been a reaction to any violence or severity demanded or imposed in the name of religion. In this particular instance it was given great impetus by the peculiarly violent forms which official Catholicism appeared to be taking with regard to the Revocation of the Edict of Nantes, and as it was largely coloured by a

† Every act of friendship, tenderness, recognition, generosity and benevolence is a feeling of pleasure.

woman, Jeanne Guyon, who was in every way outside the Church, it had much of the character of a heresy. The religion of 'Pure Love', as it was known, was fostered by Alexandre Piny, Père Caussade and Père Milley, in the last decades of the seventeenth century. In Piny's *Pur Amour* (1682), its character is already clearly defined: 'By pure love one should first understand a self-abandonment, but an amorous self-abandonment, which causes the soul, convinced of the merit, the excellence, and the infinite grandeur of God, to abandon itself like an amorous victim to the will and pleasure of its God.' But from the point of view of this study, the interest is heightened when it becomes monopolized by two women, Marie Alacoque and Jeanne Guyon. The first was a country saint who had visions at the age of four, the second a young widow who suddenly renounced her children to follow the Barnabite father, Lacombe, on his mystic journeyings in the foothills of the Alps, came to Paris, converted Mme de Maintenon and Fénelon, and was finally condemned by Bossuet. (It is interesting to note that Greuze had a particular devotion to Marie Alacoque, of whom he painted a portrait for Prince Yussupov in 1789. It is also tempting to think that the rapturous female heads he painted in his later years are in fact experiencing a state of '*pur amour*'.) In the hands of these two women, the element of love predominates; it becomes a love not sufficiently refined or understood, an indiscriminate love, more passionate than reflective, and in the ultimate analysis more sensual than sensuous. Père Lacombe teaches Mme Guyon this prayer: 'How I love you, O my God! O my God, how I love you. Your love, your love, your love, is enough. Your love and nothing more. Make me love you, O God of charity, O God of love, force me to love you as you would have it, as much as you command it; with all my heart, with all my soul, with all my spirit and with all my strength. O love, teach me to love you, give yourself to me, and I want nothing but that my beloved should be mine and I his. So that he should ever have his face turned towards me, O to do all, O to renounce all, O to lose all in order to save love alone'.[10] Marie Alacoque outlines its methods as follows: 'Say often, I want to live like a carefree child in the sacred heart of my good father, letting him dispose of me according to his pleasure, with no other care than to abandon myself to him and his amorous Providence'.[11]

This is unassailable, for this is the language proper to mystics. Yet there are signs of carelessness. Marie Alacoque is violent in comparison with an earlier Quietist, Antoinette Bourignon, whose writings caused a stir, yet who, although unlettered, was careful in her choice of words. From an excess of mystic confidence the later Quietists permitted themselves certain licences which the church could not condone. Mme Guyon in particular writes without reflection. Note, for example, the carnal quality of this poem, taken from the curious *Ame amante de son Dieu*, published in Cologne in 1717:

> *Aie pitié de moi, mon adorable Maître,*
> *Mon corps est faible et languissant;*
> *Chaque moment détruit mon être,*
> *Toi seul peut me guérir, O mon céléste Amant.*
>
> *Ah! le mal du dedans m'est plus insupportable*
> *Que les maux que souffre mon corps;*
> *Si je pouvais t'être agréable*
> *Je rirai des maux du dehors.*
>
> *Guéris, change mon coeur; que je serai contente*
> *D'endurer chaque jour mille tourments divers,*
> *Si je puis être ton Amante*
> *Je défierai tout l'univers.*
>
> *Je n'appréhends plus ni l'ennui ni la peine*
> *Si j'appartiens à mon amour.*
> *Si je pouvais porter sa chaîne*
> *Je perdrai sans regret la lumière du jour.*

The maximum licence of language was reached when Mme Guyon managed for a time to convert Fénelon. Being two people of neurotic propensities, their mutual rejoicings verge on the orgiastic, and their *Poésies Spirituelles*[12] will strike even the most fervent admirer of Fénelon with something of a shock. They were set to current or well-known tunes and were to be sung as popular songs. Here, for instance, is Fénelon's *Enfance Spirituelle*, set to the tune, '*Taisez-vous, ma musette*':

> *J'ai le goût de l'enfance;*
> *De mon hochet content,*
> *La faiblesse et l'obéissance*
> *De moi font un petit enfant . . .*
>
> *Fruite d'une sèche étude,*
> *Austère gravité,*
> *Importuns restes d'habitude,*
> *Laissez-moi vivre en liberté*

Vérité simple et nue,
Que j'aime ta candeur,
Et que l'innocence ingénue
Est au-dessus de la pudeur! . . .

Docteurs, laissez-moi vivre
Loin de vous, loin de moi,
Laissez-moi, car je veux suivre
De l'enfance, l'aveugle loi . . .

Jadis je croyais être
Sage comme Caton;
Mais je suis sous mon petit-Maître
De docteur devenu Fanchon . . .

These verses were added in the second version:

Vice et vertu surpasse
Un enfant comme moi,
Comme au maillot, je suis en grâce,
Sans honte, sans crainte, et sans loi.

A peine je bégaie,
Je ne sais pas mon nom.
Je pleure, je ris, je m'égaie,
Je ne crains que maman téton.

La main qui dans l'enfance
Sut me mettre au berceau,
En dépit de toute prudence
Me bercera jusqu'au tombeau.

The second danger was a certain pride the Quietists felt and which expressed itself in a familiarity with the Deity, a sort of waiving of the rules for the elect. Caussade says, 'Nothing so easy as sainthood'[13]. Mme Guyon announces, 'It seems to me that holy communion has nothing to add to what I already possess'.[14] In actions as well as words, the readiness was all. For if true mystics meet God in a state of non-thought, these people deliberately emptied their minds in order to meet God. And an example such as the following was exalted: 'A chaste girl was impelled by the spirit of God to expose herself to evil in a place of perdition and she went along generously in obedience to the Sovereign Ally'.[15] A moral system was built up on a process which should have been a state of grace but which was too often a spasm of autosuggestion. 'As far as the future is concerned', says Fénelon, 'settle your deepest heart, for your heart will control your entire conduct.'[16] And more, 'Begin to love and love will do more than you yourself could; love, and love will be your memory'.[17] Thus, in contrast to orthodox Christian teaching, one's love should over-ride one's repentance; one may be re-admitted to the fold without penalties being exacted. If, in fact, one's love is sure enough, one may sin within the fold itself.

The third danger was that Quietism was for a time adopted as a basis to education. Mme de Maintenon, when under the influence of Mme Guyon, made it the official religion for the girls in her school at Saint-Cyr. The desiderata of 'poverty of spirit' and 'childlike simplicity' resulted in education being subverted and the outcome was moral anarchy. Mme du Péron, in chapter 19 of her *Mémoires de tout ce qui est passé de plus remarquable depuis l'Etablissement de la Maison de Saint-Cyr* (quoted Masson, op. cit.), paints this interesting picture: 'Almost the whole house became Quietist without noticing it, the only talk was of the pure love of God, of self-abandonment, of holy indifference, of simplicity; this latter virtue masked the search for many small personal satisfactions, one behaved with the holy liberty of children of God; one did not bother about anything, not even one's salvation'. These girls, when grown into women, must have had a tremendous influence on the orientation of *sensibilité*. They had experienced the supreme pleasure of being '*sensible*' to God, and this pleasure, originally quite adventitious, became the raison d'être of the thing which occasioned it.

That Quietism was not merely a religious movement but had an actual living posterity in the eighteenth century, when Greuze was at the height of his fame, can be seen in the writings of Jean-Jacques Rousseau. Rousseau is an outstanding example of the way in which the Quietist mentality was perpetuated. He was formed by Mme de Warens, who, it has sometimes been suggested, was herself a Quietist. This cannot be proved, but one thing is certain: Rousseau's early years were spent in the Mme Guyon country where traces of her doctrine must surely have persisted. Looking back on this period, he speaks of 'a very calm and even sensual state' and says, 'The country solitude in which I passed the flower of my youth, the study of the good books to which I devoted myself, strength-ened my natural disposition towards affectionate feelings and made me devout almost in the manner of Fénelon'.[18] Later in his life, orthodox Christian principles disappeared until resuscitated in the *Rêveries d'un Promeneur Solitaire* but Jean-Jacques retained a profoundly religious spirit. His religion was simply inverted. For the orthodox Christian, man was good until corrupted by his own sin, and was ultimately restored to grace by a life of striving pleasing to God. For Rousseau, man was good until corrupted by society, and ultimately restored by conformity to the ways of nature. The former entails a lifetime of effort and insecurity, the latter of *laisser-aller* in the hope that one's innate goodness will eventually be given an opportunity to triumph.

This belief evolved in a curious way. In the first place, Rousseau, like the Quietists, considers himself of value only when his emotions are aroused. Conversely, the strength of these emotions, when aroused, prove his moral value in comparison with which his sins are of no account. 'Am I not a worthy worshipper of the divinity when my eyes are wet with tears and when my heart finds in its emotion more and even sweeter tears?'[19] Religion is in fact the climax of his own *sensibilité*. The extreme casuistry with which this theory was developed can be seen in a letter to Sophie d'Houdetot, written in March, 1758: 'I am weak, I know; my life is full of faults, because I am a man; but what distinguishes me from all the other men I know is that in the midst of my faults I have always reproached myself. My faults have never led me to neglect my duty or to despise virtue. And finally I have fought and conquered for virtue at the moment when all the others have forgotten her'. And he sums up his affair with Sophie in these words, 'I protest, I swear, that if sometimes led astray by my senses I have tried to render Sophie unfaithful, I have never truly desired it'.[20] Mme Guyon said to Fénelon, 'Never resist, but never suffer'. This cosy feeling of sinning from within the fold, this religion without repentance, guilt, or even temptation, is the basis of *La Nouvelle Héloïse*. Nothing need be lost. 'Very well! we shall be guilty but we shan't be bad; we shall be guilty, but we shall always love virtue; far from exhausting our faults . . . we shall redeem them by being good.'

The way in which Rousseau differs from the Quietists is that he develops the logical consequences of the above argument and thus provides the doctrine with a positive corollary. Not only does a state of emotional excitement indicate the presence of God, but God is now the patron of emotional excitement. In another letter to Sophie, he speaks of '. . . the witness without reproach, the Eternal Eye, which no one deceives, seeing perhaps with some pleasure two peaceable souls encouraging each other mutually to virtue (Rousseau had wooed Sophie from her lover Saint-Lambert but allowed her to return to him) and in a delicious outpouring nourishing all the purest sentiments with which he has endowed them . . .'. Similarly, in *La Nouvelle Héloïse*, Lord Bomston describes Julie and Saint-Preux in these terms: 'Two beautiful souls are made for each other; a senseless prejudice interferes with the traditional outcome and upsets the harmony of thinking beings . . . This chaste knot of nature is not under the jurisdiction of sovereign power or paternal authority but only under that of our Common Father who knows how to speak to our hearts and who, ordering them to mingle, can constrain them to love one another'. Since Julie loves Saint-Preux, her desire to remain honourable, in all senses of the word, 'is little more than madness'. 'Turn your face towards Heaven . . . swear to live and die for each other . . . Let us not inflict this wrong on humanity.' In other words, let us not contain ourselves. And so great is Julie's exaltation after the event that her cousin Claire says to her, 'Although I have not submitted, I am less chaste than you'. At a remove of several degrees, but on fundamentally the same level of feeling, Rousseau is, like Mme Guyon, united to grace by a *'coeur sensible'*. The words *'délices'* and *'supplices'* occur frequently and with the same implications in their respective works.

Rousseau's writings have a secondary importance: the sensational enthusiasm which they aroused, and in a largely feminine public. He became a sort of spiritual guide; for if his behaviour in real life were questionable, as Bachaumont said, echoing no doubt the opinion of others, *'Que ne pardonne-t-on pas à qui sait émouvoir?'*.† In 1763 an edition of his *Pensées Choisies* appeared and letters poured in containing statements like, 'I dare not do anything without consulting your book'. Interesting too is the way in which Rousseauism had its outcome in fashions of behaviour, for example, the nursing of children preached in *Emile*. 'When Jean-Jacques spoke, maternal sentiment was reborn in the mother's breast; from the ardour with which they sought to fulfil this most tender of functions, one would say that they were paying much more attention to Rousseau than to nature herself.'[21] (This is a good example of *sensibilité* passing from one level to another.) And the satisfaction value was enormous, transparent only to the eyes of a less gullible generation. 'When one has read M. de Buffon, one feels incredibly

† What will one not forgive the man who has the power to move one's emotions.

learned', said Joubert at the end of the eighteenth century. He added, 'One feels virtuous when one has read Rousseau. Nevertheless, one is neither the one nor the other'.

It will now be apparent that the circumstances operating at the end of the seventeenth century and the beginning of the eighteenth century brought about a changed attitude to religion, found its teachings to be incompatible with what was considered to be solid reasoning and self-evident material fact, and thus caused a division in men's minds with regard to moral duty and self-respect, and a nostalgia for the simplicity of a less sophisticated, less advanced religious state. A broad spectrum of beliefs grew up independently of, but were all based on, this extremely fluid situation. These doctrines represent roughly a division between reason and emotion, the two faculties which in the earlier seventeenth century had been united in the worship of God. At one end of the scale stands the purely intellectual, dispassionate, and material philosophy of Voltaire; at the other, the fervent and un-organized emotional activity of the Quietists. Between the two extremes lies the attempt at reconciliation, the realm of *sensibilité*. Even in this area there are confused trends. Leaning towards reason, Toussaint and d'Holbach try to create an abstract code of morality based on human needs and desires. On the side of emotion, a number of people draw the conclusion that since the accomplishment of a worthy action is usually accompanied by a pleasurable sensation, the converse must also be true, and that if the emotion be cultivated, it will inevitably work its own salvation in the form of a worthy action. In a surprising number of cases this did happen but the majority of people merely felt a sensuous and sentimental pleasure in their reaction to such touching and uplifting ideas as the new laws of family morality, or for that matter to the sight of Greuze's first famous picture, *Un Père de Famille expliquant la Bible à ses Enfants*.

Sensibilité, which is essentially a fashion in ways of feeling, is the broad plateau on to which these trends converge in about 1760. Yet from the beginning of the eighteenth century, it is the shadow accompaniment to many an intellectual exercise. Voltaire is *sensible*, Marivaux is *sensible*, the Abbé de Saint-Pierre is *sensible*, but their *sensibilité* is intellectual, social and material. The solidly reasoned and sincerely felt philosophy of d'Holbach, the peaceful material world of Chardin, the sad and moving reflections of Vauvenargues, all partake of *sensibilité* at rather more close quarters. At the heart of the movement is the school of *sensibilité* and the genres it actually

17

creates: in literature, the *'comédie larmoyante'* and the *'drame bourgeois'*, and in painting the art of Greuze and his numerous followers. The most extreme outcome of *sensibilité* was the dynamic mysticism of Rousseau and the intensity of Julie Lespinasse. Perhaps its final stage was the swearing of the Oath of the Jeu de Paume in 1789.

It is the school of *sensibilité* and the trends that it actually created that must now be examined.

Sensibilité in Literature

So far, *sensibilité* has only been surveyed on its highest and most abstract level. Now it is to be removed from the studies of philosophers and religious reformers, to be given a wider audience, and to be dealt with as a fashion in social behaviour. It has been stressed that *sensibilité* was an essentially literary movement. It was, after all, through the medium of literature that both the concepts of the salons and the new philosophy were popularized. It was through the medium of novels and above all plays that an audience was conditioned and prepared to accept their pictorial equivalent in Greuze's paintings. The literary history of the eighteenth century is full of names that are now forgotten, and of works which are no longer read and performed. Written for a strictly contemporary public, they have not survived the passage of the years. Yet anyone trying to understand a topical success such as that enjoyed by Greuze must examine a parallel phenomenon in a closely associated field. From about 1730 onwards, with the help of the Abbé Prévost and Nivelle de la Chaussée, *sensibilité* moves out of the study and into the theatre, and the emotive and moralizing influences usually connected with religion become entrenched in the novel. From these two precedents develops the later course and direction of *sensibilité*, and it is in the novel, the '*conte moral*', the '*comédie larmoyante*', and the '*drame bourgeois*' that it finds its most powerful and original expression.

At the beginning of the eighteenth century the literary situation looked rather blank, for in a sense Corneille, Racine and, above all, Molière had exhausted the resources of the French theatre and therefore the stream of literature as the seventeenth century had known it, for poetry had little independent existence and the novel was not yet a recognized genre. Yet perhaps because of the fact that it had never been subjected to rules and regulations, it was the novel which first went beyond the boundaries of classical literature and in the hands of Courtilz de Sandras and Le Sage, less important for their literary merits than for their innovations, sought out and described a variety of ways of life, thus satisfying that delight in anecdote which later inspired the search among the collectors for the paintings of Teniers and Wouwermans. But it was not the novel of the picaresque type which was to win the devotion of the reading public in eighteenth-century France. The picaresque was soon rejected in favour of the sentimental, and the future of the French novel of the eighteenth century is foreshadowed by the appearance in 1696 of the *Histoire des Amours de Cléante et de Bélise* by that little known writer, the Présidente Ferrand. The story opens with the following statement: 'I was born with the most impressionable and tender heart that love has ever formed . . .'. It is a rambling, shapeless work but it contains new elements: an intensity and a refusal to hide behind allegorical symbols which bring it nearer in feeling to Julie de Lespinasse than to Mlle de Scudéry, to the *sensibilité* of the eighteenth century than to the preciosity of the seventeenth. And the note of voluntary confession, the emphasis on the vulnerability of the confessor, were seized upon by men as disparate as Marivaux ('I was born the most human of all men'),[1] and the Abbé Prévost.

The Abbé Prévost was far more to his contemporaries than the author of *Manon Lescaut*. His many novels, which form the basis for the development of the genre right up to Benjamin Constant, are the first to deal with passion, not the dignified amity of the seventeenth century but real human passion, often grotesque in its progress and disastrous in its end. He deals only with the period of crisis, never dropping to a lower emotional plane to show, for example, the later life of the Chevalier des Grieux, as Rousseau continued with Saint-Preux. There is much that is Romantic in his work, many elopements, deaths and crepe-hung mortuary chambers, and, like Marivaux, he often pins his plot on an incident, such as meeting a man in a stage coach and hearing the story of his life and adventures. But no one can deny in Prévost a quite superior power of describing emotion and the single-mindedness of the true story teller. He represents the sentimental novel in its purity. His characters were commonplace and insignificant before the crisis described in their lives, and they find it hard to assume heroic stature; the story is usually formless and irregular but only because of the essentially human level on which it is being told.

Prévost was for a time lionized by a society lady, Mme de Tencin and introduced into her salon. An interesting point which emerges from the preface to *Manon Lescaut* is the way in which he made this very brutal story acceptable to the tender readers of the early eighteenth-century salons. He does this by an adroit mixture of flattery and warning. 'Distinguished spirits know that tenderness and humanity are amiable virtues and are therefore likely to possess them', but, adds Prévost, these people may be too far removed from the exigencies of everyday life to know when these virtues should be put into practice. They can only benefit from examples, and it is to be hoped that a novel such as *Manon Lescaut* will serve as one. 'It is precisely for this sort of reader that works such as this can prove useful.' Thus, even before the much more renowned Samuel Richardson, Prévost makes a stand as a novelist with a message, a sort of lay-preacher whose appeal is above all to the sympathy of his audience. Diderot felt the appropriate response when he stated that 'every line of *L'Homme de Qualité*, of *Le Doyen de Killerine*, of *Cleveland*, stimulates in me an interest in the misfortunes of virtue and brings forth my tears'.

We sometimes fail to realize that Prévost's fame in his own day was completely overshadowed by that of a man whose books he translated into French, Samuel Richardson. In the same way we tend to overlook a fact which in the eighteenth century must have seemed one of great significance: Prévost was as important an anglicizing influence as Voltaire. Both men were forced to use England as a refuge, Voltaire in the 1720s and Prévost in the late 1720s and early 1730s. Both men came back to France filled with enthusiasm. Two of Prévost's novels, the *Mémoires d'un homme de qualité* and *Cleveland*, were written in England and it is therefore fitting that he should translate the works of Richardson, one of the most popular English novelists of the day, into French. *Pamela* appeared in 1742, *Clarissa Harlowe* in 1751, and *Grandison* in 1755–6. It is no exaggeration to say that their effect was to determine the course of French literature until the Revolution and the course of *sensibilité* until, perhaps, the advent of Beaumarchais. For here was something outside French experience, the novelty of which was to last for some forty years. The embryo of the eighteenth-century novel in France was the high-flown and idealized love story; in England it was the edifying religious tract. Richardson's novels have the spurious uplifting quality inspired by his almost professional assurance that virtue will triumph, and the detail with which he describes Pamela's struggles was guaranteed to afford his readers sympathy, tears, and more than a little excitement. Moreover, one was expected to read his novels in the virtuous anticipation of being instructed. This habit was even more widespread in France than it was in England. As Saint-Lambert was to state, quite seriously, '*C'est pour entretenir en nous la passion de la vertu et pour en trouver sûrement la route que nous lisons beaucoup les romans de Richardson*'.[2]†

The novels of Richardson were an innovation in more ways than one. Firstly, there is the question of form. The letter form brings narrative direct

† It is to instil in us a passion for virtue and to find a sure road that we read Richardson's novels so much.

to the reader; it is a kind of autobiography in instalments. It had of course been known in France in the seventeenth century but when applied to this sort of subject matter it took on a novelettish thrill. Diderot, Rousseau, Rétif de la Bretonne and Choderlos de Laclos were to use it with this intention. Secondly, Richardson's three novels, *Pamela* in particular, set a certain seal on the spirit of *sensibilité*. For *sensibilité*, passivity or pure love in the religious sense, now settled down in the moral sphere, for the benefit of a large number of willing readers, at least, to abandonment to the consciousness of one's own goodness. We may now castigate Pamela's behaviour as foolish, unhealthy or downright immoral, but to her readers the blamelessness of her intentions was sufficient to transform her into a paragon of virtue. Superficially, this is near to Rousseau. It has been shown how *La Nouvelle Hélosïe* stands on a serious if inverted ethical basis. Richardson's story is just an awful warning. Yet in intention at least the two books are the same, and the success which *Pamela* met with in France goes some way to explain the enormous and unanimous response to the more complex yet more moving testament of Rousseau.

It is a mistake to represent Rousseau as proceeding directly from Prévost or Richardson, for he was a man, who, in the last analysis, wrote only under the stimulus of his own imagination. Yet his debt to both these writers is obvious. He had known Prévost in 1751, had shed many tears over his *Cleveland*, and had read Richardson in his translation. The first part of *La Nouvelle Héloïse* has the same intensity of emotion as that which characterizes the novels of Prévost. The second part, however, has a bourgeois serenity which is completely English in origin. Like Richardson in *Pamela*, Rousseau goes on to describe the married life of his heroine. There is the same lower middle-class approach, the same preoccupation with conjugal fidelity and the servant problem. But here the wheel has come full circle. Richardson had concentrated his energies on putting down vice (which to him is the most powerful part: his virtuous characters, like those of Greuze, are born victims); Rousseau directs his to uplifting virtue. In her interminable letters, Julie reforms everything in the realms of society, politics, science and art. Her good sense and her noble intentions, one is given to understand, have something to do with the fact of her being married. Marriage, in addition to providing her with her full stature as a woman, has brought her new moral distinction (fundamentally the same sentiment as that which clogs the second part of *Pamela*). And in a curious way, Rousseau comes very near to Voltaire's enthusiasm for England in the two-dimensional character of

Milord Edouard Bomston. Bomston, it will be remembered, is all enthusiasm and open-mindedness, which to the French of the eighteenth century were typical English virtues. In fact he offers Julie and Saint-Preux a home in Yorkshire with these words: 'Come and honour with the example of your virtues a country where they will be adored'. It is not surprising that when Jean-Jacques visited England some five years later he developed acute signs of persecution mania.

Rousseau's influence was felt until the last years of the century. Novels inspired by him fall roughly into three categories. There is firstly the novel dealing with a grand passion, such as Baculard d'Arnaud's *Les Epreuves du Sentiment*, Imbert's *Les Egarements de l'Amour*, Mme de Beauharnais' *Lettres de Stéphanie*, and the novels of Mme Riccoboni, so widely read in the eighteenth century and now forgotten: *Lettres de Milord Rivers, Histoire de Miss Jenny*, etc. Secondly, there is the country versus town thesis, destined to prove the superior worth of simple country folk, an important theme also with Greuze. This usually works out in the form of pastorals such as Florian's *Estelle et Némorin*. A good example of this genre is Saint-Lambert's story *Sara Th...*, based on that part of *La Nouvelle Héloïse* which deals with the married life of Julie de Wolmar. The theme is too big for Saint-Lambert; he is forced to condense his material, and the result is somewhat elliptical but eminently Lockeian: '*Le repas était simple et excellent, les convives sobres et sensuels*'. Thirdly, there is the story with a moral, based on the didactic element in the letters from Julie de Wolmar to Saint-Preux. This was thought to be excellent for young people and was done to death by Berquin in his *Idylles*. It was also the favourite method of a later writer, Mme de Genlis, whose stories have a welcome touch of acerbity. But she was a governess by profession and her *Annales de la Vertu* (1781), *Veillées du Château* (1784) and stories like *Alphonsine, ou la Tendresse Maternelle* and *Eglantine, ou l'Indolent corrigée* have an all too obviously didactic motive.

Many of these works made an additional bid for popularity by using English themes, names, or even pretending to be translations from the English. As early as 1756, Mme Riccoboni produced *Lettres de Mistress Fanny Butlerd à Milord Charles Alford, duc de Cantonbridge* (this announced itself as a translation). She followed this in 1759 with *Lettres de Milady Juliette Catesby à Milady Henrietta Campley*. In 1764 came the *Histoire de Miss Jenny*, and in 1774, *Lettres de Milord Rivers à Sir Charles Cardigan*. Baculard d'Arnaud was perhaps the most conscientious in this field. In 1764 he produced *Fanni, ou l'heureux repentir*, to be followed by *Fanni, ou la nouvelle Paméla*, and in 1766, *Sidnei et*

Silli, ou la Bienfaisance et la Reconnaissance, histoire anglaise. Then in 1767 came *Nancy, ou les malheurs de l'imprudence et de la jalousie, histoire imitée de l'anglais*, followed in 1769 by *Anne Bell, histoire anglaise*, and many others.

Older writers on this subject see a reaction to Rousseau in the persons of Rétif de la Bretonne and Choderlos de Laclos. This is surely incorrect. Rétif was an uncontrolled and illiterate Rousseau but his themes are very orthodox. His *Paysan perverti, ou les dangers de la ville* needs no underlining. His '*comédie larmoyante*', *Sa mère l'allaita*, although ribald and obscure, is of the stock of *Emile*, while his novel, *La Malédiction Paternelle*, inspired by Greuze, is an extraordinary tribute to a painter by a writer of parallel sympathies. The pornographic content which weighs down his books and for which he has been isolated is typical not only of Rétif but of the later development of *sensibilité* as a whole. Most significant of all is the importance in his writings of his own sensibility. Married to the same sort of woman as Rousseau's Thérèse Levasseur or Greuze's Anne-Gabrielle Babuty, exhausted by poverty and manual labour, Rétif produced six-, eight-, and ten-volume novels almost effortlessly and with incredible speed, and in all of these his own personality is inseparable from his treatment of the subject. It is the essentially autobiographical nature of Rétif's work which makes of him an authentic Rousseauist.

Choderlos de Laclos is quite the opposite. In sharp distinction to the novels of the preceding twenty-five years, his masterpiece, *Les Liaisons Dangereuses*, is a masterpiece of art, and the detachment and discipline which a work of art entails has had its effect on the subject treated, so that at a first reading love would appear to be transferred from the moral sphere to that of the intellect, and men and women, their spontaneity killed, reduced to simple combinations of sex and intelligence. The situations of *Les Liaisons Dangereuses* are very orthodox; its theme, that of desire without motive, moral obstacle, or very much lust, is notably far from Rousseau, but in outline at least how very near to Richardson. Grandison, once the villain, is now the hero, and Clarissa the unimpeachable has sunk to the status of a simple prude. Laclos, in fact, belongs to his period in more ways than one. The impressive fin de siècle quality of *Les Liaisons Dangereuses*, which represents man merely as a joyless mind ruminating vast fields of sexual possibility, stands out in high relief from other contemporary productions because the author is more of an artist than a moralist and refuses to explain his intentions. He does however write a preface which too often and for too long has been lightly dismissed. Moreover, in his other writings, notably *De l'Education des Femmes*,[3] he reveals himself as a fervent Rousseauist. It is therefore illogical to isolate him from the development which has been briefly described.

It is interesting to note that the novels of Fielding were also translated into French but received scant attention. Satire, as is twice proved in the persons of Fielding and Hogarth, was not so much rejected as not understood. Richardson's novels, far-fetched and of poor quality in any language, evidently answered a specific demand. French writers have pointed out that the lacuna left by the disappearance of religion and of simple unquestioning piety was filled by moralizing, by a preoccupation with virtue, and by a mystical excitement derived from things not mystical. The positive hunger exhibited by the French in the eighteenth century for domestic detail, pietistic sentiment and moral exhibitionism, swelled to a quite disproportionate climax. The novel became the stock book of reference; it was read with the same desire for instruction as that usually devoted to the reading of the gospels. In fact in 1777 Mistelet pronounced that the reading of novels should precede the reading of history.[4] Richardson had satisfied this hunger on one level; Rousseau had transformed it into a positive doctrine, and many forms of art felt the impact.

An offshoot of this development in the novel was the '*conte moral*'. The long short story was a favoured art form in the eighteenth century. Voltaire and Montesquieu had used it for didactic purposes but the function of the '*conte moral*', or story with a moral, echoes that of the novel and often takes its themes straight from it, as is witnessed by the example of Saint-Lambert quoted above. Indeed there is so great an interchange of theme between the story and the novel, the story and the '*drame bourgeois*', and the story and painting, that it is often difficult to tell which is the original source.

The most charming and accomplished of these writers is Marmontel, who is also the most original and the one best remembered today. All his stories have the character of fairy tales, of an earthly paradise where all is virtue and *sensibilité* yet nothing is outrageously exaggerated. This statement, for instance, is familiar but lacks the theatrical intensity with which it is usually uttered: 'It is not in the midst of society that an honourable woman finds her happiness but in the intimacy of her home, in the bosom of her family, and in close contact with decent people'.[5] This sentiment, no doubt unbearable to the twentieth century, was exactly suited to the mood of the eighteenth.

The lovely *Bergère des Alpes* is a good example of the interdependence of the arts in the eighteenth century. It was read by Marmontel to Mme

Geoffrin's circle of artist and philosopher friends and then published anonymously in the *Mercure de France* in 1759. Mme Geoffrin commissioned a picture of it from Joseph Vernet who was probably present at the original reading, and the painting, now in the Museum at Compiègne, was exhibited at the Salon of 1763. The sculptor Falconet did a group of the hero and heroine, Fonrose and Adelaide, in *biscuit de Sèvres* which was reproduced in a cruder form by the Derby works in England. The theme was also illustrated by Angelika Kauffmann (engraved by Bartolozzi in 1785) and given its loveliest expression by the French genre painter Aubry in 1775 (the picture is now in the Detroit Institute of Arts). Aubry's picture, however, would not have been possible without the developments in genre painting made by Greuze and Lépicié. The story also inspired a play, by Desfontaines, which passed to England in the form of a comic opera by Charles Dibdin, *The Alpine Lovers* of 1780, and this in its turn inspired the watercolour by Francis Wheatley (London, British Museum).[6]

A similar connection of ideas can be traced between Marmontel and the radical playwright Louis-Sébastien Mercier, who took one of the tenets of his theory of the drama from Marmontel's short story, *La Bonne Mère*. This tells of a mother who, anxious to procure a good husband for her daughter, takes two of her suitors to the theatre. One remains insensible to the performance; the other weeps from start to finish ('. . . when virtue and beauty are combined, I cannot answer for my actions'). This shows him to be morally superior to his rival and he gets the girl. Mercier, in his *Essai sur l'Art Dramatique*, states, 'One can judge each man's soul by the degree of emotion he shows at the theatre'.

Baculard d'Arnaud, whose *Délassements de l'Homme Sensible* consist of twelve volumes of stories with titles such as *L'Amour Filial*, *Le Pouvoir de l'Amour Paternel*, *Exemple de l'Amour Conjugal*, *La Douleur Maternelle*, *Le Respect Filial*, *La Tendresse Conjugal*, *L'Amour Fraternel* and so on, obviously draws most of his themes from the '*drame bourgeois*'. He was a friend of Greuze and it is interesting to see how alike their respective methods are. Like Greuze, Baculard d'Arnaud has a feeling for moral explosions. *L'Amour Filial*, for example, tells of a hard-hearted financier who finally cancels his debtor's bills with these words: '. . . there is my conqueror, the one who revealed to me the power of nature and *sensibilité*. Lormeuil, your son has made a man of me'. Like Greuze he has a certain form of hand-rubbing salaciousness ('What a spectacle is that of a charming creature in the throes of grief! How her looks show off to their best advantage!'),[7] and the same ability to invoke tears as an expression of virtue. In difficult moments, the characters of Baculard d'Arnaud 'have only the strength to release a torrent of tears'.[8]

In the hands of Florian the short story comes near to German *sensibilité* and the idylls of Gessner. It also degenerates into a sickly sweetness and becomes markedly decadent. This *'nouvelle allemande'*, for example, from an edition of 1786, shows the bathos to which *sensibilité* could descend—'You were in your cradle, Gertrude; you were asleep; your pink and white face was the picture of innocence and health. Aimar looked at you and tears rose to his eyes. I took you in my arms and held you out to him—"She is still your daughter", I said. You woke up at that and as if Heaven had inspired you, far from crying, you began to smile; and stretching your little arms towards old Aimar, you clutched his white hair in your hands and brought his face close to yours. The old man covered you with kisses, clasped me to his bosom, and taking you with him and holding out his hand to me, cried, "Come, son, let us go and find my daughter" '. This complicated but irresistible denouement crystallizes a long and boring story of a family estrangement, ending happily in a reunion. Florian is the master of the happy ending. He is willing to sacrifice anything to *sensibilité*, even the most hallowed traditions. The transformation undergone by Harlequin in his plays is a good example of this. Far from being the wily figure of the Commedia dell'Arte, he now 'has no sense, only *sensibilité* . . . he is a great child'.[9]

The significance of the short story is its fluidity as an art form, the number of influences it received and passed on, its wide publicity (stories were published in journals such as the *Mercure de France*), and its popularity. There is no need to underline the significance of the novel. Yet for a complete understanding of both the novel and the story, and in order to gauge the overall importance of *sensibilité* in literature, one must now examine the only two genres which it did actually create: the *'comédie larmoyante'* and the *'drame bourgeois'*.

The eighteenth century felt an overwhelming respect for the theatre of the seventeenth and in particular for Molière who was now considered exclusively as a champion of good conduct. Although a natural repertoire of comic effects, the wider and more general appeal of his plays lay in the didactic element they contained. He retained his immense popularity right through to the 1780s, by which time Corneille and Racine had foundered beneath storms of popular and democratic disapproval. Molière, in fact, was the dramatist par excellence and it remained the wish of many eighteenth-century writers to emulate him. A popular writer like Destouches, for example, does his best but without success; he is incapable of conceiving a dramatic situation with the right blend of comedy and truth-telling and his good intentions are confined to his prefaces which are copious: 'I think that the art of writing drama is only estimable if its intention is to instruct as well as to entertain. I have always held it as an incontestable maxim that however amusing a comedy might be, it is an imperfect and even dangerous work if the author does not intend to correct manners, to deride pretension, to condemn vice and to show virtue in so favourable a light that it becomes the focus of public esteem and veneration'.[10]

The peculiar relation of the eighteenth-century theatre to that of the seventeenth is exemplified in this preface of Destouches which seems to anticipate certain of Diderot's remarks when he was examining Greuze's pictures in the Salon. In the same way, Destouches' verbose and unamusing comedies have a wider significance; they are symptomatic of the modifications which took place in dramatic genres in the first half of the eighteenth century. The theory of the '*drame bourgeois*' can be traced back to the seventeenth century, in fact to Corneille himself who had outlined a form of tragedy in which the protagonists did not have to be kings, princes, or men of high rank in order to illustrate the conflicts of the human situation: 'Tragedy should excite pity and fear... Now if it is true that this latter sentiment is not aroused unless we see people like ourselves suffering and worry that their misfortunes might find an echo in our own lives, is it not true that the fear might be stronger if we saw misfortunes befalling people of our own class rather than the kind of troubles that depose kings from their thrones—kings with whom we have nothing in common apart from the fact that we are all susceptible to human passion but not always to their kind of preoccupation?'.[11]

Corneille, however, had seen no need to act on his idea and indeed there was no point in so doing. As long as there was a living stream of monumental tragedy, a compromise tragedy could have no existence. By the beginning of the eighteenth century circumstances had changed. Firstly, the tragedy had received its final and most perfect form at the hands of Racine; after his death there could only be a decline. Crébillon and Voltaire, the two major professional tragedians of the first half of the eighteenth century, are incapable of continuing in the spirit of the seventeenth; they increase the peripeteia, the language becomes more forced, and the externals more highly coloured and obtrusive.

Secondly, a change was taking place in the choice of dramatic material. The ethos of the seventeenth-century tragedy relied to a great extent on a particular idea, that of the '*honnête homme*', an ideal which has never been satisfactorily analysed but which was of its essence aristocratic. The virtues extolled were generally stoical and the softer sentiments were deplored. The whole tendency of the eighteenth century was middle-class and empirical: indeed the two conditions were often interdependent. Thus the traditional form of tragedy was no longer in accord with the dictates of the day.

And thirdly, a reaction had set in against the rigidity of the traditional genres. As Lamotte, a minor dramatic writer of the period, said, 'The heart is not subject to rules which reason has codified without her consent: there is no harm in the heart taking pleasure in a few illusions'. This argument was taken up vociferously by Fontenelle, Voltaire and, eventually, Mercier. It should be remembered that this would weigh as an additional argument against the perpetuation of classical tragedy, the most stylized and disciplined art form of the seventeenth century.

Comedy, however, remained fairly free from rule. Yet for some reason, possibly because there was a dearth of true comic dramatists, comedy was found to be lightweight and unsatisfying. The eighteenth century was self-conscious and a self-conscious age is rarely a very humorous one. 'Generally speaking,' said the Abbé Du Bos, 'people prefer to cry than to laugh when they go to the theatre.'[12] One school of theorists, indeed, held that the only aim of the theatre should be to excite emotion. The great inaugurator of emotion on the eighteenth-century stage and the man who reflects most faithfully this interim period between the destruction of one rule and the evolution of another is Nivelle de la Chaussée with his '*comédie larmoyante*', literally, tearful comedy. The '*comédie larmoyante*' contains no comic element whatsoever, although it has a happy ending. It is as declamatory as classical tragedy. Its entire merit consists in resolving an enormously complicated plot into a tender and uplifting dénouement. It is the first dramatic form to be based on the conventions of *sensibilité* for the characters step outside the bounds of their roles to give gratuitous evidence of their tender-heartedness and the intensity with which they *feel*. '*Plus je sens vivement, plus je sens que je suis*',† cries the hero of *Mélanide*, and of a character of *La Fausse Antipathie* it was said, '*Ses moindres mouvements sont des*

† The more deeply I feel, the more I feel that I exist.

29

convulsions'.† Moreover, La Chaussée knows how to flatter his audiences by making them feel they share with his characters a fund of irrepressible goodness. True virtue is natural, instinctive, needs no prompting: '*Les vertus qu'on acquiert sont si peu naturelles*'.[13]†‡

The genre, which was accepted as a genre outside the traditional conception of comedy aroused discussion; the motives were declared to be praiseworthy but the actual plays were not considered up to standard. This is not surprising, for Nivelle de la Chaussée's characters, constantly changing their identity, losing and recovering their fortunes, and marrying by mistake their uncles, mothers and sisters, spring from the stock repertoire of the '*comédie précieuse*', while their seedy aristocratic activities are altogether artificial. The '*comédie larmoyante*' contained valuable elements, notably its misdirected seriousness and its desire for change; but as a genre it led nowhere.

The first man to grasp the facts of the eclipsed tragedy and the inadequate comedy and to devote himself to the task of bringing the theatre up to date was Diderot. He took his lead, however, from Grimm, who wrote in 1754, 'I imagine a type of comedy much more tragic than the merely tearful type. Why should I not let my Gambler or my Spendthrift kill himself at the end of my play in that mood of despair which ordinarily is the consequence of his kind of excess? A well constructed comedy of this kind would be more natural than many of our tragedies and I think would produce an astonishing effect'.[14] In his lengthy writings on dramatic theory, the *Essai sur la Poésie Dramatique* and the *Entretiens sur le Fils Naturel*, Diderot evolves his theory of the '*tragédie moyenne*', 'which would have as its subject our domestic misfortunes'. The reading of *Pamela*, it should be remembered, had inspired an interest in domestic misfortunes which Diderot quite seriously considered to be effective from a dramatic point of view. 'In every moral object there is a centre and two extreme points. It seems to me that as every dramatic action has a moral object, there should be genres corresponding to the centre and the two extremes. We already have the extremes, comedy and tragedy, but men are not always in a tragic or comic situation. There is therefore a middle range which separates comedy from tragedy . . . if there were a genre for this middle range, there would be no condition in society, no important action in life that could not find a place somewhere in the dramatic system.'[15] Thus the '*drame bourgeois*', breaking completely with the unities and canons of the

† His least movements were convulsions.
†‡ The virtues which one acquires are so unnatural.

classical theatre, is to deal with domestic misfortunes, everyday happenings in the lives of the middle classes. 'A man's duties and obligations are as fertile a dramatic field as his follies and vices, and decent, sincere plays will be successful everywhere, but more particularly in a corrupt society than anywhere else.'[16]

Diderot's two dramas, *Le Fils Naturel* (1757) and *Le Père de Famille* (1758), although unactable and practically unreadable today, are significant or important in the history of the eighteenth-century theatre. Firstly, they inaugurate a new kind of comedy character. The hero of *Le Père de Famille* has no function other than that of being a *père de famille*; the other characters in the play are without personality, distinguishable only by their gestures. It is the exact equivalent of rhetorical painting of the style of Greuze's *Malédiction Paternelle* and is doubtless an important source for it. The hero of the *drame bourgeois* is usually a judge, a lawyer, a merchant or a broker, and the qualities of his class or his profession are more important than the personal and spiritual qualities of the man himself. The idealized bourgeois with his idealized bourgeois virtues now replaces the aristocratic ideal of the previous century. Secondly, they are written in prose. And thirdly, because of Diderot's interests in philosophy, education and the fine arts, his drama shoulders a new weight of morality and relies on extra-dramatic effects. He prefers the optically impressive to the dramatically fitting and often uses an enormous tableau to colour his emotional content. Visualize for a moment the final curtain of *Le Fils Naturel*:

'*Dorval! Rosalie!*' *En disant ces mots le vieillard tend ses bras étendus vers ses enfants qu'il regarde alternativement et qu'il invite à se reconnaître. Dorval et Rosalie se regardent, tombent dans les bras l'un de l'autre et vont ensemble embrasser les genoux de leur père. Lysimond, leur imposant ses mains et levant les yeux au ciel . . .*

Clairville, sans oser approcher, se contente de tendre les bras à Rosalie avec tout le mouvement du désir et de la passion. Il attend. Rosalie le regarde un instant et s'avance. Clairville se précipite et Lysimond les unit . . .

Constance et Dorval s'approchent gravement de Lysimond. Le bon vieillard prend la main de Constance, la baise, et lui présente celle de son fils que Constance reçoit.†

† 'Dorval! Rosalie!' With these words the old man stretches out his arms to his children whom he scrutinizes in turn and whom he urges to acknowledge each other. Dorval and Rosalie look at each other, fall into each other's arms, and go forward together to fall at their father's feet. Lysimond, laying his hands on them and raising his eyes to heaven . . .

Clairville, not daring to approach, merely holds out his arms to Rosalie with an expression of fervent desire and passion. He waits. Rosalie looks at him for a moment and approaches. Clairville rushes forward and Lysimond unites them . . .

Constance and Dorval approach Lysimond with an air of gravity. The good old man takes Constance's hand, kisses it, and gives her in exchange the hand of his son.

From the two dramas of Diderot develops the 'drame bourgeois' as we know it. In describing it, there is little to add to what Diderot has said about it himself. Its plot turns upon some domestic misfortune, although this is usually inflated to a dimension which would remove it from the life of any normal family. Consequently the dramatic element quickly turns to melodrama. The characters who, if they spoke in character would bore any audience to tears within five minutes, express themselves rhetorically and with a great deal of seemingly unprovoked passion. The subject matter is undistinguished, the situations hackneyed, but the marked recurrence of certain themes shows that the public responded more to these than to others. Perhaps the most popular of all is that of the tender-hearted and upright old father and his curiously complicated relations with his equally tender-hearted children. Contemplation of this theme of filial and paternal piety sent Diderot into raptures: '*Un père de famille! quel sujet dans un siècle tel que le nôtre où il ne paraît pas qu'on ait la moindre idée de ce que c'est qu'un père de famille!*'[17] It is the theme of Sedaine's *Philosophe sans le Savoir* of 1765, perhaps the best play of the period, and of *L'Honnête Criminel, ou l'Amour Familial* (1767) of Fenouillot de Falbaire, which ends like this:

> *Lisimon* (*bénissant André et Cécile*):
> '*Puisse un hymen prospère*
> *Vous faire aimer toujours le tendre nom d'époux;*
> *Puissiez-vous, comme moi, dans des moments si doux,*
> *Remercier le ciel du bonheur d'être père.*'†
> (Act V, Scene 6).

It is the basis of Amand's *Cri de la Nature*,[18] gloomier and apparently influenced by Greuze's drawings of *La Malédiction Paternelle* and *Le Fils Puni* in the Salon of 1765:

> *Que mon exemple serve à vous faire connaître*
> *Qu'on ne punit jamais ses enfants sans effort;*
> *Quelque ressentiment que l'on fasse paraître,*
> *Le cri de la nature est toujours le plus fort.*††

We find it in Mercier's *Jenneval* (1770), and in *Joachim, ou la Piété Filiale* (1775) of Blin de Sainmore, a curious play written in the abstract language of noble sentiments and incorporating whole sentences from Corneille and Racine. We

---

† Lisimon (blessing André and Cécile): May a prosperous marriage make you always cherish the tender title of spouse. May you, like me, in such sweet moments thank heaven for the happiness of being a father.

†† May my example serve to teach you that one never punishes one's children without pain. Whatever the anger one may express, the voice of nature is always stronger.

find it in many more minor plays until Florian drowns the theme in a wash of sentiment with *Le Bon Père*, *La Bonne Mère*, *Le Bon Fils*, etc. Other favourite subjects are those of the generous lord of the manor and his loyal tenants, the action of which usually incorporates a love affair between the village beauty and her swain (*L'Erreur d'un Moment*, 1773, *Les Trois Fermiers*, 1777, both by Boutet de Monvel; *L'Epreuve Villageoise*, 1784, by Desforges). This was an offshoot of the pantomime entertainment of Dancourt, Panard and Favart, but was gradually incorporated into the '*drame bourgeois*' and finally given republican status in Collé's *Partie de Chasse de Henri IV* of 1781. There is also the theme of the broken marriage, generally caused by gambling or lack of *sensibilité*, and its terrible results (*L'Ecole des Moeurs, ou les Suites du Libertinage*, 1776, by Fenouillot de Falbaire; *La Femme Jalouse*, 1784, by Desforges).

In addition to this, the intentions of dramatists are marked by an increasing desire to provide a useful lesson for their audiences and to raise the standard of public morality. Beaumarchais introduces his drama *Eugénie* (1767) with these words: 'The subject of my drama is the despair to which the imprudence or the malice of another can lead a young person in the most important action of human life'. (This action is marriage.) Moissy uses the theatre as a means of moral instruction, devoting to each age a little piece in which he resolves human difficulties from the cradle to the grave. This is his epic *Jeux de la Petite Thalie, ou nouveaux petits drames dialogués sur des proverbes, propres à former les moeurs des enfants et des jeunes personnes depuis l'âge de cinq ans et jusqu' à vingt* (1769), followed in 1770 by *L'Ecole dramatique de l'homme, âge viril, depuis vingt ans jusqu' à cinquante*. Moissy is perhaps the most dogmatic, the most willing to subordinate dramatic effect to the making of a moral point, of all the eighteenth-century dramatists. His play, *La Vraie Mère* (1771), for instance, is entirely given over to the encouragement of maternal breast-feeding. The cast consists of Mme Félibien, 'a mother for seven months, nursing her child', Mme de Villepreux, 'pregnant and nearly at term', Mme des Aulnes, 'a mother for nine and a half months', and their respective husbands. Mme Félibien, doing her best to convince an unbelieving and somewhat disrespectful husband, delivers herself of a statement which defies translation: '... *tiens-tu assez à la grossièreté de tes sens pour ne regarder ces mamelles, respectable trésor de la nature, que comme un relief de pur embellissement, destiné seulement à orner la poitrine des femmes?*' No less highminded but with a more concentrated sense of theatre is Fenouillot de Falbaire, whose *Ecole des Moeurs, ou les suites du libertinage* evidently had its effect, for according to the preface, 'the moment this work was announced, alarm spread through houses of ill fame . . . the tocsin sounded in the temple of Pleasure; the plumes of the doves of Venus stood on end; her priestesses and her warriors, even the veterans, took up their arms, and all rushed to the theatre to fight for their domain'.

And in all these plays the virtues are attendant on a softening process. '*Sois sensible, sans l'âme il n'y a point de génie*',[19] says Le Mierre. Here is a typical, though late, example of a tender scene, beloved of author and audience alike. It is taken from Desforges' *La Femme Jalouse* and it illustrates a meeting between two girls in different walks of life who turn out to be half-sisters:

Eugénie: *Je sens, en vous voyant, une joie infinie*
         Mademoiselle, mais

Clémence: *C'est un grand bien pour moi.*

Eugénie: (*à part*) *Ah! tant mieux. Mon coeur bat, je ne sais pas pourquoi.*
        Eh! quelle est-elle donc, cette jeune étrangère?
        Qui, depuis un instant—(*Haut*) *Rassurez-vous, ma chère,*
    (*à part*) *Pourquoi donc, à la voir ai-je tant de plaisir?*
        Que de la voir toujours, j'ai déjà le désir?
    (*Haut, après un temps*)
        Tenez, embrassons-nous—*car je m'en meurs d'envie.*

Clémence: *Ah! d'un si doux acceuil que mon âme est ravie!*
    Je sens couler mes pleurs.

Eugénie: *Je vais pleurer aussi.*
    C'est singulier—*qui peut nous attendrir ainsi?*

Clémence: *Vous, c'est la pitie*—*moi, c'est la reconnaissance.*

Eugénie: *Vous ne m'en devez pas*—*Je cède à la puissance*
    D'un sentiment bien doux qui n'est point la pitié,
    Et je croirais plutôt que c'est de l'amitié.†

† Eugénie: I feel at the sight of you a great joy, Mademoiselle, but . . .
Clémence: I am glad of it.
Eugénie: (Aside) So much the better. My heart beats strangely, I know not why. Who is this young stranger who suddenly—(Aloud) Don't worry, my dear, (aside) why do I enjoy seeing her so much that I want to go on seeing her always? (Aloud, after a moment). Come, let us embrace, for I am dying to do so.
Clémence: Ah! My soul is ravished by such a tender welcome. I feel my tears flow.
Eugénie: Mine too. How extraordinary—why are we so moved?
Clémence: With you it's pity—with me, gratitude.
Eugénie: You owe me nothing. I yield to the force of a sweet sentiment which has nothing to do with pity and I should say that it is more likely to be friendship.

This softening process reacted on author as well as on audience. Diderot's remark after a performance of *Le Philosophe sans le Savoir*—'I must be an honourable man for I feel the merit of this work most keenly'[20]—is a little too good to be typical. More significant is the impulse which moved Beaumarchais to make this statement: 'Sometimes, in the middle of an agreeable scene, a charming emotion brings forth abundant and easy tears which mingle with the grace of the smile and give to the face an expression of compassion and joy. Is not such a conflict the finest triumph of art and the sweetest of states for the heart which experiences it? Compassion has an additional advantage over laughter: whenever it is felt it has a powerful effect on the person who feels it'.[21]

A new and more lurid note was introduced by Greuze's friend Louis-Sébastien Mercier. Mercier, whose noisy iconoclasm would appear to date him in the 1830s rather than in the 1780s, has definite political and humanitarian reasons for upholding the '*drame bourgeois*'. In fact the accent in his plays is less bourgeois than proletarian in appeal: 'However perfect a drama, it is useless if it does not appeal to the people'.[22] Mercier, like Diderot, produced an enormous wealth of critical writing to serve as introduction to his plays. He repeats in more emphatic terms the theories of his predecessors. 'What is dramatic art? It is the art which, above all others, exercises our *sensibilité* . . . teaches us to be decent and virtuous . . . no appeal to the soul of man by impressions of pity and compassion can be too strong.'[23] Like Diderot and like Rousseau, the effect on himself is tremendous ('I weep and I feel with ecstasy that I am a man').[24] But no less important is the fact that the drama is more democratic than tragedy for it speaks to 'the multitude which contains a host of uncorrupted and impressionable souls who are only waiting to hear the voice of nature in order to be moved'.[25] Mercier wants the drama to be 'a school of the virtues and the duties of the citizen'[26] and to contain 'healthier ideas on politics and legislation'.[27] Only, however, in *La Brouette du Vinaigrier* (1775), which has the authentic 'two nations' touch, does this appear, but the inflammable prose of the prefaces seems at least a generation in advance, while his dramatic intentions anticipate those of Victor Hugo.

The success, popularity and moral effect of the '*drame bourgeois*' cannot be over-estimated. That it was negligible as literature was overlooked; its impact was irresistible. As La Harpe very rightly said of Diderot, '. . . his theatrical poetry and dramatic efforts have contributed to the decadence of the theatre and of taste. He made a curious mistake in thinking that people

35

would prefer nature in the raw, which is the antithesis of art, to refined and embellished nature which is the material on which art is built. He has left dreadful warnings and examples by showing confident mediocrities how to turn out these monstrous productions known as dramas, without choice or dignity of subject matter; without correctness, without manners, and above all without style'.[28] Yet La Harpe himself, in addition to being a fervent admirer of Greuze, produced one of the most pathetic dramas of the period (*Mélanie*, 1770). The significance of the '*drame bourgeois*' lies less in the play than in the audience. As Grimm remarked, 'All men are friends when they emerge from the theatre. They have jeered vice, applauded virtue, wept together, and developed side by side everything that is good and just in the human heart. They are much better people than they thought they were; they could easily fall into each other's arms'.[29] The enjoyment of a good cry automatically suggested one's own tender-heartedness; this had been done by the novel. The theatre brought it into the public sector and inevitably competition arose in ways of proving it. The excesses of *sensibilité*, the swooning reactions and rapturous tears, can all be traced to this source. And incidentally the pictures of Greuze would seem incomprehensible if we did not understand that the public sought for a pictorial equivalent of its favourite plays.

Sensibilité in Painting

The development of *sensibilité* in painting is hardly as clear-cut as the movement in literature. It leads a curiously independent existence until the middle of the century when it undergoes an almost unconditional surrender to the '*drame bourgeois*', and to a lesser extent the novel. Generally speaking, two trends should be kept in mind: the development, under the influence of the little Dutch masters, of the painting of anecdote, and the enjoyment of sentimental painters such as Correggio, Guido Reni and Murillo. These two trends were eventually combined by Greuze into the sentimental genre of which he was a master, but before his advent it will be necessary to take into account a number of cross-currents without which his work would not have been possible.

It should be stressed that here we are dealing with a resolutely democratic art which, it must be remembered, occupied a minor position in the overall hierarchy of painting. The primary position was represented by the art of the Académie and the Court, and the official commissions that accrued. During Greuze's working life, Carle van Loo was King's Painter until 1765, to be succeeded by Boucher until his death in 1770; Boucher was then succeeded by the almost universally disliked Pierre, who reigned until the Académie was dissolved in the Revolution. Their art is irrelevant to the productions of Greuze, although he became so popular that at one point he was summoned to Versailles to paint portraits of the Dauphin and Dauphine. Apart from a brief moment in the late 1750s and early 1760s, when Greuze appears to take Boucher's art into account, and, of course, the fiasco of 1769 when Greuze's bid to become a history painter failed, their two worlds do not connect. The kind of art which formed Greuze's style is a distinctly middle- or even lower-class art which ignores the standards of Italy, supreme in the French Académie until 1690, has its origins in Dutch seventeenth-century painting, rose to its apogée in the 1760s and 1770s, and then faded away, leaving the field clear for the radically different style of David. It is all too readily forgotten that this democratic or plebeian genre is as representative of eighteenth-century France as is the frivolous and technically immaculate art of Boucher and Fragonard.

The origins of genre painting in France in the eighteenth century must be sought in the victory of the Rubenists over the Poussinists which set up an interest not only in the work of Rubens and his followers but of painters such as Rembrandt and his school who were even more independent of academic influence. For the first years of the century the Flemish school was in the ascendant; it was, after all, the figurehead of an official argument, and it influenced not only the work but the training of several artists. The influence of Rubens is evident in the work of such transitional painters as Antoine Coypel and Charles de la Fosse, who was said to be 'very much in favour of Rubens and Van Dyck, saying that these painters had even surpassed the Venetians in certain aspects of their colour'.[1] Jouvenet and Largillière did not go to Rome at all; they went to Antwerp, and Largillière frequently upheld this action as one of extreme importance for his artistic career. Oudry reports, 'M. de Largillière told me many times that he had been trained in the School of Flanders and that he owed his success to its teachings: he often expressed regret at the little importance which our own school seemed to accord to lessons which could be of immense service to it'.[2] Similar sympathies can be traced in Rigaud and Desportes. Rigaud possessed eight Van Dycks and seven Rembrandts. It is important to remember that the first wave of enthusiasm for Rembrandt dates from very early in the century. In the Salon of 1704 Louis de Boullogne showed '*une teste dans la manière de Vandeck at une autre dans le goust de Rimbran*'. Charles Coypel possessed ten pictures by Rembrandt, Santerre copied his *Girl at a Window* (Orleans), while Michael Serre painted a head in the manner of Rembrandt for his Académie reception piece in 1704. Raoux, who, according to Voltaire, 'has equalled Rembrandt',[3] produced numerous pictures in his style, for example, the *Rabbin méditant sur la Bible* which passed through a sale in 1786, while a preoccupation with Rembrandtesque lighting is apparent in Grimou's *Pilgrim* (Louvre), *Portrait of a Girl* (Karlsruhe), and many others.

The influence of the little Dutch masters, which was to be of primary importance for both the painting of genre and the painting of *sensibilité*, began to make itself felt in the second and third decades of the century. La Font de Saint-Yenne and the Marquis d'Argens, both of whom upheld the grand style of painting, wrote bitterly of this change of taste: 'Today, to the enduring shame of the arts, one sees so-called lovers of painting forming large collections of little Dutch pictures which they buy at exorbitant prices, although the only merit such pictures have is a servile imitation of the lowest form of nature, offering the spirit images incapable of inspiring those virile and sublime ideas that the great history painters provide for those who examine their works with attention'.[4] That this taste was not exclusive to the less elevated classes of society is proved by the fact that the most important collector of the day, the Duc d'Orléans, owned nine pictures by Teniers, five by Poelemberg, three by Dou, four by Wouwermans, four by Breenbergh, and seven by Netscher. In order to get some idea of the esteem in which such masters were held, it is necessary to reverse the historical order and study catalogues of sales from about 1760 to 1780 when most of the great collections seem to have broken up.

Three points emerge from such an analysis. The first is that Dutch pictures were preferred to Flemish. At the Gaignat sale of 1768, a Van Dyck portrait (*President Richardot*) was sold for 9,200 livres, while a Wouwermans *Horse Market* went for 14,560 livres. The important collection of the Comte de Vence contained a preponderance of Dutch over Flemish pictures. At the Choiseul sale of 1772 a Rubens landscape (*The Storm*) was sold for the ridiculous sum of 2,401 livres, while two *Philosophers* by Rembrandt went for 14,000 livres. A similar scale of prices operated at the Randon de Boisset sale of 1777; a Dou interior fetched only 2,500 livres less than the great Rubens *Hélène Fourment and her children*, while the Van Dyck *Richardot* was sold for 4,500 livres less than a village scene by Isaac van Ostade.

A second point that emerges is the preference for small genre independent of artistic renown. The subject assumed an increasing importance, and an unvarnished domestic scene was often more in demand than a picture by a well-known or famous artist. For example, at the Gaignat sale, a Rembrandt *Holy Family* went for 5,450 livres, and an Adrian van Ostade *Farmyard Scene with Men drinking* for 10,800 livres. At the Blondel de Gagny sale (1776) a Metsu *Herb Market* fetched 25,800 livres, as against a Rembrandt *Vertumnus and Pomona* which went for 13,700 livres. At the Choiseul sale, Rembrandt's *Saying Grace* was sold for 4,200 livres and a Dou *Game Merchant's Stall* for 17,300 livres. In the Randon de Boisset sale, Terborch, Wynants, Adrian van Ostade, Dou, Berchem, Potter, Frans Mieris, and Adrian van de Velde were fetching the same prices as Rembrandt (about 10,000 livres), while Teniers and Wouwermans were fetching more. Rembrandt seems to have appealed far more to artists than to collectors. He was studied and copied by Raoux, Grimou, Cazes, Santerre, Vleughels, Fragonard and Greuze, but his style was perhaps too serious and unembellished for a picture of his to be the prize of an eighteenth-century French collection.

Thirdly, sales catalogues show an astonishing and almost universal slump in Italian pictures. The prices quoted above are exclusive to the northern schools, with one or two exceptions which are discussed later in this chapter. In the immense collection of the Comte de Vence, four or five paintings only are by Italian masters. The Duc de Choiseul had half a dozen, one of which was Titian's portrait of Roberto Strozzi's daughter. At his sale, this picture was sold for 1,000 livres, which should be compared with other prices at the same sale: Greuze, *Petite Fille en camisole de nuit*, 7,200 livres (the highest price for a picture of the French school); Adrian van der Werff, *Dice Players*, 12,150 livres; and Paul Potter, *A Hunting Party near the Hague*, 27,400 livres. At the sale of Blondel de Gagny, Pietro da Cortona's *Herminia and Clorinda* fetched 1,000 livres, as against Teniers' *Village Festival* which went for 11,000 livres. In the Randon de Boisset sale, a *Holy Family* by Annibale Carracci was sold for 76 livres only, while a Dou *Self Portrait* went for 12,900 livres. In the same sale, an Albani *Triumph of Venus* and a Salvator Rosa *Landscape with Tobias and the Angel* fetched 5,600 and 7,200 livres respectively. For these artists, through the agencies of Boucher and Vernet, had to a certain extent been assimilated into the current French style. No use, however, could be found for the grand subject in the Bolognese manner, or for portraits or allegories in the manner of the High Renaissance.

It should be remembered that between 1704 and 1737 there were no official Salons and the Parisian public's knowledge of works of art become confined to two sources: engravings of pictures in private collections, and the only exhibitions not controlled by the Académie, those of the Académie de Saint-Luc and the Exposition de la Jeunesse, where the inspiration was mainly Flemish. The popularity of Dutch genre pictures was greatly spread by means of engravings, which reached a high standard in the hands of Aliamet, Basan, Le Bas and Jean-Georges Wille. These men occupy an extremely important position as being the agents by means of which knowledge of the finest examples in private collections was diffused and popularized. To give a small but secure example of this, Moitte, in 1754, engraved the entire collection of the Comte de Brühl, which included Mieris' *Broken Eggs*. Greuze knew Moitte and it is likely that the latter's engraving after Mieris was the basis of Greuze's picture of the same name dating from 1757. Artists collected engravings by the hundred, as is attested by Wille's diary; they were their major means of study in default of immediate examples.

In the collection of engravings by Aliamet in the Bibliothèque Nationale in Paris, Berchem and Teniers preponderate. The *oeuvre* of Basan fills five large folio volumes. Of these, pictures by French and Italian masters fill perhaps two-thirds of one volume. The rest are given over to Teniers (above all), Molenaer, Steen, Both, Craesbeck, Brouwer, Brekelenkam, the Ostades, Kalf, Berchem, Terborch, Dou, Metsu, Netscher, Schalcken and others. Le Bas' edition of his work (1789) is interesting; it contains engravings of over ninety pictures by Teniers, all from private collections, the rest after Wouwermans, Van Falens, Van de Velde, Paul Potter, Karel du Jardin, Brouwer, Miel, Bril, Breenbergh, Ostade, Rembrandt, Ruysdael, Pynacker, Lingelbach and Wynants. There are a handful of engravings after Rubens, two after Chantereau and five after Parrocel (both these men painted in the Dutch style), one or two after Descamps, illustrating scenes from a *'drame bourgeois'*, two after Besnard, a genre painter of the Académie de Saint-Luc, half a dozen after Le Bas himself on subjects generally treated by Teniers and Wouwermans, and very little else. Wille's favourite artist was apparently Dou, whom he engraved very beautifully, and it is significant to note that the typical Dou motif of an open window with a figure leaning out passed into French genre painting in the 1740s, and became a commonplace in pictures by Chardin, Jeaurat, Schenau, and many other minor artists.

It will now be obvious that certain artists were favourites. According to the Marquis d'Argens, writing in 1752, *'Téniers a été pendant longtemps en vogue; après lui vinrent Wouwerman, Poelembourg, Gerar-Dou, Mieris; mais aujourd'hui c'est Ostade, Mezu, Potter, van de Velde, van der Werff qui remportent le prix'*. As a matter of interest, the younger Teniers enjoyed a continuous run of popularity and his pictures fetched fantastic prices until the end of the century. At the Gaignat sale of 1768, his *Bon Vieillard distribuant du Pain aux Pauvres*, with its wealth of pietistic elders and mothers nursing their children, was sold for 7,200 livres against a Titian portrait which went for less than half the price; while at the Blondel de Gagny sale, his *Enfant Prodigue* fetched the enormous sum of 30,000 livres, more than the combined prices of all the Italian pictures in the sale. An almost disproportionate number of his works are to be found in the collections of the Comte de Vence, the Comte de Brühl, the Duc de Valentinois, the Marquis d'Argenson, Jullienne, Blondel de Gagny, Randon de Boisset, the Duc de Choiseul, and the Prince de Conti.

41

Diderot pronounced, 'I would give ten Watteaus for one Teniers', and 'the French Teniers', a term applied successively to Watteau, Chardin, Greuze and Lépicié, became the highest praise to which a French genre painter could aspire. Teniers was closely followed by Wouwermans,

> . . . 'cet heureux Wouwermans,
> Qui peignit les coursiers jusqu'aux hennissements'[5]†

as Le Mierre so unfortunately put it. Wouwermans was excellently imitated by Pater and Parrocel the younger, and was followed in his turn by Dou and Mieris, who remained firm favourites, and finally by Terborch and Metsu, the point of departure of such derivative artists as Pierre-Alexandre Wille and, later in the century, Marguerite Gérard.

The stream of *sensibilité*, before channelled by Greuze to the painting of anecdote, trickled through indirectly. The source was perhaps Correggio, seven of whose paintings, including an ecstatically melting Magdalen, were exhibited at the Orléans gallery at the beginning of the century. The influence of Correggio is apparent in Santerre and becomes acute in the Annunciation of Antoine Coypel for the chapel at Meudon. Equal in importance was Guido Reni, who was now classed as a master on the same level as Raphael and Titian. The Duc d'Orléans possessed no less than fifteen of his works, including two Magdalens. Guido Reni's heads of female saints are of course an important source for Greuze who seems to have been the first artist in the eighteenth century to respond to the appeal of this master. Other artists, whose emotional content is now considered excessive, suddenly boomed. An outstanding example of this is Murillo. It has been suggested that the emotional character of mature *sensibilité* has something in common with the sensual and operatic emotionalism of Baroque, and that a parallel could be drawn between the head of Bernini's *Saint Theresa*, and, let us say, the *Colombe Retrouvée* of Greuze. Be that as it may, this dualism of sensuality and sentiment is well expressed in the paintings of Murillo, and the tremendous esteem in which his work was held cannot be explained by any factor other than that of fulfilling a particular need at a particular time. At the Jullienne sale of 1767, his *Marriage at Cana* was bought by the Prince de Conti for 6,000 livres, the highest single French bid for a painting of the southern schools of the entire sale, and at the Blondel de Gagny sale of 1776, his *Bohémienne*, which had just the right touch of self-conscious *gaminerie* for a French public, fetched 12,000 livres, an infinitely higher figure than any paid

† Happy Wouwermans, who painted horses down to the last whinny.

for an Italian picture, putting him in the same class as Teniers and Metsu. Grimou made copies after Murillo, and there were Murillos in the collection of the Duc de Tallard, Gaignat (a *Holy Family* which fetched the highest price of the entire sale—17,535 livres), Choiseul, Calonne, Randon de Boisset, and many others.

The Salons of 1699 and 1704 had contained a number of genre paintings but these were produced by relatively few artists: Parrocel, Bon Boullogne, and Alexandre in 1699; Alexandre, Bon Boullogne, Van Schuppen and Mlle Chéron in 1704. Certain of their subjects are easily traceable to Dutch sources, such as Bon Boullogne's *Jeune fille qui cherche des puces à sa compagne*, or Alexandre's *Vieille qui remet un billet à une fille touchant de la viole*, and are therefore fundamentally imitative in character. Others, such as Bon Boullogne's *Amour embrassant un pigeon*, spring naturally from the conventions of decorative painting. The only original themes are those which cannot be grouped under any convenient heading but which have been variously characterized as '*sujets galants*' or '*sujets d'agrément*', such as Mlle Chéron's *Deux jeunes filles qui accordent un clavecin* or the indefatigable Bon Boullogne's *Jeune fille essayant d'attraper un oiseau envolé*. (Bon Boullogne is the most important genre painter of this generation; in addition to producing a considerable volume of work, he was the master of Christophe, Cazes—who trained Chardin—Bertin, Tournières, Raoux and Santerre.) Most of these early genre paintings have disappeared and one has to rely for proof of their existence on Salon catalogues, but it is possible to say that this original, if temporary, style makes a definite contribution to the art of the Régence period and the years immediately following, and in the 1730s becomes elaborated into the upper-middle-class genre of Jean-Francois de Troy, Eisen, Cochin and Carle van Loo.

For a time, genre painting was swamped by the highly individual interpretations of Watteau and the continuation of his style by his pupils, Lancret, and Pater. Watteau, a Fleming by inheritance and made susceptible to the Dutch influence by training (he had served an apprenticeship in a shop on the Pont Notre Dame where he was employed to copy Dou's *St Nicholas* and *Vieille femme lisant*), managed nevertheless by virtue of his own strong artistic personality to incorporate these trends into a style which belonged completely to his own time and his own surroundings. Several genre trends can be distinguished in Watteau. There are single figures in the tradition of the popular and anonymous prints of street cries of Paris and fashion plate engravings, such as the early *Fileuse* (known only by an engraving) and the

43

Montreur de Marmotte (Leningrad, Hermitage) which became metamorphosed into *La Finette* and *L'Indifférent* (Louvre). There are scenes inspired by the theatre and by plays such as Dancourt's *Les Trois Cousines* and *La Foire de Bezons*, yet curiously enough this relationship reacted more on stage décor than on painting: an example that springs to mind is that of the extremely painterly stage directions given at the beginnings of Favart's comic operas. There are the military scenes of 1710, unheroic, unprofessional, totally different in style from those of his predecessors Parrocel the elder and Van der Meulen. And finally there are scenes like *La Vraie Gaieté* (London, private collection), and *L'Accordée de Village* (London, Soane Museum), which are unmistakably inspired by Teniers.

The Teniers element in Watteau was appropriated by his ephemeral followers Octavien and Bonaventure de Bar and is very evident in the work of Lancret, for example, in the right half of *La Vieillesse* (London, National Gallery), last in the series of *Les Quatre Ages de la Vie*, and on a larger scale in the *Fête dans un Bois* (London, Wallace Collection), *Fête en Plein Air* (Potsdam), and *Festin de Village* and *Repas de Noce de Village* (Angers). A more robust and purely Dutch note appears at the end of Lancret's life. The *Montreur de Boîte Optique* (Potsdam) is nearer to Ostade, and the *Chercheuse de Puces* (London, Wallace Collection) and *Le Galant Valet* (Hermitage) seem to have been based on either Dou or Kalf. That he had at some time studied Kalf is evident from this note in the catalogue of the Montesquiou sale (1786): '*Kalf et Lancret: intérieur d'une laiterie, richement ornée de divers accessoires; l'on voit sur la gauche un puits entouré de poterie, pot à lait et autres ustensiles de ménage; sur la droite sont placés quatre figures sur différents plans par Lancret*'.†

Pater, a painter of lower vitality, reflects the influence of Teniers in his large pieces but is also interested in Wouwermans. His various *Haltes* and *Marches de Troupes* are perhaps the most faithful interpretation of this artist to be found in the painting of the eighteenth century.

Apart from Watteau and his school, the artistic situation as a whole and the development of genre painting in particular were static in the extreme in the second and third decades of the century. Cochin, speaking of this period with relation to the life of Chardin, paints a very different picture from that popularized by the brothers Goncourt: 'At that time the art of painting languished without support or protection. With the exception of M. le

---

† Kalf and Lancret: interior of a dairy richly decorated with various objects; on the left one sees a well surrounded by earthenware pots, milk churns and other household articles; on the right are four figures placed on different levels by Lancret.

Moyne, M. de Troy, and a few portrait painters, all the others lived in a state of mediocrity verging on poverty. Very few pictures were executed for private collectors; the churches rarely gave commissions and if they did the price was so low that one could barely live on it. Pictures for Notre Dame, which had to be done in duplicate, one large, one small, were only paid 400 livres. It was the same with those done for the abbey of St Germain des Prés. Nevertheless they were highly sought after for they were a sure method of advertising one's talents. The custom of exhibitions at the Salon was not yet in force and one can say that this fortunate establishment saved painting, by a prompt showing of the most worthy talents and by inspiring with a love of the arts a number of people who, without the exhibition, would never have given them a thought.'

It says much for the vitality of the genre trend that when the Salon re-opened in 1737, the list of exhibits showed that not only had the volume of genre paintings increased but that there were more genre painters: Cazes, Carle van Loo, Jean-Francis de Troy, Charles-Antoine Coypel, Huilliot, Lancret, Chavanne, Boisot, Bouys, and the two outstanding artists of the period, Chardin and Aved. Genre painting now tended to fall into two categories, refined and plebeian, the first consisting of the followers of Watteau, together with Van Loo, Coypel, De Troy, Oudry and Desportes; the second of Chardin and Aved and their followers. It would seem as if the future lay with the first group through sheer weight of numbers, yet the second group had behind it the vitality of the Flemish settlement in Paris of the seventeenth century, the Exposition de la Jeunesse and the Académie de Saint-Luc, and those amateurs of Dutch and Flemish pictures whom the Marquis d'Argens upbraided so bitterly.

Actually the situation remained stalemate for several years, and the Salons of the 1730s and 1740s show little variation; Chardin, Aved, Tocqué, Desportes, Oudry, Parrocel and Lancret are the most constant names, while Francisque Millet establishes himself as a landscape painter. The only incursions are by minor artists such as Delobel, Poitreau and Autereau, with one solitary visitation by Portail. By the end of the 1740s, however, the situation had been reversed by the enormous esteem which had grown up around Chardin, who, by his example, had won the first victory of prestige for lower-middle-class genre painting. It seems invidious to speak of Chardin (who made his début in the Place Dauphine) in terms of influences. He is the moment of equilibrium; he marks the point of assimilation of foreign influences and transforms them into a style that is purely French. Mariette, indeed, speaks of him as continuing the tradition of the Le Nains. Yet from our point of view, it is necessary to remember that the source of his genre paintings is usually Dutch; *Le Bénédicité* and *La Pourvoyeuse* stem from Maes, *Les Bulles de Savon* from Dou, and the technical devices of *Le Jeune Dessinateur* and *La Petite Fille aux Cerises* from Vermeer. Chardin was after all a pupil of the early popularizer of Dutch genre, Cazes. Perhaps no artist in the eighteenth century was so universally admired by his colleagues. From his first appearance in the Salon (1737), his pictures aroused nothing but enthusiasm. Gougenot, who called him 'the French Teniers', made this significant remark: '. . . the genre of M. Chardin comes very near to history painting'[6]. This was in 1748, an important date in the history of French genre painting, for the first time accepted in its unvarnished simplicity and not parading as a piece of agreeable illustration.

The posterity of Chardin is interesting. He was engraved by F.-B. Lépicié, Charpentier, Cochin the elder, Surrugue, Dupin and Filloeil between 1738 and 1757, after which date there are no more announcements in the *Mercure de France*. His engravings were popular, setting a fashion all their own, and this statement of Mariette's shows the importance of his career not only for itself but for the wider aspect of French painting as a whole: '. . . they are the engravings most in favour at the moment and together with those of Teniers, Wouwermans and Lancret they have put paid to the serious engravings after Le Brun, Poussin, Le Sueur and even Coypel. The general public is delighted with the sight of actions which it sees every day in its own home, and without hesitation prefers them to more elevated subjects which demand a certain amount of hard work'.[7]

Chardin had many imitators: Jeaurat in certain moods, N.-B. Lépicié, Dumesnil of the Académie de Saint-Luc, J.-B. Charpentier, painter to the Duc de Penthièvre, and, later in the century, Martin Drolling. Yet all of these, good artists in their way, mark a falling off from the calm and solidity of Chardin's style. Perhaps his most faithful imitator is Pierre-Louis Dumesnil, most of whose work is now known only through the medium of Le Bas' engravings. He specialized in scenes of children with their mothers, nurses or tutors, quiet, unpretentious, and with considerable charm. He exhibited at the Académie de Saint-Luc from 1751 to 1774, after which date nothing is heard of him. J.-B. Charpentier, who has an infinitely lighter touch, seems also to have been influenced by Boucher and Baudouin. He is a constant plagiarist, never bothering to find a new theme, but an agreeable artist, as his *Espièglerie près d'une fontaine* (Chartres) demonstrates. Drolling, with his constant desire to embellish, seems to proceed from Charpentier, but all refer back to the standards and patterns set originally by Chardin.

Charpentier, in fact, is the first of the second generation of French genre painters, men like Schenau, Pierre-Alexandre Wille, Bounieu, Bénazech, Quéverdo, Moreau le jeune, Demarne, Freudeberg, Peters and Chodowiecki, who exist by painting slight variations on themes made popular by bigger men. A study of genre painting before Greuze must therefore end with Charpentier. It is interesting, however, to note in this connection that the trend of straight imitation from Dutch models lingered on among painters of humble pretensions, as can be seen in the list of exhibits at the Académie de Saint-Luc from 1751 until it was closed in 1774. In 1751, Besnard showed a *Cuisine* and a *Cuisine dans le goût flamand*, and in 1772 a *Mangeur d'Huitres*. In 1756, Lemercier showed a *Soldat revenant de campagne avec un congé de semestre* and a *Dormeuse*. In 1764 Delepine showed *Un Patissier et un cabaretier, deux sujets de nuit*, Bernou, *Un jeu de sifflet* and *Un vieillard disant la bonne aventure à une jeune fille*, and as late as 1774, Dumesnil, *Deux femmes, l'une brûlant du café, et l'autre occupée à le moudre*.

One more abortive influence remains to be dealt with: that of England and of Hogarth. An American writer, dealing with this subject, has made a very elliptical and misleading statement which, through sheer wishful thinking, many people are inclined to accept: 'Genre painting served its purpose in establishing materialism as a valid aesthetic creed, but it was incapable of serving as a weapon in a social struggle . . . from the Dutch the French assimilated genre painting, and from the English they borrowed the philosophical and moral concepts of the bourgeoisie, together with its literary and sentimental ideas'.[8] This is far from being the whole truth, for *sensibilité* in France remains throughout a distinct and unincorporated movement with strong social and historical roots, but it is undeniably true that the attention of French artists in the late 1740s and early 1750s turned to England and to Hogarth.

The problem of how much Hogarth's work was known in France in the first half of the century is one which needs a great deal of investigation. Nor has his visit to France in 1743 ever been subjected to a rigorous and searching enquiry. There are no French engravings after Hogarth in the Bibliothèque Nationale in Paris, although it is obvious that his own engravings must have been brought back by French artists visiting England. A striking example of his influence is to be found in the work of Etienne Jeaurat who, in pieces like the *Place Maubert* (Earl Beauchamp collection) or the *Place des Halles* (Salon of 1757), has an English model in mind. His *Carnaval des rues de Paris* (Salon of 1757) and *Enlèvement de Police* (Earl Beauchamp collection) are obviously connected with Hogarth's *March to Finchley*, and his *Déménagement du Peintre* (Earl Beauchamp collection) with Hogarth's *Distrest poet* or *Enrag'd musician*. Yet Jeaurat is completely blind to the essence of Hogarth's work; he seizes only on the picturesque aspect and ignores the weight of moral teaching which it carries. Just as the French failed to enjoy the novels of Fielding, they failed to enjoy the satires of Hogarth. It was precisely the element of social satire that was outside their mental range. The essence of Hogarth's work was to be made known to the French not in the form of engravings but by verbal descriptions, those of J.-A. Rouquet, whose *Lettres de M. X à un de ses amis à Paris pour lui expliquer les estampes de M. Hogarth* were published in 1746, and, more important, *Etat des Arts en Angleterre* in 1755. From these we learn that, 'M. Hogarth has provided England with a new type of picture; these contain a considerable number of figures, usually seven or eight inches high. These singular works are properly speaking the story of various vices . . . They are sometimes a little overcrowded for foreign eyes but always full of wit and novelty. He is adept at introducing into his works an opportunity of censuring ridicule and vice by means of a strong and purposeful delineation which springs from a lively, fertile, and judicious imagination . . . He does not so much seek to make fun of vice as to render it odious.' Greuze was the first to incorporate this moral teaching into his work in the drawings of *La Malédiction Paternelle* and *Le Fils Puni* exhibited at the Salon of 1765. These did not meet with very great success. True to the native French tradition, Greuze's more serious moralizings were deplored (see below). But his strong connection with Hogarth is doubly proved by the existence of a scenario, entitled *Bazile et Thibault, ou les deux éducations* (see Appendix), for a series of pictures or more probably engravings clearly based on Hogarth's series of the *Idle and Industrious Apprentices*.

These were the external influences which shaped French genre painting in the eighteenth century. We have now to deal with an internal influence which not only developed a public for it but which formed an entirely new school of taste and appreciation.

The outstanding characteristics of French eighteenth-century writings on art is their empiricism, a reflection of the philosophical movement which in some cases is brought to our notice with surprising clarity. This statement, for example, is made not by a writer on philosophy or the new morality but by the Comte de Caylus in his *Discourse on Harmony and Colour*: '... it is certain that we have no innate ideas and that the gifts of nature consist in a greater or lesser aptitude, or a more ready disposition of the fibres in certain persons to receive an impression and to make it bear fruit'. French writers have underlined the parallel existing between the aesthetic of Le Brun and the philosophy of Descartes and have given many examples of the rigidity of the system which these interdependent teachings brought into existence. The emancipation of philosophy and the supercession of Descartes which took place at the turn of the century were bound, if not to create a new aesthetic, at least to invalidate the old one. It is a sign of surprising vitality that by 1720 we find a new attitude not only in existence but most explicitly and most forcibly expressed.

The new attitude originated inside the Académie, possibly in the teachings of Antoine Coypel who made statements such as: '... The principal object that the arts should set themselves is to give pleasure...'. Yet this is too general, has too much the character of an *obiter dictum* to arouse much discussion, and until Tocqué's *Réflexions sur la peinture et particulièrement sur le genre du portrait* (1750), this remains the character of most Académie pronouncements. Until given the benefit of a wider appreciation, the new attitude could not hope for independent status. This was provided in 1719 by the Abbé Du Bos and his *Réflexions sur la poésie et sur la peinture*.

Du Bos is the outstanding aesthetician of the eighteenth century, the Le Brun of the new situation. La Font de Saint-Yenne, Le Blanc, Bachaumont and D'Alembert are but pale reflections of him; Diderot merely describes his principles in practice. The attitude of Du Bos is that later elaborated by Helvétius, namely that natural instinct is the motive factor in any situation, spiritual, moral or aesthetic: '... aesthetic taste and physical taste are the same'. Consequently, innate ideas, or in this case, aesthetic principles are out of the question. 'Now, feeling is a better guide to whether a work moves us and makes the desired impression on us than all the dissertations composed by critics to explain its merits and to work out its perfections and defects. The method of discussion and analysis is certainly good when examining the causes of whether a work does or does not give pleasure but this method does not compare with that of feeling when we have to decide, 'Does this work please us or not? Is the work generally good or bad?' It is the same thing. Reason should therefore not intervene in the judgement we make on a poem or a picture except to justify the decision that feeling has already decreed.'

How can 'feeling' derive the maximum satisfaction from a work of art? Not by contemplation but by participation. Painting and poetry procure for us passion without its sometimes disagreeable accompaniments. Passion is the highest state to which man (i.e. natural man) can rise. Therefore that which in a work of art can procure for man the same emotional excitement as a parallel situation in real life shall be called good. 'Of all the talents that give one influence over others, the most powerful is not superiority of intellect and learning; it is the ability to move them as one wishes.' And when the object of a work of art is to excite the emotions, a new weight of responsibility falls on the subject matter. 'The moment the principal merit of a poem or a picture consists of the representation of objects capable of arousing our emotions if we were involved in the real situation, it is easy to realize how important the choice of subject is for painters and poets. In fact it cannot be too important.'

The importance of the subject is therefore supreme, as it was in the seventeenth century, but it has a different set of duties to fulfil, those duties being to satisfy the moral and emotional conscience of '*l'homme sensible*'. Treatment of the subject is irrelevant; technique must find its own level. This dualism of narrow inventive scope and extreme technical freedom persisted until the advent of David. Diderot's conception of the artist as a man of intense and tumultuous feelings has its origin in the doctrine of the Abbé Du Bos. The standards of appreciation which Diderot upheld—'Move me, astonish me, unnerve me, make me tremble, weep, shudder, rage, then delight my eyes afterwards, if you care to'—are merely a more explicit version of the requirements of the Abbé Du Bos who stated: 'Since the primary object of poetry and painting is to play on the emotions, poems and pictures are only good if they move and involve us. A work which moves us a great deal must be excellent from every point of view'. It was precisely this sort of standard which assured the success of the pictures of Greuze.

Du Bos had laid down rules both for the artist and the spectator. Writers of the 1740s and the 1750s concentrated on the reactions of the latter, and *sensibilité* became firmly established in the aesthetic code: '. . . that natural quality called feeling . . . it is this feeling which is the basis of taste',[9] said La Font de Saint-Yenne, and D'Alembert defined taste as 'the talent of discerning in works of art those elements which please tender hearts and those which displease them'.[10] The Abbé Le Blanc reflects in a curious way something of the preciosity of earlier writers on drawing room *sensibilité* when he says, 'Sensibility to the beauty of nature requires more qualities than most people suppose. Only souls of a certain quality are affected by the Beautiful'. He says this not in a drawing room context but when discussing the pictures exhibited in the Salon of 1753. It was in 1753 that another manifesto of *sensibilité* in painting appeared, Baillet de Saint-Julien's *Lettre à M. Chardin sur les caractères en peinture*. Here Saint-Julien makes a plea for more characters in painting, for the equivalent in art of the *'drame bourgeois'*. 'Characters are to passions what drama is to tragedy. A totally different art is needed to paint the one and the other.' The writer wants less 'art' and more 'nature'; less fantasy (in the style no doubt of Watteau and his school since he says, 'As long as pictures contain a few pretty women's faces, the public is happy') and more humanity. He ends with this statement, 'I know that the composition of a picture is important, its colour affects me infinitely, its drawing even more; but more than all this, its truth, its character and its expression. I want my heart or my understanding to be involved in my pleasures'.

A convenient way of estimating changes both in style and appreciation during the first fifty years of the century is to follow a persistently popular theme in painting and note the modifications it undergoes. In great demand, and in strict contrast to the more uplifting themes of the seventeenth century, was that of the village wedding. Watteau produced two versions of *La Signature du Contrat, ou la Noce de Village*, and four *Mariées de Village*, one of which (the picture in the Soane Museum, London), showing a number of small idealized figures on a large village green, takes its inspiration more or less directly from Teniers. In 1721 Pater painted a *Noce de Village* for the Duc de la Force at the Château de la Boulaye, and in 1724 was admitted to the Académie on the strength of three drawings, two of which were *Festins de Noces de Village*. He also painted a *Cortège de Fiançailles de Village* (Dresden) which, despite its musicians from Teniers, relies almost wholly on its pantomime quality for its pictorial effect. In the Salon of 1737, Lancret showed a *Noce de Village* (Angers) which returns more fully than the other examples to its Flemish model, although the result is suburban rather than rustic. In December of the same year he was paid for three pictures, one of which was a *Noce de Village* for the château of Fontainebleau. The description from the accounts reads, '... the priest at table with the young bride seems to be giving her some advice; Charpentier, an excellent musician ... is playing his instrument for a shepherd and shepherdess to dance to against a landscape background'. (At the same time, Lancret was paid for three

Fêtes de Village painted for the Petits Appartements at Fontainebleau). In the Salon of 1753 Jeaurat exhibited a *Noce de Village*, again a kermesse type of composition in a Teniers setting, which called forth criticisms consisting mainly of a sententious dissertation on the origins of virtue, to the tune of, 'One must look to cottage life for happiness when one wishes to see it at table and in moments of celebration', while the picture itself is dismissed with these words, '. . . the execution of this picture is certainly too serious. The ideas are not but the manner is . . . The heads have not enough expression or enough sweetness'.

Retrospectively, this seems to be the point of departure for Greuze, whose own version of this theme, *L'Accordée de Village*, appeared in 1761. The period of study and assimilation of foreign influences is over, the reign of sentiment is about to begin. The artistic situation embraces on the one hand an uneasy alliance between the Netherlands and certain southern masters and on the other the emergence of a new genre corresponding to the empirical and sentimental predilections of the French bourgeoisie. Greuze replaces Lancret as Diderot replaced Nivelle de la Chaussée. The major requirement of a picture is to satisfy the tastes of '*l'homme sensible*', who is a sensualist and a sentimentalist. As an extreme outcome of the teaching of the Abbé Du Bos, all pictures are now submitted to a test for sentiment. Even the little masters of the Dutch and Flemish schools, once valued for their anecdote and pictorial qualities, did not escape. This is how a tender-hearted journalist named Bastide describes an interior by Pieter de Hooch:

> Devant moi, j'aperçois dans une chambre obscure
> Une mère, fidèle aux soins de la nature,
> Prêchant son fils et peignant ses cheveux;
> Je la vois, je l'écoute, et je lis dans ses yeux.
> La leçon est sans art; la simple créature
> N'a pas appris ces discours éloquents
> Dont on accable les enfants;
> Et dont la suite la plus sûre
> Est de les ennuyer et de les rendre méchants
> En les mettant à la torture.
> Tout est senti dans ce discours;
> Et si jamais il se plonge et s'oublie
> Dans quelque triste égarement,
> Cette leçon empreinte pour la vie
> Lui servira de premier châtiment;

Il écoute sa mère, il la croit, il l'adore;
Le discours déjà long serait plus long encore
Qu'il n'y verrait aucune importunité;
Pouvoir du sentiment et de la vérité!
Tu fais sentir ici ce charme qu'on ignore
Quand on nous prêche avec sévérité . . .
Des chaises, une alcôve, un duvet, une table
Sont tout le bien de cette mère aimable:

La vanité ne fait pas le bonheur,
Et la richesse sert à corrompre le coeur.
Ici la properté supplée à l'opulence;
Dans les palais souvent il ne règne pas;
Et l'on méprise une abondance
Qui n'entraîne qu'un vain fracas
Marqué par tant de négligence;
Tous les sorts sont égaux quand on est vertueux . . .
Jamais illusion ne fut plus agréable;
Jamais description ne fut plus véritables;
Et la mère et le fils respirent à mes yeux.[11]†

Obviously, the time is ripe for a new departure.

† Before me, in a dark room, I see a mother who, faithful to the laws of nature, instructs her son while she combs his hair; I see her, I hear her, I read the message in her eyes. The lesson is artless; the simple creature knows none of those eloquent sermons to which children are too often subjected and whose most predictable outcome is to bore them and make them naughty out of sheer exasperation. In this speech everything comes from the heart; and if ever he forgets himself and plunges into some disastrous adventure, this lesson, learnt for life, will be his first punishment; he listens to his mother, he believes her, he adores her; even if the speech were twice as long it would not worry him; O power of feeling and of truthfulness! You demonstrate the charm one misses when one is preached at with severity . . . Chairs, a bed, a quilt, and a table constitute the sole wealth of this charming mother: vanity does not make for happiness, and wealth only corrupts the heart. Here cleanliness takes the place of opulence, although it is frequently absent in palaces; and an abundance which leads to shoddy show is worthy only of contempt. All destinies are equal when one is virtuous . . . Never was illusion more agreeable, never was description more truthful; and both mother and son come to life before my eyes.

Greuze's Life 1725–1769

Jean-Baptiste Greuze, the sixth of a family of nine children, was born at Tournus, near Chalon-sur-Saône, on 21 August 1725. His god-daughter or niece, Mme de Valory, whose account of his life, embellished with highly inaccurate detail, appeared in 1813 as a preface to her comedy, *L'Accordée de Village*, says that the Greuze family came originally from Bussy, and counted among its ancestors a '*procureur du roi*' who was also lord of the manor of La Guiche, a property near Icilly.[1] No evidence of a direct connection with these bygone glories can be found, but an indication that Greuze was not satisfied with his father's station in life can be seen by comparing his birth certificate with the version he gave when he published the banns for his marriage. In the first,[2] the profession of his father, Jean-Louis Greuze, is given as '*maître-couvreur*' or master tiler, that of his godfather, Jean Bezand, also as '*maître-couvreur*', while his godmother, Antoinette Auboeuf, is described as the wife of the local baker. In the second version,[3] however, Greuze has promoted his father's profession to that of '*entrepreneur-architecte*', his godfather to '*architecte*', and his godmother to '*épouse d'Hugues Brulet, marchand*'.

Very little is known about Greuze's childhood and early youth. According to Mme de Valory, from the age of eight years old he showed a passion for drawing which he had to conceal from his father. On the latter's saint's day, however, he presented him with a pen drawing of Saint Jacques which was so accomplished that the elder Greuze took it for an engraving, and on being enlightened, consented to his son's wish to become an artist and sent him to the studio of Charles Grandon in Lyon. So much for Mme de Valory; there is no means of knowing how the introduction to Grandon was made, nor do we know the date when Greuze entered his studio. Contemporary writers on Greuze state that he was self-taught, and this is probably true to judge from two very stiff and immature works still in Tournus, the *St Francis of Assisi* in the church of the Madeleine, and a *Portrait of Mme Piot* (plate 2), a local inn-keeper who died in 1747. These works, which show no signs of the sophistication which would come with studio practice, will be discussed in the next chapter.

Charles Grandon, born in about 1691, was made '*peintre-ordinaire de la ville de Lyon*' in 1749, and for the years 1749–50 was '*maître de métier pour les peintres de Lyon*'.[4] It was no doubt on the strength of these appointments that the elder Greuze decided to send his son to the best painter in the nearest big town, so that we must date his entry into Grandon's studio some time after 1747, the date of the Piot portrait, and the early 1750s, when Greuze left Lyon for Paris. There is not a trace of evidence as to whether he had another master before or after Grandon, who was one of a dynasty of painters established in Lyon since the seventeenth century. Grandon's work, which has almost totally disappeared, seems to have consisted of portraits of local personalities, as his appointment would imply. There is a very charming small oval portrait by his hand in the museum at Lyon, an elegant painting rather like an enlarged miniature. Greuze may have laid the foundations for his excellent portrait style in Grandon's studio, but from a technical point of view received no major inspiration. According to Mme de Valory, 'Greuze said laughingly that Grandon ran a painting factory. Grandon was delighted with the eagerness and talent of his young pupil and made him paint a picture a day'.[5] It was probably Greuze's dissatisfaction with the inevitable hackwork he was made to do which determined him to strike out for Paris. Greuze's works of this period remain undiscovered.

The only other information we have on this time in Greuze's life is a highly misleading paragraph in the memoirs of the composer Grétry, who married into the Grandon family in 1771: 'Greuze, although still a child and pupil of Grandon, my wife's father, often said, 'I must paint a *père de famille*'. And he did'.[6] This corroborates Mme de Valory's statement that *La Lecture de la Bible, ou un père de famille expliquant la Bible à ses enfants* (plate 6), which brought Greuze immediate fame in Paris, was painted in Lyon. The picture will be discussed stylistically in the following chapter; its content, which is Protestant rather than Catholic, indicates an immediate Lyonnais or Mâconnais background.

Greuze, then, came to Paris at an unknown date but some time before 1755 and was enrolled at the Académie. His beginnings were not propitious. 'When he went to draw at the Académie his talent was ignored and he was given the worst place; his proud and sensitive soul rebelled against this injustice, and, taking his works in his hands, he went to see Sylvestre, former drawing master to the royal children, who, astonished and delighted

55

by his talents, ordered that Greuze be given a decent place . . . and was the first to encourage him with a smile of approbation . . . Unfortunately, Greuze followed no school and no master, and this gave him a bad name among artists whom he might have had as supporters had he been wise enough to recognize them as his superiors'.[7]

Certain of these statements are borne out by direct evidence. He was indeed befriended by Sylvestre, whose portrait he painted and exhibited at the Salon of 1755, and also by the sculptor Pigalle, on whose advice he submitted several works to the Salon of 1755: *L'Aveugle Trompé* (Moscow, Pushkin Museum), *Un père de famille qui lit la Bible à ses enfants* (Paris, private collection), *Un Écolier endormi sur son livre* (Montpellier), *Portrait de M. Sylvestre, directeur de l'Académie* and *Portrait de M. Lebas, graveur du cabinet du roi*. On the strength of these works he was admitted to the Académie on 28 June 1755. These pictures, together with the portrait of the Académie servant and model, Joseph (Louvre) which must date from the same time, have an energy and strength which will rapidly disappear from Greuze's work. Apart from the advice of Sylvestre and the passing influence of Boucher, he had no masters, but early made the acquaintance of the engravers Moitte and Le Bas, both of whom were instrumental in popularizing Dutch genre painters of the seventeenth century.

The *Lecture de la Bible*, for its touching sentiment and the novelty of its subject matter, had an immediate success. It had been bought by the influential collector La Live de Jully, who exhibited it in his home before it was sent to the Salon.[8] Encouraged no doubt by such success, Pigalle, who seems to have been genuinely concerned about Greuze, introduced him to his friend the Abbé Gougenot, a rich amateur. Gougenot was the author of the *Lettre sur la Peinture* of 1748 (quoted in the previous chapter) and had helped to map out the iconography of Pigalle's monument to Louis XV at Rheims and that of the Maréchal de Saxe at Strasbourg. On 24 September 1755 Greuze was given leave of absence, and departed for Italy under the aegis of the Abbé Gougenot.[9] He thus made this almost obligatory journey independently of the Académie, although through the agency of the Abbé Barthélémy he was soon made known to Mme de Pompadour's brother, the Marquis de Marigny, who held the all important position of *Surintendant des Bâtiments* and was thus able to supply Greuze with a lodging in the Palazzo Mancini. Greuze, remarkably fortunate in his early patrons, was thus able to take his place by the side of the other *pensionnaires* of the French Academy in Rome.

Thanks to a work entitled *Voyage d'un Français en Italie* by Jean-Jacques François de La Lande, published in Venice and Paris in 1769,[10] our knowledge of the Italian journey is remarkably full. La Lande joined company with Gougenot, who, he tells us, 'insisted on being accompanied everywhere in Rome by a painter, a sculptor, an architect, and an antiquarian'. Their itinerary, according to La Lande, was as follows: Chambéry, Turin, Milan, Lodi, Cremona, Piacenza, Parma, Reggio, Modena, Bologna, Livorno, Lucca, Siena, Florence, passing through Rome to Naples, via Velletri, Terracina and Capua, visiting Herculaneum and Pompeii, and returning to Rome on 28 January 1756, as is attested by a letter from Natoire, the director of the French Academy in Rome, to Marigny.[11] In May Gougenot proceeded north to Venice, Padua, Verona, Mantua, Brescia, Bergamo, Pavia and Genoa, but Greuze had other plans.[12] The Abbé Barthélémy, writing to the Comte de Caylus on 12 May 1756, tells us, 'Creuze (sic) is staying in Rome, although the Abbé Gougenot wanted to take him home. He replied that as the Académie had done him the honour of admitting him he should repay the debt by redoubling his efforts . . . he would find in the vistas and ruins of Rome arresting accessories for his compositions; and who knows whether the sight and study of the works of Raphael might not raise him above his present level? . . . It is therefore decided that he will stay in Rome in order to shine even more brightly in Paris, and after a stay of several months he will go to Venice for another few months.' Mme de Valory gives another reason for this prolonged stay in Rome, a love affair with a Roman girl of high birth (the daughter of the Duke dell'Orr . . ., according to Mme de Valory, a Pignatelli according to the Vicomte du Peloux[13]) to whom she refers as Letitia. Greuze gave her drawing lessons and later painted a portrait of her entitled *L'Embarras d'une Couronne*, which has been wrongly identified with the *Prière à l'Amour* in the Wallace Collection. The full story can be read in the biographies of Mauclair and Hautecoeur.

The itinerary given by La Lande is borne out by a series of engravings entitled *Divers habillemens suivant le costume d'Italie dessinés d'après nature par Jean-Baptiste Greuze, peintre du roi, ornés de fonds par Jean-Baptiste Lallement et gravés d'après les dessins tirés du cabinet de M. l'abbé Gougenot* . . . These show girls in regional costume from Chambéry, Asti, Genoa, Parma, Bologna, Florence, Pisa, Lucca, Naples, Frascati, etc.

La Lande's book is also useful for supplying us with information as to Gougenot's capacity as a patron of the arts. After the latter's death, La

Lande obtained from his brother Gougenot de Croissy the manuscript of his notes made on the Italian journey, and in his book quotes Gougenot's judgement extensively. From the text Gougenot emerges as one of those men whose opinions are so moderate that they are almost useless. He was conventional to the point of insignificance, carefully playing the role of patron and amateur. He admires Sacchi and Guido Reni, points out the 'faults of drawing' in Correggio's *Madonna of St Jerome*, considers Michelangelo 'a bad painter but a tremendous draughtsman', approves of Veronese, and surprisingly enough of Ribera and Luca Giordano, and makes this sort of remark about the painters of Herculaneum: '. . . they had little knowledge of local colour, less of the magic of chiaroscuro, for which they had, practically speaking, no use at all'. He considers a work of art from the point of view of the story, describing it down to its smallest detail, which has led some writers to present him as a precursor of Diderot.[14] It is doubtful, however, whether Gougenot, despite his advice to Pigalle on the Rheims monument of Louis XV and the monument of the Maréchal de Saxe at Strasbourg, was ever anything quite so positive.

Greuze appears to have made no friends in Rome, although he was there at the same time as Fragonard and Hubert Robert. That he knew Fragonard is attested in a later letter to Prince Yussupov which is quoted below. But Greuze did not go in for the sort of camaraderie normally practised among artists. Ferociously independent, rancorous, proud, and quick to take offence, he seems to have moved suspiciously through a milieu so very different from the one in which he grew up. He retained from his early background a mighty ambition for his works and a desire to make people pay for them, in every sense of the word. He was probably a humourless man, certainly puritanical in feeling: for all the voluptuous heads he was later to paint, he seems to have regarded sexuality as something reprehensible. Not for Greuze the healthy fantasies—they are hardly fantasies—of Boucher and Fragonard. He seems rather to have been inspired by a wistful vision of the ideal family in which children are begotten easily, remain devoted to their parents, and are always there at the death. This vision, which usually reaches parody in his works, betrays great loneliness, and in the light of his experiences with his wife and children is little short of tragic.

Meanwhile, in Rome, Greuze, a man of little sentiment as far as his career was concerned, was cultivating his garden. He painted the portraits of the French ambassador and his wife, M. and Mme de Stainville. They in their turn provided him with another patron, M. de Stainville's sister, the

Duchesse de Grammont, who bought *Les Oeufs Cassés* (New York, Metropolitan Museum). Marigny, interested in Greuze's very public statements conveyed to him by Natoire, that he wished to benefit from Rome, wrote from Versailles on 17 June 1756 as follows: 'I am delighted to learn, Monsieur, that M. Greuze is striving hard to develop his talent for painting; I have seen in Paris pictures which he has sent from Rome and which please me so much that, knowing his fortune to be extremely limited, I have resolved to provide him with opportunities to support himself by his work and thus become even more adept in his art'.[15] This materialized in the first instance into new lodgings in the Palazzo Mancini, from which Mme Vleughels, the widow of the defunct director of the French Academy in Rome, was removed, and in the second, into a commission for two oval paintings, of which Greuze was at liberty to choose the subject, to adorn the apartments of Marigny's sister, Mme de Pompadour, at Versailles. Greuze asked whether he might execute these after his return to Paris; they are the pictures known as *La Simplicité* (Salon of 1759) and *L'Ingénuité* (Salon of 1761).

In December 1756 Greuze began to complain about his health; and in January 1757 Marigny wrote again to Natoire: 'Since M. Greuze, Monsieur, proposes to leave Rome any day for Paris . . . I shall await his return to collect the two pictures which I commissioned from him. He can be assured of the pleasure I shall take in encouraging him and doing what I can for him'.[16] Greuze left Rome in April 1757. In the Salon of the same year he exhibited a number of pseudo-Italian pictures (plates 13–16): *Les Oeufs Cassés* (New York, Metropolitan Museum), *Le Geste Napolitain* (Worcester Art Museum, Mass.), *La Paresseuse Italienne* (Wadsworth Atheneum, Hertford, Conn.), *Un Oiseleur accordant sa guitare* (Warsaw, National Museum), *Un Matelot Napolitain* (Leningrad, Hermitage), together with a portrait of Pigalle, a portrait of an unnamed man, *Un Ecolier qui étudie sa leçon* (Edinburgh, National Gallery of Scotland (plate 1)), two heads of a boy and girl, and a drawing of Italians playing the game know as *morra* (Moscow University). The Abbé Gougenot was elected an honorary free associate of the Académie for his pains but heard no more from his protégé. As his biographer, Gougenot de Mousseaux, puts it, 'Cherished, loved and esteemed by all who knew him, he was forgotten only by Greuze who nevertheless always found him indulgent and anxious to be of help'.[17]

From 1757 to 1759 Greuze worked steadily. He had acquired the patronage of such men as La Live de Jully, Jullienne, Damery, Marigny, the Comte de Vence and the Duc de Choiseul, and the friendship of the engravers Le Bas and Jean-Georges Wille. These two men influenced his choice of subjects and his contribution to the Salon of 1759 contains pictures which are outstandingly Dutch in character, notably *Silence!* (HM The Queen), *La Tricoteuse Endormie* and *La Dévideuse* (New York, Frick Collection). In addition, there were *La Simplicité, une jeune fille interrogeant une fleur* (Morrison collection), *Une jeune fille qui pleure la mort de son oiseau, Portrait de M. XXX* (La Live de Jully) *jouant de la harpe* (Washington, National Gallery, Kress Collection), *Portrait de Mme la Marquise de XXX* (Bezons) *accordant sa guitare* (Baltimore Art Museum), *Portrait de M. XXX, docteur de la Sorbonne, Portrait de Mlle XXX* (Barberie de Courteille) *sentant une rose* (Paris, Heim Gallery), *Portrait de Mlle Amicis en habit de caractère* (Mentmore, Lord Rosebery collection), *Portrait de Babuty, libraire, beau-père de Greuze* (Pierre David-Weill collection), seven '*têtes de caractère*', three of which belonged to Sylvestre, two to the engraver Massé, and one to his friend Wille, and two sketches in Indian ink, one of which represented an *Ecole de Filles* or *Mme Geoffrin, maîtresse d'école* (see below). To these years also may be attributed the many genre drawings based on Dutch models: *La Cuisinière debout, La Marchande de Marrons* (these two belonged to Wille), *La Marchande de Pommes Cuites, Le Bénédicité, Les Enfants Surpris,* and the pictures, *La Fille Confuse* (Paris, Musée Jacquemart-André), *Les Ecosseuses de Poix, La Savonneuse,* etc. Pictures such as these are not the ones which made him famous or by which he is remembered. They are dark in tonality like their Dutch models and have none of the slippery liquidity of the so-called mature Greuze. This can be seen especially in *La Fille Confuse* (plate 18) and *Un Ecolier qui étudie sa leçon* (plate 1). His portraits, however, were fresher and more rugged in handling. Both these traits were noticed. 'Who is this young rival of Teniers and Braur (Brouwer) whose bold and rapid progress seems so sure to lead to glory?'[18] This comparison with Dutch and Flemish masters is a considerable compliment which annexes Greuze to that stratum of middle-class appreciation so intimately bound up with the popularity of the Netherlandish schools. Another critic remarked: 'The heads of M. Greuze are attractive in colour and are pleasing to everyone; in this limited genre he holds his own against several great men because he knows and cherishes nature: in his desire to avoid dark tones, however, he has gone to the opposite extreme; I myself should give him the palm for portraiture'.[19]

More remarkable still is a notice in the catalogue of the sale of the Comte de Vence which took place in 1761. 'In the second room . . . on the wall beside the fireplace and in the uppermost row are five portraits, that in the middle is by a French painter named Greuze and is not in any way out of place beside its neighbours which nevertheless have a mighty reputation.' To the left of the Greuze hung a Porbus, to the right a Rembrandt; and beyond these, two more Rembrandts. The portrait in question is probably of the Academy model, Joseph, painted, according to Munhall, in 1755 and now in the Louvre (plate 11).

In 1759 Greuze became linked with two people who were to have a major influence on the rest of his life, his wife and Diderot. The painful story of his marriage has been told by Greuze himself in his *Mémoire de Greuze contre sa femme*[20], with a great deal of literary gloom straight from Baculard d'Arnaud: 'Citizen, I must reveal to you, despite my distaste, matters over which I had thrown a veil of darkness ... Shortly after returning from Rome, I know not what fatality prompted me to walk down the rue Saint-Jacques in Paris, where I noticed Mlle Babuty at her counter ... I was overcome with admiration for she had a very beautiful face; I asked for some books in order to have an opportunity of examining her more closely ...'. Anne-Gabrielle Babuty, born in Paris on 12 December 1732, was the elder daughter of a bookseller in the rue Saint-Jacques. She was twenty-seven when she met Greuze and looking for a husband. According to Greuze, she manoeuvred the marriage by the simple expedient of announcing the engagement and then begging Greuze not to ruin her pride by denying it. Her appearance is familiar to us: she is the heroine of *L'Accordée de Village*, of *La Mère Bien-aimée*, of *La Dame de Charité*, and of so many '*têtes d'étude*'. Diderot, whose vindictive comments in later years imply that she had been his mistress, describes her in a delirious sentence as '*poupine, blanche et droite comme le lys, vermeille comme la rose*'.[21] Her character is no less famous. She was greedy and dissolute; she neglected her children and seduced Greuze's sitters; she corrupted his pupils (which explains why the ones that survived were usually women); she extorted payment for commissions and is largely responsible for the atmosphere of bad faith which surrounds his dealings with engravers (see below). Even Greuze, proud and ambitious as he was, quailed before her harsh insistence. They were married on 3 February 1759 at the church of Saint-Benoît. The first child, a daughter, Marie-Anne-Claudine, was born in November of the same year and had as godparents her maternal grandmother and the engraver Claude Drevet.[22]

It is not certain where Greuze met Diderot, possibly at the bookshop, possibly at the home of Mme Geoffrin whom Greuze knew before 1760[23] and whose remarkable salon, held every Monday and Wednesday, was famous for its artistic as well as its literary attendance. Diderot's career as art critic for Grimm's *Correspondance Littéraire* had begun in that year. Their friendship was not instantaneous; in the Salon of 1759, Diderot dismisses the Greuzes with a few words—'the Greuzes are not much good this year'—although warmly appreciative of such genre painters as Chardin, whom Greuze was at that moment emulating, and Mme Vien. Greuze had not yet become a popular artist: he still studied sources which interested him, his handling was careful, he had great belief in himself, and he was brusque and uncompromising in manner.[24] It was not until he had the responsibility of an exacting wife and a small daughter that he began to compromise these qualities by painting scenes which he knew would please the public and bring him easy popularity. When seconded by the combustible prose of Diderot and rewarded by public acclamation, the character of Greuze's work changed entirely.

1761 marked the beginning of the change. To the Salon of that year Greuze submitted portraits of the Dauphin, of his father-in-law Babuty (Pierre David-Weill collection), of himself (Louvre), of his wife *'en vestale'*, *Une petite blanchisseuse*, *Un jeune berger qui tente le sort pour savoir s'il est aimé de sa bergère* (probably the picture originally painted for Mme de Pompadour), a *Tête de nymphe de Diane*, two pictures of children, *L'Enfant qui boude* and *L'Enfant qui se repose sur sa chaise*, and three drawings, *Des enfants qui dérobent des marrons*, *Le Fermier incendié*[25], and *Le Paralytique secouru par ses enfants, ou le fruit de la bonne éducation* (Leningrad, Hermitage). Then, when the Salon had already been open for a month, on 20 September, he exhibited the picture known as *L'Accordée de Village* (plate 29), of which the exact title is *Un Mariage, et l'instant où le père de l'Accordée délivre la dot à son gendre*.[26] It was given a rapturous reception. Diderot, after an enthusiastic description which contrasts strangely with his remarks on the other Greuzes, sets his seal of approval: 'His composition is full of wit and delicacy. His choice of subject is a proof of *sensibilité* and good conduct ... Teniers paints truer scenes, perhaps ... but there is more elegance, more grace, a more agreeable nature in Greuze'. The Swedish engraver Floding, in Paris at that time, ranks him with the masters of the classical school. 'I make so bold as to say that this great man is far superior to the famous Le Brun'.[27] The Abbé de la Porte was moved by the utter decency of the whole thing: '... the picture so long awaited in the Salon has as its subject an honest rural family ... the father ... an old man whose open face shows all the nobility of his station in life. There is nothing so touching and so apt as the figure of the betrothed girl. The graceful suppleness of a pretty waist which is the work of nature not of art is painted with a delicacy beyond all praise'.[28] Greuze was acclaimed as having created a new genre: 'his brush can ennoble the rustic genre without altering its essential truth'.[29]

From 1761 to 1765, Greuze, now living in the rue de Sorbonne, knew a period of great success. His second daughter, Anne-Geneviève, born in April 1762, had as godparents the Chevalier de Damery and the widow of the lawyer Pierre-Jean de Mozart.[30] In the same month he received his first pupil, Pierre-Alexandre Wille, son of his friend, the engraver, Jean-Georges Wille. His enthusiasm for the Dutch school was replaced by an emulation of the Flemish masters, Rubens for flesh tones and Van Dyck for portrait style.[31] Teniers and small genre painters are now ignored for Greuze is no longer a genre painter in his own estimation: he is the painter of *sensibilité* and good conduct, and as a sideline the idol of a sentimental and perverted public. From an aesthetic point of view the Salon of 1763 is notable only for a superb portrait, that of the *Comte d'Angivillers* (Metz) (plate 31), which was deplored for its 'coldness'.[32] The other pictures exhibited were portraits of the *Duc de Chartres* and of *Mademoiselle* (on the same canvas), of *Mlle de Pange*, of *Mme Greuze* and of *Watelet*, a *Tête de pêtit garçon*, two *têtes de petite fille*, one of which was the portrait of the daughter of the Russian ambassador,[33] and the great *Paralytique secouru par ses enfants, ou le fruit de la bonne éducation* (Leningrad, Hermitage). *Le Malheur Imprévu* (London, Wallace Collection), *Le Tendre Ressouvenir* (London, Wallace Collection), and *Une petite fille lisant la Croix de Jésus*, were all announced but not exhibited. Diderot, blind to the qualities of Greuze's portraits, was rapturous about the *Paralytic*: 'Greuze is really the man for me'—and with this judgement gave his fame a new orientation. 'To begin with, the genre pleases me, it is moral painting. Well! hasn't the brush been consecrated to debauchery and vice for long enough—for too long? Should we not be pleased to see it compete with the drama in an effort to touch us, to instruct us, to correct us and to invite us to virtue? Courage, my friend Greuze, paint moral pictures and go on painting them.' Other critics were overcome by the pathos of the story which they could not resist embroidering; for example, the boy holding a cup became 'another (who) brings a cupful of vintage wine which they were reserving for important occasions'.[34] It was a picture painted for a sentimental public, a death-bed without pain or tears—'it is not an old man dying, it is a paralytic who blesses the care and piety of his son'[35]—artificial in content, cold and deliberate in handling. The fact that it was an essentially literary piece of work if anything increased its appeal. Influenced by the contemporary drama, the audience concentrated on the 'cast'. 'The principal personage is a venerable old man of 80 . . . his daughter-in-law, a woman of about 23 . . . his wife who looks about 60 . . . a boy of 18 adjusts a coverlet over the old man's legs . . . another of his grandsons, aged 15, brings him a drink . . . a child of 3 has brought a bird to show him . . . a girl of 14 or 15 supports his head.'[36] Great excitement was raised in one quarter because the picture was thought to be a sequel to *L'Accordée de Village*—'this work is the final instalment of a pastoral poem of which the author had provided earlier episodes in preceding Salons'.[37] In 1766 the picture was bought by Catherine of Russia, a country to which Greuze, with his astute business sense was now directing his attention.[38] In May 1764 a third daughter, Louise-Gabrielle, was born.

The peak of Greuze's popularity was probably reached in 1765. In the pictures submitted to the Salon of that year can be seen an exploitation of every point on which he had ever won public approbation—uplifting, sentimental, and decently pornographic, with a number of portraits for good measure. They were *Une jeune fille qui pleure la mort de son oiseau* (Edinburgh, National Gallery of Scotland), *L'Enfant Gâté* (Leningrad, Hermitage), *Petite fille qui tient un capucin de bois* (Montauban), two *têtes de fille*, one of which may be the lovely, faintly Neoclassical head in the Wallace Collection, a sketch for the picture *Les Sevreuses* (Kansas), portraits of Watelet, of Wille (Paris, Musée Jacquemart-André), of Caffieri, of Guibert, of Mme Tassart, of La Live de Jully (pastel), a pastel of Mme Greuze and three drawings of the first importance, the first sketches of *La Mère Bien-aimée* (Laborde collection), *Le Fils Ingrat* and *Le Fils Puni* (Lille, Musée Wicar). These last two show Greuze moving into the realm of noble passion, and incidentally playing an important part in the reaction towards historical painting then taking place.[39] The reception verged on the rhapsodic. The enormous delight of Diderot over the girl mourning the loss of her canary is too well-known to need more than a reference; his appreciation of the head of Mme Greuze, which may be a study for *La Mère Bien-aimée*, is rather more astute since the picture is a good deal more perverted: 'That half-open mouth, those swimming eyes, that relaxed position, that swollen throat, that voluptuous mixture of pain and pleasure, obliges all decent women in the place to lower their eyes and blush with shame'.[40] Yet despite all this, because the propaganda of the picture was praiseworthy, Diderot hailed him as '. . . your painter and mine, the first to decide to endow art with morality and to serialize events in such a way that one could write a novel about them.'

1. *Un écolier qui étudie sa leçon*

Before the two sketches of the prodigal son his emotion was overwhelming: 'I don't know how I shall fare with this one, let alone the next... My friend, this Greuze will be the ruin of us'. Mathon de la Cour,[41] a good example of *sensibilité* in art criticism was speechless. 'It is impossible to convey to you, Monsieur, the extreme emotion occasioned in me by this figure (*Jeune fille qui pleure son oiseau mort*)... These two fearful scenes (*Le Fils Ingrat, Le Fils Puni*) are rendered in the strongest possible manner. I should not advise M. Greuze to execute them. One suffers too much at the sight of them. They affect the soul with a sentiment so profound and so terrible that one is obliged to turn one's eyes away'.

Yet Greuze was not altogether satisfied. For the first time, in 1764 or 1765, he had been passed over for a commission. The Duc de la Rochefoucauld wanted a picture of himself arriving on his estate and being received by his family. Greuze offered as a project a great apotheosis of happy family activity in which the men busied themselves with experimental physics, the women worked, the children played, and cohorts of tenants, tearful with joy, were seen approaching the gates.[42] But the idea was not accepted, and his two friends, Watelet and Marigny, saw to it that the commission was given to the Swedish portraitist Roslin. Secondly, there was trouble with the Académie. Greuze, admitted in June 1755 on the strength of his *Lecture de la Bible*, had never presented his formal reception picture, although ten years had elapsed since his entry into the Académie. He was now required to do so or forfeit his right to exhibit in further Salons. As it was, he exhibited nothing in 1767. He considered that on the strength of his stature as a public moralist he should try for the title not of genre- but of history-painter: his reception picture would therefore have to be a piece in the classical tradition. Diderot proposed as subject *The Death of Brutus* and was annoyed when Greuze rejected the idea. Having been ever successful with the theme of filial piety (*Père de famille expliquant la Bible à ses enfants, Père de famille qui vient de payer la dot de sa fille, Paralytique secouru par ses enfants, La Mère Bien-aimée, La Malédiction Paternelle, Le Fils Puni*) he searched in the annals of classical antiquity for a subject on this theme and found one in the story of Severus and Caracalla.

Diderot was at first enthusiastic, yet there was a certain amount of bad feeling all round. Angered by the Roslin incident, Greuze refused in 1767 when asked to paint a picture of the death of the Dauphin. The commission was given to La Grenée, thus augmenting a long-standing rivalry between the two artists.[43] He had antagonized Watelet and Marigny by his behaviour

65

over the two commissions; he was disliked by his fellow-academicians, especially by Cochin[44] who had informed him of the Académie's decision and received a rude letter in reply, and he was losing the support of Diderot. How instrumental Diderot was in sabotaging the plan to send Greuze to Saint Petersburg as court painter to Catherine of Russia has never been proved, but since Diderot was *persona grata* at the Russian Court, the following statements may be significant: 'Listen, my friend, all things considered, I think we shall not be sending Greuze to Russia. He is an excellent artist but a bad-tempered fellow. One should collect his drawings and his pictures and otherwise leave him alone. And then his wife is by universal consent—and when I say universal I include both herself and her husband—one of the most dangerous creatures in the world. I still have hopes that one day Her Imperial Majesty will send her off to Siberia'.[45] Moreover, the family situation was deteriorating. In 1767 Mme Greuze took as her lover the engraver Blondel d'Azincourt, and Diderot, openly delighted at the direction things were taking, seems to have fanned the flames: 'I love to hear him talking to his wife. It's a performance in which Punch lays about him with an artistry which makes his partner even more furious. I sometimes take the liberty of favouring them with my opinion on these goings-on'.[46] Most serious of all, in the Salon of 1767, Lépicié exhibited a *Tableau de famille* which showed that Greuze no longer had a monopoly of this subject.

Greuze's contribution to the Salon of 1769 was large in quantity and serious in content, as befits a future history painter. In addition to his reception picture, he showed *Une jeune fille qui fait sa prière au pied de l'autel de l'Amour* (London, Wallace Collection), *Une petite fille en camisole de nuit qui tient entre ses genoux un chien avec lequel elle joue* (England, private collection), portraits of Jeaurat (Louvre), of the Prince of Saxe-Gotha and of a man unnamed, three *têtes d'enfant*, *La Voluptueuse* or *Jeune fille qui envoie un baiser par la fenêtre appuyée sur les fleurs qu'elle brise* (Baron E. de Rothschild collection), and a selection of drawings: *La mort d'un père dénaturé abandonné par ses enfants* (Tournus), *L'Avare et ses enfants*, *La Bénédiction Paternelle* (Chicago, Art Institute), *La Consolation de la Vieillesse*, and *Le Départ de la Bercelonette* (Louvre Inv.26.954). The finished *Mère Bien-aimée* was announced but removed by its owner the Marquis de Laborde and therefore not shown. Leaving aside *Sévère et Caracalla*, criticism of the other pictures was very brisk indeed. The child playing with a dog was recognized by all as a masterpiece.[47] The girl praying to love was the victim of caustic comments.

According to Diderot, 'The shoulder is too small. The right leg is badly drawn. The foot is too big. The figure is badly draped. The landscape is heavy and tired-looking. The accessories are neglected', etc. M. Raphael[48] is patronizing. 'What a pretty child it is saying its prayer to love! What a pretty face! What an ugly body! What a pity the dear creature has no right shoulder!' *La Voluptueuse* was regarded by some as indecent—'The author has been unwise in making free with an expression which should be reserved for happier moments'[49]—and by others as insipid, e.g. M. Raphael, who wanted 'something lascivious and sparkling'. With the drawing of the wicked father Greuze had taken too big a step forward into the sublime, for it was regarded as too awful to be natural, and was viewed with something approaching indignation. 'I can't stand that wicked youth who wanted to kill his father—such ugly stories bring bad luck. It is a pity that this painter has such bad dreams, like the other one being kicked out of bed ... (probably *L'Avare et ses enfants*).'[50] 'The death of an unnatural father abandoned by his children forces the spectator's attention, tears out his soul, and makes his hair stand on end ... The strong, profound, and revolting impression made by such a spectacle has caused several spectators to recoil in horror.'[51] 'This subject is a scandal. I am annoyed that a Frenchman is responsible for it', etc.

The *Sévère et Caracalla* (plate 41) was a fiasco. The records of the Académie are discreet on this matter and give no hint of the drama which took place. 'The sieur Jean-Baptiste Greuze, genre painter, admitted on 28 June 1755, has presented his reception picture, the subject of which is The Emperor Severus reproaching his son Caracalla for having tried to assassinate him. Having taken a vote, the Académie has received and does receive the sieur Greuze as an academician, able to take part in its meetings and to enjoy the privileges, prerogatives and honours of that state, with the obligation of observing the statutes and rules of the Académie, which he has promised to do, swearing his allegiance before M. Le Moyne, director and rector. (Signed) Le Moyne, Caffieri, Cochin, and Dumont le Romain.'[52] Contemporary accounts paint a different picture. According to Diderot, Greuze was received by the Académie and then told, 'Monsieur, the Académie receives you but as a genre painter; we have taken into account your former productions, which are excellent, and shut our eyes to this one which is worthy neither of the Académie nor of you.'[53] In fact Cochin, the Secretary of the Académie, allowed Greuze to take the oath before announcing to him the embarrassing news that he was still a genre and not a history painter, and it was only the whispered comments of his colleagues that alerted Greuze that something was amiss.[54]

Once the facts were known to him, Greuze 'lost his head'[55] and tried to point out the excellences of his picture, then became overwrought, and leaving the picture in the Salon, retired to his home where an even more furious wife was awaiting him. Greuze was by this time sufficiently deranged to accuse her of plotting with her lover Blondel d'Azincourt for his downfall,[56] but this conflicts with Diderot's statement: 'Have I told you that Greuze has just been paid back for his disdain he has hitherto shown for his colleagues? . . . His wife is biting her nails with fury'.[57]

There is no doubt that many people, tired of Greuze's pride and insolence, were delighted to have this opportunity of humiliating him. Chardin was a little over-surprised: 'Chardin told me twenty times or more that he simply couldn't understand it'.[58] La Grenée triumphed over his old rival by producing a piece of chalk from his pocket and correcting the drawing of the heads. Diderot was patronizing. 'Greuze is out of his class; a scrupulous imitator of nature, he has not been able to rise to the sort of exaggeration demanded by history painting. His Caracalla would fit very well into a rustic or domestic scene . . . In the whole picture there is not a single principle of art.' One critic, in a not otherwise unfair article, was facetious: 'Certain people without much education have understood this mournful scene as some domestic quarrel in the life of his Paralytic'.[59] Bachaumont was almost as severe as the academicians. 'M. Greuze's first mistake is to have chosen to paint a speech and not an action.' The second was that there was insufficient expression in the heads. The third, 'enormous faults in the drawing'. The fourth, that the action was portrayed in a bedroom instead of inside a tent. His final verdict was that the picture was 'strangulated, poor and mean'.[60] M. Raphael endorsed Bachaumont's second and third points: '. . . the son is an idiot; I say an idiot because he is not stricken, as an illustrious criminal would be, but shamefaced, as if he had been caught stealing lead from a roof . . . The emperor stretches out an arm a yard long and in the process dislocates his wrist; in order to establish a certain proportion between the emperor's arm and his thigh, the painter has lengthened the latter beyond all reason; the right thigh and leg seem to go on for ever'.[61]

A rearguard action was fought in the *Avant-Coureur*, whose article on the Salon appeared on 18 September and took Greuze up on a rather injudicious comparison he had made between himself and Poussin. 'If Poussin had been faced with such a subject he would have imparted to the face of the prince

(Sévère) a calmer and more tranquil expression, more in keeping with the character of an Emperor . . . he would have indicated his displeasure by a simple movement of the eyebrows . . . Moreover, Poussin would have tried to emphasize his subject by a broader handling', etc. In answer to this, the *Avant-Coureur* of the following week (25 September) printed a letter from Greuze which, although published by Mauclair, deserves to be quoted once more in full:

Monsieur.

En continuant de rendre compte dans votre dernière feuille des tableaux exposés au Salon, vous avez commis à mon égard deux injustices, qu'en galant homme vous devez réparer dans la prochaine. D'abord, au lieu de me traiter comme les autres peintres, mes confrères, dont vous vous contentez de rappeler les productions, en payant à chacun d'eux, dans un petit nombre de lignes, le tribut de louanges qu'ils méritent, vous vous êtes étendu avec affectation sur mon tableau d'histoire, pour apprendre au public comment le Poussin, selon vous, aurait traité le même sujet. Je ne doute pas, Monsieur, qu'il n'en eût fait un tableau sublime, mais à coup sûr, il s'y serait pris autrement que vous ne le dîtes. Je vous supplie d'être persuadé que j'ai étudié aussi bien que vous ne l'avez pu faire les ouvrages de ce grand homme et que j'y ai surtout cherché l'art de mettre de l'expression dans les figures. Vous avez porté, il est vrai, vos vues plus loin, puisque vous avez remarqué qu'il mettait les agrafes des manteaux du côté droit tandis que j'ai mis celle de la robe de Caracalla du côté gauche; voilà une erreur bien grave, j'en conviens, mais je ne me rends pas si aisément sur le caractère que vous prétendez qu'il aurait donné à l'empereur. Tout le monde sait que Sévère était le plus emporté, le plus violent des hommes, et vous voudriez que lorsqu'il dit à son fils, 'Si tu désires ma mort, ordonne à Papinien de me la donner avec cette épée', il eût dans mon tableau, comme aurait pu l'avoir Salomon en pareille circonstance, un air calme et tranquille; j'en fais juge tout homme sensé, était-ce là l'expression qu'il fallait peindre sur la physionomie de ce redoutable empereur?

Une autre injustice bien plus grande encore, c'est, après vous être étudié à deviner comment le Poussin aurait traité ce sujet, d'avoir voulu imaginer que j'eusse eu l'idée de peindre Géta, frère de Caracalla, dans le personnage que j'ai placé derrière Papinien. Premièrement, Géta n'était pas présent à cette scène; c'était Castor, chambellan et le plus fidèle domestique de Sévère, suivant Moreri. Secondement, en supposant gratuitement, comme vous le faîtes, que j'ai eu le dessein de représenter Géta, vous auriez dû me reprocher de le peindre trop vieux; il était le cadet de Caracalla. Troisièment, j'aurai eu tort de ne pas le peindre en habit de guerre. Voyez, Monsieur, que d'absurdités vous me prêtez, pour avoir voulu exercer votre critique? Je vous crois trop honnête pour me refuser la satisfaction de rendre ma lettre publique dans votre feuille de lundi. Il doit m'être permis d'expliquer mon tableau, tel que je l'ai conçu, et de redresser l'interprétation que vous en avez donné sans me consulter, sans consulter l'histoire.

Auriez-vous envie de décourager un artiste qui sacrifie tout pour mériter les bontés dont le

*public l'a honoré jusqu'à présent? Pourquoi, dès mon premier essai, m'attaquer si ouverte-
ment sur un genre nouveau que je me flatte de perfectionner avec le temps? Pourquoi
m'opposer seul entre tout mes confrères au plus savant peintre de notre école? Si vous l'avez
fait pour me flatter, le tour n'est pas heureux, car je n'ai vu dans tout cet article qu'un
dessein marqué de me désobliger. Je ne reconnaîtrai que vous n'avez pas eu cette intention,
indigne de tout écrivain impartial, que quand vous aurez bien voulu imprimer ma lettre dans
vos feuilles.†*

Greuze, then, had cut himself off voluntarily from the Académie. The
question of his lodgings in the Louvre needs a certain amount of investigation. The brothers Goncourt, in their study of the artist in *L'Art du
dix-huitième siècle*, state that Greuze lived in the Louvre from March 1769 to
February 1780, when he was replaced by Allegrain, taking as evidence an
Etat-Général des Bâtiments du Roi of 1775 which mentions 'the sixteenth
apartment, Greuze, King's painter—March 1769'.[62] This evidence, however,
is not conclusive. A *brevet de logement* was made out to Greuze on 26
February 1769,[63] although an earlier nomination had been made when

† Monsieur.
   In continuing to review the pictures exhibited in the Salon in your most recent edition, you have been
unjust to me on two accounts and as an honourable man should be prepared to rectify this in your next
number. In the first place, instead of treating me as you treat the other painters, my colleagues, whose
works you simply enumerate in passing while at the same time devoting a few lines to paying each one the
compliment he deserves, you go into great detail over my history painting, in order to teach the public how
Poussin, according to you, would have treated the same subject. I do not doubt, Monsieur, that he would
have painted a sublime picture, but I am quite sure that he would have gone about it differently from the
manner you describe. I beg you to believe that I have studied, every bit as closely as you may have done, the
works of this great man and that I have above all studied the art of making the figures expressive. You have
gone farther than I have, I must admit, since you remark that he put the clasps of the cloaks on the right
whereas I have put that of Caracalla on the left; I admit that this is a very serious mistake but I do not give
in so easily as to the character you would have given the Emperor. Everyone knows that Severus was the
most hot-headed and violent of men and you decree that when he says to his son, 'If you desire my death,
order Papinian to run me through with this sword', I should make him look as calm and peaceful as if he
were Solomon giving judgement; I appeal to all men of good sense, is that the kind of expression I should
have painted on the face of this terrifying Emperor?
   Another even greater injustice is that after having imagined how Poussin would have treated the subject,
you assume that I intended to paint Geta, Caracalla's brother, in the character I place behind Papinian. In
the first place, Geta was not present at the scene; it was Castor, Severus' chamberlain and most faithful
servant, according to Moreri. Secondly, in assuming, quite gratuitously, as you do, that I intended to paint
Geta, you should have reproached me for making him look too old; he was Caracalla's younger brother.
Thirdly, I should have had to paint him in uniform. Come now, Monsieur, you have saddled me with many
absurdities in order to write your article. I believe you are too honourable to refuse me the satisfaction of
seeing my letter printed in your Monday edition. I have the right to explain my picture, as I intended it, and
to correct the interpretation you have given without consulting either myself or the evidence of history.
   Do you wish to discourage an artist who sacrifices everything in order to deserve the favours with which
the public has honoured him until now? Why, at my first attempt, do you attack me so openly on a new
genre which I flatter myself I shall perfect with time? Why pick me out from all my colleagues to set up
against the cleverest painter of our school? If you meant to flatter me you did not succeed for I see in this
article nothing more than a marked intention to offend me. I shall not believe that you did not have this
intention, which is unworthy of any impartial writer, until I see my letter printed in your pages.

Greuze had been proposed as successor to a clockmaker, the Abbé Nollet, who had moved into other lodgings and installed a relative of his in the ones he had left. 'If these considerations persuade Your Majesty to deprive the Abbé Nollet of this lodging as soon as he is established in the one he has rented, may I humbly request that he be succeeded in the galleries by the sieur Greuze, one of the painters of the Académie.'[64] The Abbé Nollet's successor was not Greuze but a certain La Roche, on whose death Greuze's nomination was again put forward and confirmed by the King verbally [65] and in writing[66] on 6 March 1769. On 31 October 1769 a report was made by Soufflot to Marigny that the rooms were in too bad a condition to be lived in and that a sum of 5,000 to 6,000 livres would be needed to repair them. Correspondence ensued.[67] Marigny refused to put up more than 2,000 livres, which he knocked down, in his letter to the King, to 1,500. 'The lodging in the galleries of the Louvre that Your Majesty was good enough to give to one of his painters, the sieur Greuze, a little while ago, is in a state of dilapidation all the more severe in that no repairs or improvements appear to have been made since his predecessor occupied it. According to the estimate submitted to me, the expenditure necessary to get the lodgings into a reasonable condition amounts to about 1,500 livres. Would Your Majesty be good enough to authorize this expenditure.' In the meantime, Greuze had made his own moves. In October 1769 he was living in the rue Pavée, near Saint-André-des Arts,[68] by 1774 in the rue Thibotodé,[69] while in 1778, Maurice Tourneux, in his biography of La Tour, states of the latter, '. . . with Greuze and his wife he signed a lawyer's document, according to the terms of which he took possession of their apartment, the third after the entrance of Saint-Thomas-du-Louvre'. Also, in an *Etat des pensions de Messieurs et Mesdames peintres, sculpteurs, et graveurs de l'Académie* of 1780, Greuze is not mentioned. In 1789 Angivillers wrote to Brebion, 'Monsieur, as it is empty, I have been asked for the lodging formerly belonging to sieur La Roche . . . first given to M. Greuze, and on his resignation to M. Caffieri . . .'[70] However, in 1801 Greuze wrote to Lucien Bonaparte (see below) giving his address as 'rue des Orties, Galleries du Louvre 11'. It can only be assumed that Greuze kept his studio in the Louvre, in which he exhibited the major pictures of the 1770s, while actually living in various parts of Paris with his family. When forced to by the extreme poverty of his old age, he moved back into his studio, where he died in 1805.

Greuze's Life 1769-1805

In 1769 or 1770 Greuze appears to have left Paris. According to Michel Florisoone (*Le dix-huitième siècle*, Paris, 1948) he went to friends in Angers where he would have painted the portrait of *Mme de Porcin* (plate 53) still in the Museum at Angers. It is more likely, however, that he went back to Tournus. The evidence for this is a drawing of good pedigree in the Pierre David-Weill collection which bears the inscription, *Greuze retrouvant sa mère après vingt ans d'absence*, which corresponds in style with the *Bénédiction Paternelle* of 1769. On his return to Paris he found himself enjoying a precarious wave of popularity based, as he was well aware, on a public delight in any sort of scandal. He knew that in order to maintain this he would have to stir up a little excitement from time to time. He began by holding a private Salon, always timed to coincide with the real one, in his studio. 'He threw open his studio whenever he finished a picture.'[1] He followed this up by trying to provoke another quarrel with the Académie, which was unsuccessful. 'He was sufficiently obsessed to go to the Académie and demand that he be struck off the list of academicians, saying that he belonged not to the King but to himself.'[2] He insisted that his name should no longer be connected with the Académie, 'upon which M. Pierre told him that His Majesty decreed it'. For a while this publicity was successful, and pictures painted by Greuze fetched high prices. At a sale at the Hôtel d'Aligre in February 1777, a *tête de femme* by Greuze went for 2,599 livres as against two landscapes by Hubert Robert which went for 900, and on the third day of the sale, the famous child with the dog went for 7,200 livres, an extraordinarily high price for a picture by a contemporary artist.[3]

The 1770s were therefore profitable years and they started in a distinguished manner. In 1771 King Gustav III of Sweden, in Paris for confidential political talks with the Duc de Choiseul, visited Greuze in his studio.[4] In the pictures of this period Greuze had the good sense to abstain from controversial subjects and instead concentrated on what would be sure to please. The early 1770s saw *Le Gâteau des Rois* (Montpellier (plate 57)), a family piece in the vein of

L'Accordée de Village, and *La Dame de Charité* (Lyon), a picture of unimpeachable morality. His absence at the official Salon had been regretted in 1774[5] and these pictures did much to redeem his status in the eyes of the general public. As La Harpe put it, 'Everyone asks if there is anything by M. Greuze; it is like the ceremony in which all the portraits of the great men of the Republic were carried in procession except those of Brutus and Cassius; and according to Tacitus everybody thought about them precisely because they were not present'.[6] These same pictures, which are discussed in the following chapter, undoubtedly enhanced his stature as a moralist. 'M. Greuze has all the more right to the admiration of the public in that all his pictures are a lesson in morality. He inspires virtue through the eyes and devotes to the good of society an art which of late has considered itself justified in emphasizing vice.'[7] 'In vain do they accuse the artist who interests and moves us of having draped his figures carelessly, of having painted linen in a hard and uncomfortable manner; when the expressions touch us so deeply, when the effect and truth of the whole make our tears flow, a little carelessness in the accessories is a minor fault, and the painter who can move us in this manner is, for us, a second Raphael.'[8] In 1777 he revealed to the public his most notorious work, *La Cruche Cassée* (plate 49), a picture painted and engraved in 1773 and based on the French proverb, *Tant va la cruche à l'eau qu'à la fin elle se casse'*. Mme Roland, who was delighted with it, says that Greuze pointed it out to her *'avec une honnêteté toute particulière'*.[9]

In the years 1777–8 Greuze brought off a great coup. 1777 saw the arrival in Paris of two distinguished visitors, Benjamin Franklin and the Emperor Joseph II, brother to Marie-Antoinette, travelling under the name of Count Falkenstein. Greuze, determined to mark the occasion, worked up a theme which had brought him the premonition of tremendous success twelve years earlier, *La Malédiction Paternelle* (plate 61). 'Instructed of the Emperor's arrival, he hurried to finish his work in order to show it to this Prince in a perfect condition.'[10] Also, due to the good offices of the Abbé de Véri, he was able to get Franklin to sit to him. In the September of that year, Greuze exhibited in his studio a portrait of Benjamin Franklin (Mrs Lamont du Pont Copeland collection), *La Malédiction Paternelle* (Louvre) and, a month later, *La Cruche Cassée* (Louvre).

The success of *La Malédiction Paternelle* surpassed anything that had gone before, showing that a change in public taste had taken place since 1765, when the drawings had called forth a shudder. 'The masterpiece that M. Greuze has now on view . . . is stronger than anything in the Salon . . .'[11] 'Madame, I was not able to sleep all night because of the profound impression made on my senses by the superb picture of *La Malédiction Paternelle*, etc.'[12] Greuze was now reaping the fruits of his isolationism; already in the May of that year Métra had noted, '. . . a crowd of people is besieging the studio of the celebrated Greuze to see his new picture of *Le Fils Ingrat* which he has recently finished; but this artist only opens his doors to his friends and to princes of the blood'.[13] The picture was held by some to merit for its author the title of history painter, e.g. 'Do you seriously think that *La Malédiction Paternelle* . . . which calls forth tears of compassion should be put on the same level as the still lifes on show at the Salon and is not as much a history painting as an Amphitrite or an Aurora and Cephalus ?'[14]

A year later another stir was caused by the pendant, *Le Fils Puni* (plate 62).[15] 'The whole of Paris is going to see M. Greuze's new composition. It is the follow-up of his *Malédiction Paternelle*. No scene was ever more touching, more energetic, or more true. Connoisseurs consider that this last picture is the most perfect and the most astonishing he has ever produced. I am of the same opinion; but works like this are above all description. One must see them in order to judge them.'[16] A resounding article by Sautreau de Marsy in the *Journal de Paris* (26 November 1778) must have satisfied even Greuze. In 1779 two odes appeared in the same pages:

> *Greuze! peintre divin! La Nature outragée*
> *Semble avoir déposé ses foudres dans tes mains,*
> > *Sois satisfait! tu l'as vengée!*
> *Si j'adore ton coeur qui conduit ton pinceau,*
> > *Combien j'admire en ton tableau*
> > *La noble vigueur du génie!*
> > *A voir l'expression hardie*
> > *Et la chaleur du coloris*
> > *Qu'il étale à nos yeux surpris*
> > *On te croirait le maître de la vie.*
> > *O Greuze! si je t'ai chanté*
> > *Tu ne me dois rien; c'est l'hommage*
> > *Que m'arrache la vérité*
> > *Qui m'a frappé dans ton ouvrage†*

(11.1.1779)

† Greuze! divine painter. Outraged Nature seems to have left her weapons in your hands. Be satisfied. You have avenged her. If I worship your heart which directs your brush, how much more I admire the noble vigour of genius in your painting! To see the bold expression and the warmth of the colouring that you unfold before our surprised eyes, one would think you the master of life. O Greuze! If I have praised you you owe me nothing; it is respect that draws from me the truth which has struck me in your work.

And later in the same year:

> Poursuis, Greuze! Poursuis: la faible humanité
> Pour le peintre du coeur te réclame et te nomme.
> Ce n'est qu'en pénétrant au fond du coeur de l'homme
> Qu'on s'ouvre le chemin à l'immortalité.†

(22.6.1779)[17]

Yet these successes were based largely on inflation. Bachaumont had remarked that Greuze was to follow up *La Malédiction Paternelle* with a 'series of similar moral subjects'[18] but in the years 1779–86, he either showed only one picture—'a young person . . . opening her bodice in order to shelter two birds'[19]—or this is the only one which received notice. The latter is probably the case, for in these years Greuze lost no opportunity of publicizing his work. He joined the movement to overturn or at least discredit the Académie by exhibiting in the independent Salons of Pahin-Champlain de la Blancherie in the rue de la Harpe. This was an interesting project, designed to bring together men of learning in every field, from France and other countries as well.[20] The Salon was at first well-supported. In 1779, Greuze sent a *Tête de jeune fille* and the first version of *Le Gâteau des Rois*; in 1782, the *Jeune fille qui fait sa prière au pied de l'autel de l'Amour*; in 1783, *La Dame de Charité* and a drawing *La Marchande de Marrons*; in 1785, a *Tête de vestale*, and at some time or other a very early work, *Vénus demande à Vulcain des armes pour Enée*. The Abbé Mulot, who was present at the first meeting in January 1778, made this enlightening observation in his diary: 'The assembly was very well composed on the arts side: M. Hallé and M. Pierre, the King's principal painter, came accompanied by M. Cochin, secretary of the Academy of Painting, and they were joined by M. Greuze. The latter has an air of charlatanism which is perhaps responsible for the popularity of his works, which are in many ways estimable but which are enjoying such insane popularity that there is bound to be a reaction'.[21] In 1779 he sent a *tête d'étude* for an exhibition organized by the Société des Amis des Beaux-Arts de Montpellier; in 1781 he announced the appearance of his engraving, *La Belle-Mère*, by means of a long letter in the *Journal de Paris*,[22] and in 1786 went to the extent of sending three drawings to Lyon, which held its first Salon in that year and which had as its secretary Mathon de la Cour.[23]

The letter to the *Journal de Paris* illustrates in an unequivocal way how

---

† Continue Greuze! Continue. Feeble humanity applauds you and names you the painter of the heart. It is only by penetrating the heart of man that one can open up the road to immortality for oneself.

75

completely Greuze was involved with the literary or rather melodramatic aspects of a subject. It is hard to imagine a painter with less eye for the externals of life and with a more maniacal desire to plot and to complicate. There is of course a considerable element of publicity-seeking in this letter which seems to underline yet again that Greuze was keeping a vigilant eye on the morality of the people:

Permettez, Messieur, que je profite de la voie de votre journal pour donner une note historique de l'estampe que je dois mettre au jour le 28 du présent mois, et que j'ai fait graver par M. Levasseur. Il y avait longtemps que j'avais envie de tracer ce caractère, mais à chaque esquisse l'expression de la belle-mère me paraissait toujours insuffisante. Un jour, en passant sur le Pont-Neuf, je vis deux femmes qui se parlaient avec beaucoup de véhémence; l'une d'elles répandait des larmes et s'ecriait—'Quelle belle-mère! Oui, elle lui donne du pain mais elle lui brise les dents avec le pain!' Ce fut un coup de lumière pour moi. Je retournai à la maison et je traçai le plan de mon tableau, qui est de cinq figures: la belle-mère, la fille de la défunte, la grand'mère de l'orpheline, la fille de la belle-mère, et un enfant de trois ans. Je suppose que c'est l'heure du diner et que la jeune infortunée va se mettre à table comme les autres; alors la belle-mère prend un morceau de pain, et la retenant par son tablier, elle lui en donne par le visage. J'ai tâché de peindre dans ce moment le caractère de haine réfléchie qui vient ordinairement d'une haine invéterée. La jeune fille cherche à l'éviter et semble lui dire, 'Pourquoi me frappez-vous? Je ne vous fais point de mal'. Son expression est la modestie et la crainte. Sa grandmère est à l'autre bout de la table: pénétrée de la plus vive douleur, elle élève vers le ciel ses yeux et ses mains tremblantes et semble dire, 'Ah! ma fille, où es-tu? Que de malheurs, que d'amertume!' La fille de la belle-mère, peu sensible au sort de sa soeur, rit en voyant le désespoir de cette femme respectable, et avertit sa mère en la tournant en ridicule. Le petit enfant, qui n'a pas encore le coeur corrompu, tend ses bras reconnaissants vers sa soeur, qui prend soin de lui. Enfin, j'ai voulu peindre une femme qui maltraite un enfant qui ne lui appartient pas et qui, par un double crime, a corrompu le coeur de sa propre fille.

† Permit me, Monsieur, to avail myself of your journal in order to explain the print which is due to appear on the 28th of this month and which I have had engraved by M. Levasseur. I have long wanted to portray a character of this type but with every sketch I made the expression of the stepmother always seemed insufficiently forceful. One day, as I was walking across the Pont-Neuf, I saw two women talking to each other with some vehemence; one of them was weeping and exclaiming, 'What a stepmother! Yes, she gives her bread all right but she makes sure she breaks her teeth on it!' This to me was a revelation. I went back to my house and drew the outline of my picture which consists of five figures: the stepmother, the daughter of the dead mother, the grandmother of the orphan girl, the stepmother's daughter, and a child of three. I suggest that it is dinner time and that the wretched girl is about to take her place at table with the others; when the stepmother takes a crust of bread and holding the girl by the apron hurls it into her face. I have tried to depict at this particular moment the character of deliberate hatred which springs from deep-rooted loathing. The girl tries to escape and seems to be saying, 'Why do you strike me? I have done you no harm'. Her expression is one of modesty and fear. The grandmother is at the other end of the table; filled with the deepest sadness, she raises her eyes and her trembling hands to heaven, as if to say, 'Ah! my daughter, where are you? What misfortunes, what bitterness!' The stepmother's own daughter, quite insensitive to her stepsister's fate, laughs at the old woman's despair and points her out to her mother by regarding her as a figure of fun. The baby, whose heart is not yet corrupted, holds out loving arms to his sister who takes care of him. Finally, I wanted to paint a woman who mistreats a child not belonging to her and who is doubly wicked in that she corrupts the heart of her own daughter.

It becomes evident throughout the 1780s that Greuze, as well as being in search of fame, is in search of money. His pictures continued to fetch high prices but this was not enough. Gradually his place was being taken by an increasing number of genre painters whose works, on show in the Salon, were supplanting those of the more exclusive and unrelenting Greuze. A more specific cause for declining popularity at this time is one noted some months earlier in the *Lettre d'un voyageur à Paris à son ami Sir Charles Lovers demeurant à Londres*: 'Why, ask those fired by the glory of serving King and country, is this father so angry at seeing his son preferring the glorious perils of war to the peaceful labours of agriculture?' When, in 1786, Greuze announced the engraving of *La Veuve et son Curé*, the event was remarked upon only by Bachaumont, who was luke-warm in his appreciation and remarks 'that he has not sufficiently studied his subject, that the composition is vague, and that the widow and the priest have no personality; that moreover the intentions of the characters are not very clear'.[24] The pictures of *Le Retour de l'Ivrogne* (Portland, Oregon) and *Le Donneur de Chapelets* (Montclair Art Museum, New Jersey), as well as the engraving called *Le Testament Déchiré*, are not mentioned anywhere at all.

Another reason for Greuze's loss of security is that his wife was systematically absconding with his money. Her private life was deteriorating. Blondel d'Azincourt was succeeded by one of Greuze's pupils. He in his turn was succeeded by another pupil, the son of a fruiterer, to whom she gave a large sum of money, later accusing him of stealing it. She then contracted syphilis and was forced to undergo a cure for which she afterwards refused to pay. Her next lover was the Comte de Saint-Morys, whose portrait Greuze was then painting. She seems to have made over large sums of money to him and even settled some on his small son. To do this, she could only take from her husband, and we have several evidences of her participation in business, which we know from Greuze was conducted without his knowledge. Three letters in her appallingly illiterate hand exist, two accepting commissions, and a third demanding payment for twenty engravings. The person to whom the last letter is addressed is not named, but that the engravings were for export is implied by this statement: '*Le tems est si malheureux dans notre pays comme dans le votre; que l'on a absolument besoin; de ce que l'on pocede*'.[25]

More serious is the affair of the contract. Some time around 1763, Greuze, like Lancret before him, decided to form an association, in this instance with Flipart, for the exclusive right of selling engravings after his pictures.[26] Mme

Greuze was included in the contract which was drawn up in April 1764 and renewed in December 1767. Flipart was to engrave *L'Accordée de Village* and *Le Paralytique*, for which he was to receive 3,000 livres, and after which he was to return the original plates to the Greuzes who would furthermore retain all profits from the sales of the engravings. If Greuze died, the contract would hold between Flipart and Mme Greuze. If Flipart died, the contract would be automatically annulled, the plates would revert to the Greuzes, a sale made, and half the proceeds go to Flipart's next of kin, in this case his sister. The association was renewed in 1772 and 1780 with the following proviso: that if Flipart and Greuze both died, the association would hold good between Mlle Flipart and Mme Greuze, but that if Flipart died first, leaving a plate half finished, the plate would revert to the Greuzes and compensation be made to Mlle Flipart on the amount of work done.

In July 1782 Flipart died, leaving the plate of *Le Testament Déchiré* unfinished. Two months later, Mlle Flipart was summoned before a lawyer by the Greuzes who ordered her to destroy the plate. She was clever enough not to do this. Not only did the Greuzes make no mention of payment; they tried to remove her sole means of compensation, for with the plate destroyed, there would be no means of telling how much work had been done on it. Mlle Flipart, however, demanded permission to summon the Greuzes before two experts for a valuation of the plates of *L'Accordée de Village*, *Le Paralytique*, and *Le Testament Déchiré*. The expertise, by Cochin and Lempereur, took place on 3 December 1782, when it was decided that Mlle Flipart was owed 360 livres. This was confirmed in a second expertise the following month, when Cochin was replaced by Miger. In February 1783 the Greuzes were still opposing the verdict as irregular and the whole matter of judging the plate (which had been stipulated in the contract) as unfair, and agitating for a sale of the engravings with some vague promise of compensating Mlle Flipart out of the proceeds. Should this happen, of course, there could be no check on the money received. The rest of the proceedings, together with the final verdict and the Greuze's defence is unfortunately lost.[27]

The inspiration behind these proceedings can only have come from Mme Greuze. Greuze was mean but by no means dishonourable, as we know from Diderot. Mme Greuze was even more dishonourable than she was mean, and it has been proved that the greater part of her extravagances were made possible by an illicit sale of her husband's engravings. 'From that moment on I had nothing to do with the business side; everything went on without my knowledge; I had moreover a hopeless head for business matters; my love for my art has made me neglect my own interests and my children's future . . . Business had brought in 300,000 livres and 120,000 livres were missing from the house as well as the engravings I gave her for her own profit; she was supposed to take only 50 pulls from each plate for herself and our associate; but she took more than 500 which she sold privately for 3 or 4 louis each. This happened in the case of nine plates during the time we were living together.'[28] On two occasions at least she destroyed the accounts.

From the rue Thibotodé the Greuzes moved to the rue Notre-Dame-des-Victoires, where, in 1780, according to Greuze, Mme Greuze tried to poison him with verdigris from a saucepan. He was rescued by a friend, M. Ledoux. One night he awoke to find Mme Greuze, 'by the light of a lamp, about to deal me a blow with her chamber-pot'. They moved to the rue Basse, Porte Saint-Denis, and had separate rooms, but Mme Greuze was constantly receiving 'people of all kinds', and once he was insulted by a hairdresser to whom she had taken a fancy. In 1785 he made his first statement before a lawyer. In 1789 Mme Greuze is referred to as 'wife of Jean-Baptiste Greuze, living apart from her husband'. Three more *procès-verbaux* were recorded in 1793, and on 4 August the marriage was pronounced null and void. Greuze did not appear in court but made over to his wife a large settlement which must have depleted his already shrunken income considerably.

The connection with Russia, however, was now revived. The exact story of Greuze's relations with Russia remains obscure. It appears that Mme Greuze had reacted unfavourably to her husband's lost opportunities in Saint Petersburg and had taken her quarrel directly to the Russian court. On this point M. Réau[29] quotes a letter from La Condamine to Falconet dated 12 June 1773 (Archives du Musée Lorrain, Nancy). A friend of La Condamine had composed an ode to Catherine containing praises of Greuze, her favourite painter; but on second thoughts he had changed it, omitting the praises. La Condamine explained to Falconet: 'he was advised by M. Diderot, who left two days ago for The Hague and thence to Saint Petersburg, that M. Greuze, or rather his wife, had, by some vile machination, angered or displeased the Russian court . . .'

This breach stayed open for nearly ten years and was only closed by the efforts of those two specialists in international relations, La Harpe and Grimm. La Harpe, in addition to being an admirer of Greuze, was the Paris correspondent of the Grand-Duke Paul Petrovitch, heir to the Russian throne. When the latter came to Paris in June 1782, under the pseudonym of the Comte du Nord, he visited the studios of both Houdon and Greuze.[30] Mme de Valory says of the Greuze visit, 'They were so enchanted by his talent that they bought several of his pictures, including *La Veuve et son Curé*, and once back in their own country spoke so highly of him to their august mother, the Empress Catherine II, that they obtained for him the benevolence of that illustrious princess'.[31] Another, though very much smaller incident brought him to the notice of the court of Russia. Catherine had had her portrait painted by the Dane Ericson, and although not pleased with the result had sent the picture to Grimm. Greuze, visiting Grimm's home in 1782, noticed the ineffectual treatment of the head and offered to repaint it. Grimm was delighted with the result and wrote enthusiastically to Catherine, who ordered Greuze to make a copy.[32] It is therefore probable that Catherine was behind the movement to make Greuze an additional agent for the Russian court in the French art market, although this function was officially fulfilled by Grimm. It will be remembered that she had formerly used Diderot for the same purpose; at the Gaignat sale of 1768 he had bought for her a Murillo, three Dous and a J.-B. Van Loo, and in 1772 the entire collection of Crozat de Thiers.[33]

The example given by the Grand-Duke was taken up immediately by members of his court and entourage, although the Russian colony in Paris seems to have kept up amicable relations or at least re-entered them in the late 1770s. Count Andrei Petrovitch Shuvalov and his wife Catherine Petrovna, who stayed in Paris from 1776–81 had their portraits painted by Greuze. They were also the purchasers of *Le Premier Sillon* (plate 95) of 1801. The catalogue of the collection of Count Alexander Sergeivitch Stroganov contains the following statement: 'Two busts, one of my son aged 6 and another of a little girl of about the same age. These two charming and infinitely attractive works are most cleverly painted . . .'. As Paul, or Popo, Stroganov was born in 1772, his portrait, of which there is a copy by Greuze at Besancon of the original in the Hermitage, dates from 1778. From the mid-1780s date the portraits of Prince Sergei Sergeivitch Gagarin and his wife Varvara Nikolaevna, and of Princess Anna Grigorievna Beloselskaya-Beloserskaya (reproduced in M. Réau's article in *L'Art et les Artistes*, 1919). The collection of Prince Nikolai Nikitich Demidov, transported to the Palazzo San Donato and sold up in 1870 (Paris) and 1880 (Florence), contained some twenty-five pictures by Greuze, including *Les Oeufs Cassés, Le Geste Napolitain, Le Favori, Mlle Duthé en Flore, L'Ecouteuse aux Portes, L'Espagnole, La Tricoteuse Endormie, La Suppliante, Le Matin, L'Etude, L'Effroi, Le Malice, La Pudeur, La Volupté*, a self-portrait, *Un*

11. *Portrait of Mlle Barberie de Courteille*

eune paysan hollandais, *Un jeune garçon* (1802), and *Les Oiseaux Favoris* (1805). Thus Greuze numbered among his patrons the greatest families in Imperial Russia; in addition to the names mentioned above, early twentieth-century sales catalogues show that the Kouchelev-Besborodko, Troubetskoi, Orlov-Davidov and many other collections all contained pictures by Greuze.[34]

The Grand-Duke's equerry on his visit to Paris had been Prince Nikolai Borisovitch Yussupov, who for a number of years not only commissioned pictures from Greuze but also used him as a medium for commissioning pictures from other artists. A certain number of letters from Greuze to Yussupov, published in the *Bulletin de la Société de l'Histoire de l'Art Français* for 1922, give some hint as to the terms of their relationship. The first extant letter, dated 17 September 1785, is obviously written *à propos* of the Catherine portrait and is addressed to Turin, where Yussupov held the post of Russian ambassador. The commission had been interrupted by the original having been recalled, and Greuze demands either that it should be sent back or that compensation be made on the work already done. His tone is by no means obsequious:

'Does His Excellency not recall that it was through sheer gallantry that I agreed to make a copy of the Empress's picture? His Excellency might remember that I had already made a sketch of it, in other words, done one third of the work. You were to send it back for me to finish; you changed your mind. I should far prefer to paint an original picture and you would also benefit; but it would not be fair to leave me with my sketch on my hands—a complete loss from my point of view.'

Whether this problem was settled is not known, but the next letter from Greuze, dated 29 July 1789, refers to another commission. Yussupov obviously wanted a picture of *Le Bonheur*; what he got was a portrait of the Quietist saint Marie Alacoque, and in this letter, a document of outstanding interest for the historian of *sensibilité*, Greuze gives his reasons for painting it:

'My Prince.
   In order to paint the head you asked me for I consulted your heart and the quality of your soul. I have therefore painted '*une femme sensible*' [the words are untranslatable] who, when you are no longer able to make use of the weapons love has bestowed on you, will remind you that in this life real happiness is not to be found in the arms of one's mistress. I have therefore painted happiness in the head which I am pleased to send you; when you look at it, it will say to you: I am happy. Like

81

myself, I dare to think that you will say: 'this is the true reality, the rest of our existence is often little more than a bad dream'.

The title is Marie Alacoque, Quietist; she loved God as other people love mortal men ...'

The next letter (2 November 1789) is important from two points of view. Firstly, its tone reveals the same abnormal pride and sensitivity so apparent in the writings of Rousseau. Secondly, it shows Greuze acting as middleman and commissioning pictures from French artists for Russian collectors, the pictures being despatched through the medium of the Comtesse de Ségur.[35]

'Your commission was made with such indifference that one would have to be as attached to you as I am in order to bother, and I might point out that I am the only person who has bothered. Fragonard told me that no-one had spoken to him about it: M. Vincent is in the same situation; Mme Lebrun has not begun . . . M. Fragonard is about to begin your picture, as is M. Vincent.'

The tone of the next letter shows that Greuze's business streak was not entirely dormant. It announces the imminent arrival of *La Colombe Retrouvée*:

'Please tell those who see the picture that you paid 100 louis for it; moreover you can judge for yourself; it does not change the agreement I had the honour of concluding with you. Think of it as a moment of enthusiasm that I wanted to satisfy. My passion for painting and my friendship for you were the deciding factors. Even if it were worth a thousand louis it would still only cost you fifty. If it reminds you of me from time to time, I shall be amply rewarded.'

An art historical cliché would have it that Greuze was put out of work by the rise of the Neoclassical school and ruined professionally by the Revolution. This is only partly true. In 1789 he still held a position of some importance. We have seen something of his relations with Russia. He painted more than one portrait of Napoleon and of the personalities of the revolutionary government, *Gensonné* (Louvre), *Cambacérès* (Chartres), *Fabre d'Eglantine* (Louvre) etc. Prud'hon and Mme Vigée-Lebrun studied his works, probably in his studio; Romney visited him.[36] An inventory of the Greuze household in the rue Basse, made in 1793 and instigated by Anne-Gabrielle Greuze, show his appointments to have been extremely comfortable. The bedroom, for example, contained a four-poster bed upholstered in green damask, two mirrors, six tapestry chairs, four ordinary chairs, curtains, two pairs of gilt flambeaux, and 'several busts and vases'; another room, a mirror, a clock and two vases in bronze, a chiffonnier, and two tables with marble tops, two bergères, four armchairs and four plain chairs covered in Utrecht velvet, and hangings in green taffeta.[37] His work does not seem to have been upset by the Revolution. Like most revolutionary artists, he himself was of a revolutionary temper, and like Jacques-Louis David he had a considerable personal animus against the Académie. In 1790 he exhibited in the *Salon de l'Encouragement des Arts*, as is witnessed by this letter, of which the signature alone is from Greuze's hand:

Address from the painters of Paris to J.-B. F. Lebrun who had thrown his Salons open to an exhibition of their works (1790–2). [Lebrun was the husband of Mme Vigée-Lebrun and a prominent picture dealer.]

Monsieur.

We have not forgotten that when Paris and France were far from that beautiful and sublime liberty which is life itself to the arts, you generously opened your house to an exhibition of our works.

Today you are repeating this favour and it is due to your care and under your auspices that our works are gathered here. Inspired by the liveliest gratitude, we have decided to call the home you have given us 'Salon for the Encouragement of the Arts'. What better name could we bestow since the respected and virtuous head of the Commune and the General of our citizen army (Bailly and Lafayette) have honoured us by coming to see our works. May this happy event inspire our efforts for as long as our gratitude towards you will endure.

Greuze.
In the name of the
commission.[38]

In October 1793 he joined the very much more powerful and revolutionary *Commune des Arts*, of which the guiding lights were J.-B. Restout and David.[39]

The answer must be that he was on the verge of bankruptcy. His investments were placed in such a manner that they fell automatically with the Ancien Régime: '. . . his savings, bound up with the former government or with rich stockholders, were almost entirely lost in the Revolution'.[40] His patrons of thirty years ago were disappearing, he had no publicity, and his income was dependent on the number of pictures he was able to sell. A visitor to his studio, Nitot-Dufresne, who was in Paris from 1790–1802, congratulated him one day on 'the decent fortune which was the fruit of his talent' and received the following answer: 'Monsieur, a man who works with three fingers can never be rich. The money goes not to the artist but to the reproduction trade which keeps a lot of men employed.[41] A great deal of his thunder as a moralist had been stolen by David and his school, now celebrating more public virtues. Greuze made a few unsuccessful attempts to emulate this style; then, with the ideological element of his work completely superseded, he withdrew behind the lines of his sentimental-pornographic *tête de jeune fille* which, with an occasional portrait, consequently became his sole line of production.

In 1792 Greuze was awarded a pension on the Royal Exchequer. This was obviously not regularly paid, for in 1801 he wrote to Lucien Bonaparte that he was starving. In the 1790s he was also occupied with a particularly futile lawsuit, the proceedings of which read like something by Maupassant. Greuze had a brother Jacques, who was titular curé of Saint-Sorlin-les-Maurs and Nancelle, '*son annexe*'. Not having declared an oath of allegiance to the new government, Jacques Greuze was suspect, and in view of this made his will on 21 March 1792. It appears that Jacques Greuze was the sole legatee of the elder Greuze who had died in 1769 and from whom Greuze had received nothing. In his will, Jacques Greuze bequeathed the tiny sum of thirty livres to his brother and thirty livres to each of his brother's daughters, to be paid at the end of one year; then, with the exception of donations to charity, named as his legatee Jeanne-Charlotte Commerçon, foster child of the elder Greuzes and housekeeper to Jacques Greuze. The curé then fled to Switzerland, and Commerçon took over and disposed very quickly of the fortune, so much so that when, in September 1793, the Convention sequestered the property of suspects, she was forced to sell property in Tournus in order to reimburse public funds. The Greuze family had possessed two houses in Tournus, of which one had been sold ten years earlier and one remained. Commerçon had a claim in the contract of the one that had been sold as, according to her, Mme Greuze *mère* had promised her board and lodging for life.[42] This claim she now tried to transfer to the remaining house which the government had decided to requisition.

She therefore wrote to Jean-Baptiste Greuze, telling him that his brother had fled leaving nothing but debts for which she was being held responsible, and that she was now faced with the loss of her property, her sole means of support, for Jacques Greuze, according to her, was to have made her an annuity on the sale of the contents:

'When your brother left for Switzerland and saw that he was leaving me without any money after I had sacrificed my youth for him and the family and seeing that he was leaving two houses, or rather one contract and one house, without knowing what would become of these properties, he decided, for my subsistence and to

84

preserve the properties for my cousins [i.e. Greuze's children], to sell everything he owned and make me an annuity, as you will see from the copy of the document which I enclose. He was advised to keep this as simple as possible and did not add the names of my nieces, although we both wanted to do so. Consequently, this document is the only protection I have against requisition and sale ... I think it will be necessary to have this document ratified by a lawyer so that I can act more effectively, remembering that you have some interest in the matter. Try to reply as soon as possible and to provide me with the means necessary to preserve your properties. I say your properties because I must keep them for you. This is urgent as they are anxious to conclude the matter and all will be lost for both of us.'

Greuze, penniless himself, and muttering, 'I don't understand a word of this', sent the documents to his local lawyer and friend Tupinier, adding suspiciously, 'I am counting on your friendship and hope that you will do all you can to protect me from the pitfalls of chicanery'. In 1797, acting on Tupinier's advice, he cited Commerçon in court at Mâcon, charging her with appropriation of his brother's succession. Both were bound over, and five days later both went before the civil tribunal at Chalon-sur-Saône. The case was won by Commerçon who was given full rights to Jacques Greuze's succession. Greuze put in an appeal, and after a month went up for trial again at Chalon. This time he won and the case was closed. He wrote to Tupinier in an almost pathetic spirit of gratitude, entrusting him with the liquidation of the property and offering to paint his wife's portrait. As Mme Tupinier was not strong enough to come to Greuze's studio (his address is still given as rue Basse), Tupinier came himself, and the portrait, painted in 1797, is said to be still in the possession of the Tupinier family.

In 1799 Greuze wrote, 'You would be doing me a great favour if you could let me have, as quickly as possible, the house left by my brother. I have urgent reasons for asking you'. He writes again soon after, asking Tupinier to wait for the rest of his fee. Shortly after, the correspondence came to an end, although friendly relations between Tupinier and Anne-Geneviève and Louise-Gabrielle Greuze continued after their father's death.[43]

These evidences of Greuze's poverty are borne out in a letter preserved at Tournus, written by Greuze to Lucien Bonaparte in 1801:

Le tableau que je fais pour le gouvernment est à moitié fini. La situation dans laquelle je me trouve me force de vous prier de donner les ordres pour que je touche encore un accompte et que je puisse le terminer. J'ai eu l'honneur de vous faire part de tous mes malheurs. J'ai tout perdu hors le talent et le courage. J'ai soixante-quinze ans, pas un seul ouvrage de commandé. De ma vie je n'ai jamais eu un moment aussi pénible à passer. Vous avez le coeur bon. Je me flatte que vous aurez égard à mes peines, le plus tôt possible, car il y a urgence. Salut et respect.

Greuze, rue des Orties,[44]
Gallerie du Louvre 11.†

According to Delort, Lucien Bonaparte, by way of reply, commissioned from him a picture of Saint Mary of Egypt.

Greuze had lost his independence and with it his *raison d'être*. Bruun-Neergard, writing in 1801, dismisses him with these words: 'Greuze is an old man who came after Boucher. His colour is not true and his drawing is not pure. David has so accustomed us to this purity that we look for it everywhere. For the rest, Greuze's compositions are simple and have character'. Greuze, however, was not discouraged. To the re-inaugurated Salon of 1800 he sent the following pictures and drawings: *Départ pour la chasse, portrait de C. et de sa femme dans un paysage* (drawing, Louvre R. F. 1870, 2058) (plate 94), *Jeune fille qui pleure son oiseau mort* (Louvre), *Jeune fille qui se dispose a écrire une lettre d'amour* (London, Wallace Collection), *Jeune fille préludant sur un forte-piano, La Peur de l'Orage* (Leger Gallery, 1946; present owner unknown), *La Crainte et le Désir* (possibly Paris, Musée Cognac-Jay), *Le Sommeil, L'Innocence tenant deux pigeons* (the picture in the Wallace Collection is a signed copy of this), *Une jeune fille bouchant ses oreilles pour ne pas entendre ce qu'on lui dit* and two male portraits. The *Mercure de France* was condescending but indulgent: 'Greuze has adorned this year's Salon with several small pictures which show that sixty years of charming work have not exhausted the piquant delicacy of his talent or the variety and facility of his brush'[45], and extended this tribute: 'His '*Paralytic*' and his '*Fils Ingrat*', which artists still describe as genre paintings, are unfortunately history paintings for all nations'.[46] The author of the *Coup d'Oeil sur le Salon de l'An VIII* was more impartial. Of the girl with the dead bird, the subject which had once delighted Diderot, he said, 'There is something unnatural about this figure. Gessner has painted with more naivety and grace that repugnance and that sort of fear caused by the spectacle of death when one encounters it for the first time . . . It is painful to watch an old artist return to the fray and measure his strength against young athletes when

---

† The picture I am painting for the government is half-finished. The situation in which I find myself forces me to ask you to give orders that I can receive money on account and thus finish the picture. I have had the privilege of recounting to you all my misfortunes. I have lost everything apart from my talent and my courage. I am seventy-five years old, without a single commission. I have never in my life been in such a difficult position. You have a good heart. I flatter myself that you will pay some attention to my troubles, as soon as possible, for the matter is urgent. Greetings and respect.

Greuze, rue des Orties,
Galleries du Louvre 11.

taste has changed and the direction of art is no longer the same. Pleasant colours, fresh and sentimental ideas, simple compositions, a gentle and naive poetry animated all his pictures and were responsible for all his success. His drawing was not too correct and he was without doubt too mannered; but he came after Boucher and left him far behind . . . He has survived his century and the taste of his century is no longer that of our own. The defects with which we now reproach him were mainly due to his contemporaries'. These comparisons with Boucher show that Greuze was now irreparably dated in the eyes of the new generation in art. Nevertheless Greuze was sufficiently alive to changing trends in painting to admire Girodet's *Deluge*, which he must have seen in the artist's studio since it was not exhibited until 1806. Girodet's master, David, was perplexed by his most unconventional pupil's work but Greuze, according to Mme de Valory, had no hesitation in calling him a genius.

In 1801 he showed two history paintings, *Le Repentir de Sainte Marie l'Egyptienne* and *Le Premier Sillon* (Moscow, Pushkin Museum) (plate 95), and three portraits, including one of a child, probably the exquisite *Edouard-Francois Bertin* (plate IV) in the Louvre. He received only one notice, in the *Mercure de France*, which spoke of him rather as a superannuated functionary overdue for retirement: 'How can I leave the ladies without mentioning Greuze who has spent thirty successful years painting their graces and their virtues?'[47] He still kept up appearances, as is witnessed by this statement of Mme Vigée-Lebrun, who visited him on her return to Paris from Russia in 1802: 'The first visit I received the following morning was from Greuze whom I found unchanged. I would even say that he had not altered his coiffure since I went away, for ringlets still danced on either side of his head'.[48] In 1804, Greuze, now seventy-nine, exhibited the *Sainte Marie*, *Ariane dans l'Ile de Naxos* (London, Wallace Collection), a female portrait, a self-portrait (probably the superb picture in Marseilles), and two subject pieces, *La Timidité* and *La Gaieté*.

In 1805 he was still engaged on another public-spirited piece entitled *La Veuve et son Seigneur*,[49] but became ill and died on 21 March in his studio in the rue des Orties.[50] A short notice was printed in the *Journal des Débats* of 24 March: 'M. Greuze died in Paris the day before yesterday, 30 ventôse'. The funeral was sparsely attended. One incident, however, was remarked upon. During the funeral service, '. . . a young well-dressed girl, whose tears could be seen through the veil which covered her face, approached his coffin, placed on it a bouquet of *immortelles*, and retired to the back of the church to continue her prayers. The stems of the flowers were bound up in paper on which could be read these words: 'These flowers, offered by the most grateful of his pupils, are the symbol of his fame'.[51]

A few days after his death, the following letter arrived from Tournus:

'Commissaire of the town of Tournus to the celebrated M. Greuze.
Monsieur.
On the occasion of the re-naming of the streets of our town, we have no need to borrow the names of great men from history: your name, Monsieur, is synonymous with the glory of the arts and the honour of France, it was therefore natural for your native town to honour you. The street inhabited by your forebears now has your name; and in informing you of this, it is yet another homage which, in the name of your fellow citizens, I hasten to render to your talents, and to which I am flattered to be able to add my own respects

Bidau'.[52]

Greuze was honoured by a long obituary in the *Journal des Débats*, later reprinted in the *Journal des Arts, des Sciences, et de la Littérature*. Commenting on the scene at the funeral, it draws a comparison with the pomp that attended the death of Reynolds: 'The celebrated Raynolds, whose respect for Greuze's talents was such that he wished to come over in order to make his acquaintance, Raynolds lived in England a rich and respected man. When he had finished a career as long as it was successful, the esteem of his fellow citizens surrounded him right to the grave; not only all the artists in London and men distinguished in many fields but also great aristocrats attended his funeral and lavished on him those last respects which do honour both to the giver and the recipient.

'Greuze was less fortunate: the interest of which he was so worthy brought to his coffin only a very small number of artists and friends . . .'[53]

The discovery among his personal effects of a scenario for a series of moral pictures (Appendix) provided a theme for an article in the *Journal de l'Empire* and a long overdue comparison with Hogarth.[54] The comparison, however, was worthless: Hogarth was still misunderstood, and of Greuze it was said, 'he would have been well advised to stop after having painted the most picturesque episodes'. The *Société d'Emulation de Rouen*[55] made him the subject of an address in which reference was made to his frequent pronouncements on art. None of these, unfortunately, have survived, for Greuze had no biographer during his lifetime or immediately after his death.

Greuze is buried in the cemetery at Montmartre. His epitaph is in the style of the poetic tributes of the 1770s:

> *Rival de la nature, orgeuil de notre France,*
> *Il garda toujours pur l'honneur de ses pinceaux*
> *Il peignit la vertu, l'amitié, l'innocence,*
> *Et son âme respire à travers ses tableaux.*†

Anne-Gabrielle Babuty died in 1811. Louise-Gabrielle Greuze died in April 1812, and Anne-Geneviève Greuze, who made her living as a teacher of drawing, in November 1842. They share the same vault as their father.

† Rival of nature, pride of our France, he always kept the honour of his brushes pure. He painted virtue, friendship, innocence, and his soul breathes through his pictures.

Greuze's Development as an Artist to 1769

Greuze is mostly judged on a style which he adopted only in middle life and which he applied only to a restricted type of subject matter. He was thirty-seven when he painted his first *Jeune fille dans la langueur de la nonchalance*, fifty-four when he painted the full-blown *Le Désir* at Montpellier (*Exposition de la Société des Beaux-Arts de Montpellier*, 1779); but it should be understood that between these dates he had paid scant attention to this type of subject head, regarding it merely as an isolated and light-weight element in an *oeuvre* for which he had very different ambitions, or at most as a sort of experiment in the delineation of expressions much as he would have studied them in the engravings of Charles Le Brun: there exists, in fact, in the Bibliothèque Nationale a series of engravings entitled *Têtes de différents caractères*, dedicated to Wille and dated 1766. Greuze is essentially an artist who develops slowly and whose manner changes in accordance with the dictates of the day. Possibly the least known period of his life is that corresponding with his emergence as an artist, and the least appreciated that when he was not yet famous as a painter of *sensibilité*.

Much has been said about the conflict between his sensuality and his puritanism, resulting in mediocre pictures in which both qualities are uneasily muted. His curious, almost Victorian conscience made him yearn for a kind of patriarchal simplicity and obedience: sexuality is permitted only in young girls at puberty but must be instantly reprimanded and repressed into the symbol of a broken egg or a spoilt dish once these girls grow into sexual awareness. But Greuze's own sexual awareness is omnipresent; it informs the very quality of his paint, which, at its best, as in *La Laitière* (plate 71), is soft, melting, and luscious. While continuing to scold, chastise, and humiliate in his moral homilies, he cannot refrain from exploring, hinting, exposing, in his studies and genre pieces. Finally, in middle and old age, he resolved the problem by painting those profane versions of female saints in ecstasy which have given him such a bad name. He is free from mannerisms only in his portraits, which are masterly and which he produces at a high pitch of excellence throughout his long life.

There are few extant examples of Greuze's earliest period, i.e. before he left Tournus for Lyon and eventually Paris. The first in date would appear to be a *Saint Francis of Assisi* in the church of the Madeleine at Tournus, painted for the Couvent des Récollets of that town.[1] It is a large drab picture and the saint a crude imitation of the current Baroque formula for a devotional painting of this kind. Apart from a few angel heads, Greuze has made no concession to decorative effect, and the bareness of the figure, combined with the ecstatically upturned eyes, give the picture a curiously Spanish appearance. Near to this in date (for there is little difference in handling, if a greater ease in presentation) is the *Portrait of Mme Piot* (Tournus, Museum) (plate 2), a local innkeeper who died in 1747, thus providing us with a *terminus ante quem*. This is face-painting at its simplest, wooden in expression, and, with the slate blue dress and bonnet and neutral background, cold in colouring. Yet the picture is not without a certain dignity which is missing from the companion portrait of Mme Piot's son, *Pierre Piot* (Tournus, Museum) (plate 3), canon of Saint-Philibert at Tournus. In comparison this is an accomplished work. It is executed in a dull monochrome, with no positive colour at all, but the smoother painting of the flesh, the frill at the cuff, and above all, the Van Dyckian hand, indicate that a period of studying and copying has intervened. Between these two we may tentatively place the *Self-Portrait* (plate 1), also in the Museum at Tournus. Here the colouring is lighter and the painting uncomplicated; apart from these considerations, the picture is more interesting from an iconographical than from a technical point of view.

The *Saint Francis of Assisi* and the *Portrait of Mme Piot* are the only two works which we can assign with any degree of certainty to the period before Greuze entered Grandon's studio, a date which is itself problematic, as is the date when Greuze left Lyon for Paris. As he was thirty years old in 1755, and as recent research has thrown no light on the matter of his early productions, his evolution in these years is a complete mystery. Nevertheless, in view of the technical accomplishment which he possessed in 1755—an accomplishment which indicates a long and uninterrupted practice of his art—we may assume that his apprenticeship began several years before his arrival in Paris, where he continued to attend classes at the Académie. Of his activities in Grandon's studio we know nothing, but it is almost certain that a great part of his time was devoted to the study of prints after Dutch and Flemish masters which

Grandon must have collected. Mme de Valory provides us with two vague pieces of information in this connection. She states that Greuze was from his earliest years an '*admirateur de Wandyck*', and in her comedy, *L'Accordée de Village*, she makes Le Mierre apostrophize Greuze with these words: 'Greuze, have you forgotten that when you first took up your pencil in front of Rembrandt's *Benediction*, you exclaimed like Correggio, "I too am a painter" '.[2] One might mention in this connection Renouvier's story of a Marcenay engraving, dated 1754, *Man in a Fur Hat*, after Greuze, *en imitation de Rembrandt*.[3] We shall find many signs of the influence of Van Dyck and Rembrandt in Greuze's later works, but in these early formative years his mind was equally occupied by the little masters of the Dutch and Flemish schools. This can be established with more certainty. The principal engravers of these artists, Le Bas and Wille, became his friends within a very short period of time; in fact he exhibited a portrait of Le Bas in the Salon of 1755, which indicates either that he knew him when he came to Paris or, more probably, that he knew of him and wanted to further the acquaintance. Moreover, a number of pictures painted shortly after his arrival in Paris, notably *L'Aveugle trompé* (Moscow, Pushkin Museum) (plate 10) of 1755, have pure Dutch genre subjects and, lastly, his *Lecture de la Bible* (plate 6) is undoubtedly influenced by two pictures by Teniers, one engraved by Le Bas and one by Basan some fifteen years earlier.

Another work which can be tentatively ascribed to the years before 1755 is the *Triomphe de Galatée* at Aix-en-Provence (plate 4). Here Greuze, uneasy with a subject he does not fully understand, has undergone the influence of Boucher, particularly of the *Triumph of Venus* (1740, Stockholm) and the *Rising and Setting of the Sun* (1753, London, Wallace Collection). It is rigid and wooden in character—the nymph in the foreground might be a relation of Mme Piot—but there are signs of progress. Unfortunately, the photograph gives no idea of just how near this picture is to Boucher, not only in colour harmonies—the uniform blue-green décor, which is used as *repoussoir* to the flesh, the pink and whiteness of the female nudes which is contrasted with the exaggeratedly brown and muscular torsoes of the men—but in the actual handling. Some of this can perhaps be seen in the putti which seem to have been lifted straight from Boucher and painted in his manner, i.e. with thick pink brush-strokes and carmine trimmings. This picture originally had as a pendant *Vénus qui commande des armes pour Enée*, according to a note in the catalogue of the Montesquiou sale of 9 December 1789; this has now disappeared.

The *Lecture de la Bible* (Paris, private collection) (plate 6), exhibited in the Salon of 1755, is an interesting picture from many points of view. Of moderate size (80 × 64 cm) and showing none of the earlier woodenness of the Piot portraits, it is almost possible today to recapture something of the impact it made on the Paris of 1755, dominated as it was by the artistic combination of Boucher and Mme de Pompadour. It is one of Greuze's least affected paintings: a family assembled for its daily Bible reading around a *père de famille* who has not yet acquired a patina of moribund piety. Light but dull in tone, it makes few concessions to sensuousness of pigment. Indeed, the blue skirt of the kneeling girl and the blue sleeves and red bodice of the old woman on the right are the only positive colours. Mme de Valory, who states that it was painted before Greuze's arrival in Paris, is probably right, for it bears the marks of its Lyonnais origins, notably in the form of the table and the style of the room. The Protestant custom of reading the Bible aloud, which, to a Parisian public, represented the simplicity of the Golden Age, would have been quite possible in the environs of Lyon up to about 1770. As Edgar Munhall remarks, Lyon had been an active Protestant centre since 1530 and Greuze was much influenced in these years by the milieu in which he had grown up. Whether or not Greuze himself was a Protestant cannot be proved: he certainly painted Protestant subjects, notably *La Lecture de la Bible* and *L'Accordée de Village*, but he himself was married in, and baptized his daughters in, the Catholic church.[4]

Aside from the religious arguments, however, there are certain precedents for the subject matter of Greuze's picture. The Salon of 1753 had seen Chardin's *La Bonne Education*, a picture of similar sentiment. Greuze's sources, however, lie not in Chardin but in Teniers. The iconography of the picture might have been suggested by Teniers' *Le Bon Père* (plate 7), the title given to the picture by the engraver Le Bas who made a print after it in 1753. It shows a family seated at table, the father at the head reading from a broadsheet, and on the wall behind, a picture of a bird feeding her young. (Greuze was to make this form of allegory a feature of his *Accordée de Village*, *Le Paralytique*, and *La Belle-Mère*). But, as is often the case in Teniers, the intention is amusing and even scurrilous, and the inscription on the engraving reads:

> *A table entre les pots et les discours joyeux,*
> *Qu'est-ce qu'à son gendre, à sa fille*

Veut enseigner ce Père de Famille?
Vous le voyez, l'art d'être heureux†

(It is even possible that this banal little rhyme was the inspiration behind *L'Accordée de Village*.)

There is an even closer connection with Teniers. The disposition of the figures in *La Lecture de la Bible* is an almost exact copy of the disposition of the figures in Teniers' *Card Players*, engraved by Basan (plate 8). Thus this picture, which caused a sensation in Paris in 1755, is fundamentally unoriginal. It is the outcome of long and careful study, overlaid with a striking fidelity to a way of life unfamiliar to a Parisian public. Strictly speaking, all that belongs to Greuze is the wealth of local detail and the sentiment which earned him the title of '*le Molière de nos peintres*'.[5] This effect, which Greuze repeated in *L'Accordée de Village*, *Le Paralytique*, and *Le Gâteau des Rois*, won him his first fame as a painter of good conduct. The sentiment, which in time was to become imbued with a kind of sickly nostalgia, was at this stage a welcome innovation and a challenge to the more highly polished works of La Grenée, Restout, Nattier, Vien and Drouais, the most illustrious representatives of the Académie in the Salon exhibition. Such works tended to keep one at arm's length, whereas the intimacy of *La Lecture de la Bible* created an aura of empathy into which the emotional eighteenth century was immediately gathered. The apparent paradox of a sophisticated audience responding to a humble scene of regional piety is therefore not a paradox at all. For the first time during the reign of *sensibilité* a painter had emerged who was part of the vigorous emotional life of his age. His picture was as good as a novel or a play. Moreover, the autobiographical nature of such a picture, far more extensive than in the works of Chardin, for example, added a note of personal experience to the contemporary scene, a note on which critics were wise to insist, for it was to become the hallmark of this generation which included not only a Greuze but also a Jean-Jacques Rousseau. In 1755 Greuze's gifts of narrative and self-expression appear in their pure state. But the success with which *La Lecture de la Bible* was received determined Greuze's intentions for the future, and his further exercises in this genre are marred by an element of showmanship, as if the author were the only qualified guide to a simpler and better way of life which all could recognize but few could share. The brilliant but fallible Diderot, who was to be on hand to further Greuze's exercises in

† What is this father wishing to convey to his son-in-law and daughter at table among the dishes and the happy chatter? You can see it—the art of being happy.

this field from 1759 to 1769, never fully recognized this element of vainglory in Greuze's moral pictures, although he was quick enough to detect it in the character of the man himself.

Other pictures exhibited in the Salon of 1755 were *L'Aveugle Trompé* (Moscow, Pushkin Museum) (plate 10), portraits of Sylvestre and Le Bas, and one masterpiece, a *Tête d'après nature*. This is the *Ecolier endormi sur son livre* (engraved title, *Le Petit Paresseux*) at Montpellier (plate 9), one of the finest of the early, predominantly brown Greuzes (the *Portrait of Joseph* in the Louvre, plate 11, is another). In sharp contrast to his later style, with its arch mannerisms, the child is treated as so much still life, and to remove him even more from contact with living things, he is placed behind a parapet. The only positive colour is brown, which is used for the jacket, the table, the background and the hair, this last being enlivened with white highlights. The paint is uniformly thick and the head is done in a stiff, dry, creamy impasto, as is the book, where the letters are scratched in with the wrong end of the brush. It is a picture of very fine quality and seems entirely original, although the tendency to reduce the figure to still life and the preoccupation with details (finger-nails, button-holes) can be traced to a study of the Dutch masters.

This rough and vigorous technique was gently deplored. Greuze's colour was accepted as 'rich and brilliant'[6] but his modelling and chiaroscuro were thought to be too uncompromising: 'The shadows that throw the flesh into relief seem to me too hard and obtrusive; it seems to me that they would look better if they were softer and more blended'.[7] 'I should like to see more roundness in the face (i.e. that of Sylvestre) and less harshness in the drapery'.[8] Yet apart from these considerations, the criticisms of his first Salon sound the notes which were to be echoed throughout the course of his public exhibitions. Only one critic was unmoved by him and remarked simply, 'His style is half-way between those of Chardin and Jeaurat'.[9] At the other end of the scale came a lyrical effusion: 'One feels he must have a delicate and sensitive soul. One would like to know him',[10] while a grave note of warning and prophecy was sounded by the author of a *Lettre sur le Salon de 1755 adressée à tous ceux qui la liront*: 'The superior talents of M. Greuze have made all who have seen his pictures wish that the painter would elevate his Muse to a slightly more noble type of subject matter; it seems as if he might be capable of doing something grander . . . he should follow his own genius and not the desires of the public.'

It is generally recognized that the journey to Italy, which took place in

1755–7, did nothing for Greuze's art. It might almost be true to say that it wasted two years which he might otherwise have employed in following up the Dutch models which he had set himself and to which he returned in the late 1750s. Greuze, as we know, visited all the major Italian cities but did only a little desultory copying: Mme de Valory mentions copies of two Titians in the family palace of the enigmatic Letitia; there are a number of red chalk drawings in Leningrad including copies of the nude from Raphael's *Fire in the Borgo*, the *Dying Gladiator*, and a figure of Christ from a Reni-esque *Crucifixion*, together with some nudes from the Sistine ceiling, and a figure of a satyr playing a pipe. It seems, from the picture of *Un Oiseleur accordant sa guitare*, exhibited in the immediately post-Italian Salon of 1757, that he had glanced at Caravaggio and Orazio Gentileschi. His Italian productions are extremely scanty although it is to be supposed that a number of them are lost. The drawings of Savoyard and Italian girls in the regional costume, prepared to be engraved by Moitte (plate 12), are unoriginal, being a simple contin-uation of those already done by Vleughels, also engraved by Moitte, as can be seen in the *Cittadina di Frascatana* in the Bibliothèque Nationale. Greuze's taste seems from the start to have been exclusively orientated towards figure painting and no landscapes by him have survived.

Perhaps it is possible to see the influence of Fragonard in the Louvre *Danäe* (plate 5), a sketch executed in trails of fatty pigment that seem to foreshadow Fragonard's fancy portraits of the 1760s. Here Greuze, in this uncharacteristic mythology, gives full reign to his sensuality, and the result is dynamic, linking him with the main trends in the painting of his century. Masterly though it is, the Louvre sketch is inferior to the more finished picture in Metz, another predominantly tawny sketch which has a brilliance of colour rare in a work of this period. Here the nude seems to go back ultimately to the Naples Titian, and the richness of the colour, although not its harmonies which are coppery, with notes of gold, blue and olive, seems Venetian in inspiration. These pictures, together with the ones exhibited in the Salon of 1757 and a handful of academies in the style of Boucher, are the only extant works of the Italian period, always allowing, of course, for the lost portraits of Choiseul and his wife and that of Gougenot, '*à la manière de Vandyck*'.

As M. Hautecoeur remarks,[11] perhaps the most lasting legacy of the Italian journey was that curious melting ecstasy of gaze painted habitually by Carlo Dolci and Guido Reni. In later years this combines with the seventeenth-century tradition of '*têtes d'expression*' to create one whole aspect of Greuze's work, that represented by heads indicating *La Crainte*, *Le Désir*, etc. But this was a latent influence which did not receive full painted expression until the 1770s when it gave a secular or more properly speaking profane flavour to what was originally subject matter of a divine nature. This of course is what imparts to Greuze's entire work its slightly heretical character; one is aware that beneath the surface fiction of those good fathers and honest brides there lies something more traditionally hallowed. Not unnaturally, in this century of the Enlightenment, Greuze has attempted to turn religion into morality and this is perhaps the true significance of his career.

The sum total of Greuze's Italian efforts was shown in the Salon of 1757. *Le Geste Napolitain* (Worcester Art Museum, Mass.) (plate 14) is a curious work showing that mania for plotting that was to be the ruin of Greuze. A young nobleman has gained access to the house of the girl he is courting by disguising himself as a pedlar. Unmasked by the duenna, he creeps away while his beloved places her fingers to her chin in the so-called Neapolitan gesture. It is to be noted that this elevated scene takes place in defiantly ragged surroundings, with the usual complement of dogs, children, and household accessories. The child's knitted hat receives as much attention as a broken Ionic capital. One would be hard put to it to discern any Italian influence here apart from a certain Roman fullness in the bust and shoulders of the girl. Far more impressive are the companion pieces of *La Paresseuse Italienne* (Hartford, Conn., Wadsworth Atheneum) (plate 13) and *Un Oiseleur, qui, au retour de la chasse, accorde sa guitare* (Warsaw, National Museum) (plate 15). These are genuine scenes from Italian life. The slack, fuddled body of the woman who contemplates, without too much dismay, her overturned bowl of water, has a genuine appearance of things seen and for once has no undertone of sexuality reprimanded. There is enough sensuality in the picture, in the still life of the stocking and the shoe, for example, to render it wholesome. The tortuous attitude of the picturesque bird-snarer seems to derive from the *Lute-Player* by Orazio Gentileschi in the Doria Gallery and was in turn to be copied by Manet in his *Guitarrero*. One has the impression, from his suspicious face, that a living model was used. Again raggedness, clutter, falling garments—Greuze's characters seem to be at war with their clothes—but a genuine ability to fill the canvas with an attitude that has nothing to do with literature.

This is not the case in *Les Oeufs Cassés* (New York, Metropolitan Museum) (plate 16). Sexual innuendo here reigns supreme, although the picture is in fact based on an engraving by Moitte of the same subject by Mieris (plate

97

17). A mother returns home to find her daughter meditating over a basket of broken eggs; the girl's attitude and expression indicate that a more serious accident has taken place. Why this tawdry theme should have so obsessed Greuze is beyond the imagination of the twentieth-century spectator, yet in all fairness it should be emphasized that its origin is Dutch, and the inscription on the Moitte engraving is sufficient indication of the delight with which it was understood by an eighteenth-century public.

In the whole of Salon there was only one work by Greuze which might be called original, *Un Ecolier qui étudie sa leçon* (plate I) (engraved title, *La Jeunesse Studieuse*) now in Edinburgh, another tawny picture in the style of the *Ecolier endormi*. The quality of the paint in this picture is again extremely high, the technique more varied. The colours are less highly saturated, the background lightened to the typical Greuze olive-grey, and the paint thinner and smoother. Interesting passages are the thickly painted sleeves and collar, white with grey pulled through (a trick which was to become mechanical and ugly in his later work), the wonderful gold scumble on the forehead where the hairline catches the light, and in contrast the meticulous painting of the book and the hands with the 'Dutch' highlights on the fingernails. The whole picture has something of the gravity of a Chardin, and it is interesting to note that Gautier d'Agoty, in his criticism of the Salon of 1757, devoted considerable space to a comparison between the two artists.[12]

Greuze shook off the shades of Italy and reverted to the study of his favourite Dutch and Flemish masters. To the years 1757–61 we may assign a number of drawings and paintings which spring directly from this source. Certain paintings are extremely Dutch in subject, e.g. *La Femme Jalouse, ou les offres déshonnêtes* (now known only from an engraving), with its pendant, the extremely fine russet-coloured *Fille Confuse* (Paris, Musée Jacquemart-André) (plate 18), both of which have a typical Teniers or Mieris head peering through a window into the room, and *Les Soins Maternels* (Tournelle sale, 1776, now known only from an engraving), in which a mother is seen showing her daughter how to knit. Others, such as *Les Ecosseuses de Poix* (engraved 1760), *L'Enfant Gâté* (Leningrad, Hermitage) (plate 19), and *Silence!* (H.M. The Queen) (plate 20) are decorated versions of a Dutch original. All have a certain coy humour which is not to be confused with the sentimentality of the 1760s, but is possibly a dainty version of the more robust comedy of their Dutch models.

The number of paintings, however, is in inverse proportion to the number of drawings which were having a considerable vogue at this time.[13] These were either sold to collectors, the most important being the Chevalier de Damery.[14] or simply used for engravings. They are mostly single figure studies or combinations of two or three figures and their titles are revealing: *Le Bénédicité* (engraved by Laurent), *Une Cuisinière debout* (bought by Wille, November, 1759), *L'Ecureuse* (plate 21) (engraved by Beauvarlet), *La Maman ou la Jalousie* (Vienna, Albertina), *La Marchande de Poissons* (which passed through a sale in 1762), *Une Marchande ambulante se disputant avec des blanchisseuses*, *La Marchande de Marrons* (bought by Wille, 8 December, 1759), *Le Retour sur Soy-même* (Tournus), a markedly Rembrandtesque figure of an old woman sitting by a window reading the Bible, and *Le Ramoneur*, *La Grand'Maman*, *La Servante congédiée*, *Le Ménage ambulant*, and *La Marchande de pommes cuites*, all from the Damery collection.

A dwindling legacy from his Italian visit was a rather weak style of Rococo drawing based on the Vleughels of the *Cittadina di Frascatana*, etc., which can be seen in the tiny doll-like figures of *La Jeune Nourrice* and *La Petite Mère*, both at Rouen, dated 1757 and 1759 respectively. Damery also bought a number of drawings in this style, including *La Frileuse*, *Dame touchant à la guitare*, and the more literary *La Mère en Courroux* which prefigures the later *Veuve et son Curé*, and its pendant, *Le Repentir*. None of these works can properly be called sentimental except *La Bonne Education* (engraved by Moreau, finished by Ingouf, 1766), which shows a girl reading the Bible to her parents, and *Le Bonheur Conjugal*, for which there is a drawing dated 1758 at Montpellier.

The Salon of 1759 contained a number of works which were as Dutch in their accessories and spirit as those of the preceding Salon had been Italian. But Greuze seems to have risen quite suddenly to a great sophistication in portraiture. *M. de XXX jouant de la harpe* (Washington, National Gallery, Kress Collection) is his early patron La Live de Jully, while *La Marquise de XXX accordant sa guitare* (Baltimore Art Museum) is the Marquise de Bezons (plates 23 and 24). These were obviously conceived as a pair of companion portraits, although of different size. Both sitters are dressed in their *négligé d'intérieur*; Mme de Bezons sits in a Louis XV armchair, while La Live de Jully, a well-known arbiter of all that was forward-looking in contemporary taste, is enclosed by the straighter lines of what was to be known as a Louis XVI table and chair. Both turn affably to the spectator; there is not the slightest trace of affectation. Indeed, one is amazed at the ease with which Greuze has adapted himself to the manners of these sophisticated people, having formerly given no indication that he was interested in anything but resolutely humble country genre. A step further is taken in the portrait of *Mlle XXX* (Barberie de Courteille) *sentant une rose* (Paris, Galerie Heim) (plate II) in which the influence of Boucher is evident in the colouring and accessories. The painting of the pink ribbons of the bodice is thick and creamy and if the features are a little tight, the plump delicate arms and hands foreshadow those of *La Laitière* some twenty-five years ahead. The portrait of Mlle de Amicis *'en habit de caractère'* (*'peint à la manière de Van Dyck'*) would appear to be the picture in the collection of the Earl of Rosebery (plate 25); that of a *Docteur en Sorbonne* is apparently lost. The *Portrait of Jacques-Christophe Babuty* (Neuilly, Pierre David-Weill collection) (plate 27) is, together with that of *Wille* in the Salon of 1765, generally acknowledged to be Greuze's masterpiece. In addition to seven *têtes de caractère*, one of which was a girl pulling the petals off a flower, there were four pictures with recognizable subjects: *Le Repos, caractérisé par une femme qui impose silence à son fils en lui montrant ses autres enfants qui dorment* (H.M. The Queen) (plate 20); *La Tricoteuse endormie*, possibly commissioned as a pendant to *L'Ecolier endormi* of 1755; *La Dévideuse*, also known as *La Pelotonneuse* (New York, Frick Collection) (plate 22); and *Une jeune fille qui pleure la mort de son oiseau*, which is unfortunately lost. *Le Repos* (*Silence!*) is taken from a picture by Maes, now in Weimar, showing exactly the same subject except that the little boy is playing a drum instead of a trumpet. Similarly, *La Tricoteuse Endormie* is based on Maes' *Tricoteuse Hollandaise* as engraved by Wille. A precedent for *La Dévideuse* might be found in Dumesnil's *La Fileuse*, exhibited at the Académie de Saint-Luc in 1751. The young girl mourning the loss of her bird, making her appearance for the first time, remains an enigma. How nearly the picture resembled the famous one of 1765 cannot be known, but since Diderot, who was reviewing this year for the first time, did not even notice it, it is possible that it was different in style. The Salon also contained two drawings in Indian ink, one of which was an *Ecole de filles*, surely the drawing which Mme Kamenskaya takes to be *Mme Geoffrin en maîtresse d'école*.[15]

Greuze's studies of Rembrandt, which are superseded in the following decade by his study of another master, Rubens, can now be summarized. Rembrandt impressed him as an artist probably more than any other master, and although the direct inspiration of only a few works, formed his conception of chiaroscuro (see the drawings for *Le Malédiction Paternelle* and *Le Fils Puni*) and led him to his early experiments in paint and texture. The works obviously inspired by Rembrandt are the Tournus drawing, *Le*

Retour sur Soy-même, and the two fine portraits of Babuty (Neuilly, Pierre David-Weill collection) and Wille (Paris, Musée Jaquemart-Andre) (plate 28). The portrait known as *Joseph* (plate 11), which passed through the Vence sale in 1761 and was praised for its ability to stand up to the Porbus and Rembrandts surrounding it, may be mentioned in this context although it is slightly different in derivation. It has something of the angularity of the Piot portraits and can almost certainly be dated before the Italian visit. A thick yellow varnish now darkens the deep unified coppery brown-gold tonality, relieved by the white shirt and the dull green used for the coat and background. The haze behind the left shoulder, the shading of the left side of the face and the shadows in the throat are reminiscent of the chiaroscuro of the Dutch Caravaggiesques, whose pictures Greuze might have known from engravings while still in Grandon's studio. In contrast to this, the magnificent portrait of his father-in-law, which dates from 1759, is the summary of all Greuze's studies of Rembrandt. Only Diderot's marvellous sentence will do justice to this portrait. '*Et ces yeux éraillés et larmoyants, et cette chevelure grisâtre, et ces détails de vieillesse qui sont infinis au bas du visage et autour du cou, Greuze les a tous rendus; et cependant sa peinture est large.*'† The *Wille* of 1765, a deep note sounded in an essentially Rococo decade, is not Rembrandtesque in its colouring, which is predominantly yellow and grey, but the weatherbeaten face, worked up in colour to a rough and almost rugged surface, and the middle-class solidity and propriety of the figure, are Dutch rather than French in origin.

A convenient piece of information fixing this connection between Greuze and Rembrandt is provided by a Watelet engraving of 1765. It is a very bad copy of Rembrandt's *Jan Six* portrait, and the inscription reads as follows: 'This print was engraved by M. Watelet, Receveur Général des Finances, of the Académie Française and the Académie of Painting, after a drawing by the celebrated Greuze, the idea being to give a pendant to the rare and beautiful print called *The Burgomaster Jan Six*. He was the friend and benefactor of Rembrandt, M. Watelet is also the friend of the artist after whom he has himself engraved this print which is both his portrait and as it were another Six who was also the friend of the Arts and Literature'. All very flattering to Watelet, but it is probable that the idea came from Greuze, as did the drawing.

The Salon of 1761 is significant in two ways. It sums up Greuze's

† And those red-rimmed and watering eyes, and that greying hair, and those infinite details of old age around the jaw and neck, Greuze has portrayed them all; and notwithstanding his technique is broad.

activities in the 1750s and it inaugurates his second, more Rococo manner. To take the backward-looking elements first, it contained, in addition to the portrait of the elder Babuty, *Une jeune blanchisseuse*, the Rococo *Jeune berger qui tente la sort pour savoir s'il est aimé de sa bergère*[16] (for Mme de Pompadour, pendant to *La Simplicité* and known by its short title of *L'Ingénuité*), a sketch, *Des enfants qui dérobent des marrons*, and a transitional drawing, *Un fermier brûlé demandant l'aumône avec sa famille*. The *Mme Greuze en vestale* ('. . . somewhat mannered. This picture would flatter Coypel but it does not flatter you')[17] seems to have been an allegorical portrait of the type popularized by Grimou. Forward-looking elements are the pictures which come under the heading of '*têtes d'expression*'—*Une jeune fille dans la langueur de la nonchalance*, *L'Enfant qui boude*, *Petite fille qui se repose sur sa chaise* (Montpellier), and the major subject pictures, *L'Accordée de Village* and the sketch for *Le Paralytique*.

L'*Accordée de Village* (Paris, Louvre) (plate 29) is not new in sentiment for it is painted in the vein of *La Lecture de la Bible*, with its accent on a lost world of innocence and obedience, but its technique shows certain conventions which give the pictures of the 1760s a homogeneous character. Its composition is tighter, more controlled, and also more scenic than that of *La Lecture de la Bible*. The incident is presented to us as a tableau vivant, confined to its stage by the broomstick in the bottom left hand corner and the lawyer's chair on the right. Without the staircase and the view beyond the main room on the left—a device that David was to use in his *Death of Socrates*—the scene would be almost intolerably cramped. The father of *La Lecture de la Bible* has now broadened into the type of venerable old man who will reappear as the 'Paralytic', the father in *Le Gâteau des Rois*, the wrathful ancient of *La Malédiction Paternelle* etc. His rhetorical gesture is not so much an artistic convention as a dramatic one, and it should be remembered that Diderot's *Père de Famille*, first produced in 1761, had provided a most explicit precedent and one which Greuze and Diderot had no doubt discussed. The central figure of the bride herself, although exactly capturing the slightly petulant charm of late adolescence, has lost the exquisite delicacy of the drawing at Chalon-sur-Saône (plate 30). The whole picture is characterized by a wealth of preliminary studies, whereas few are known for *La Lecture de la Bible*. This was henceforth to be Greuze's method in all his large family pictures which perhaps explains their uniform lack of freshness in contrast to the spirited drawings and studies for single figures.

The palette of the picture is light and bluish in overall tonality, but above all calculated down to the smallest detail. Thus the mother (left) wears a blue skirt and brown bodice and the notary on the right corresponds with a blue coat and brown trousers. These colours meet again in the son-in-law who wears a brown jacket, blue coat, white waistcoat and mauve trousers, and are picked up again in the father who wears a brown waistcoat and a mauve-blue coat. The yellow underskirt of the Accordée is matched by the yellow breeches of the father. Her striped dress concentrates all the notes of white and has bluish reflections. The sleeves of the other girls are variations of blue, mauve or brown, and the background is a wash of these colours. Technically, the picture is uninteresting except for the thinnish ruddy painting of the flesh, a forecast of Greuze's Rubens manner. Apart from the thickly impasted blue-white linen, the brush-strokes are insignificant. There is a complete absence of bravura, as may be seen in the careful pedestrian painting of the hen and chicks.

It is, in fact, a predominantly literary picture. The subject is supreme and the technique has been subordinated to it, reduced to an adequate but none the less minimal supporting role of outline, colour, and shading. This situation is reflected in the criticisms of the Salon of 1761 with reference to Greuze's exhibits. The authors of the various 'letters' are now so much under the sway of the story that they give no technical details whatever. Diderot is the worst offender in this respect; he characterizes the subject of the sketch of the *Paralytic* as a '*tableau de moeurs*' and leaves it at that. Similarly, the author of *Observation d'une société d'amateurs sur les tableaux exposés au Salon cette année 1761* considers the picture much as a serial story, to be continued, when he says, 'The subjects that this young painter imagines and executes so well might one day form a complete treatise of domestic morality'.[18] Grimm gives a partial explanation of the success of this picture when he states, 'Greuze is young' (this myth of Greuze's youth was tenacious. He was in fact thirty-six when he painted *L'Accordée de Village*). 'He has learnt everything he knows without being a pupil of anyone and it is clear that he has none of the cheap mannerisms that ruin the present French school.' Untutored, unspoilt, and representing the solidity and morality of provincial France, Greuze was at this stage as much of a social phenomenon as an artistic one.

Edgar Munhall[19] points out that the original title of this painting was *Un Mariage, et l'instant où le père de l'Accordée délivre la dot à son gendre*, in other words that it was a Protestant marriage, for Protestants considered 'as a complete marriage ceremony the registration of a civil contract before a notary'. This discovery lends weight to the fact not necessarily that Greuze himself was a Protestant but that he was still hankering after his Protestant homeland, which was the inspiration for his moral works. This nostalgia, allied to the absence of 'cheap mannerisms' in *L'Accordée de Village*, provided a blessed alternative to the Parisian view of the world which the Parisians themselves were the first to appreciate. In the long story of the eighteenth century's fight against its own sophistication, from the collecting of Dutch genre pictures to Marie Antoinette's cottage at Versailles, *L'Accordée de Village* occupies an important position.

On 27 July 1760 Wille made the following statement in his diary: 'M. Greuze and myself went to the Rubens gallery in the Luxembourg which was specially opened for us. We went up on ladders to have a closer view of the pictures painted by this great man and we considered his manner of painting and colouring worthy of our exertions'. It has been noted that the works of the 1760s and early 1770s are marked by a certain homogeneity of style: a much lighter blonde tonality, tending to the pink and white and blue of Boucher, an increase in scale, a greater attention to flesh painting and more feeling for the soft pulpy character of the flesh. All these characteristics, together with technical details such as strokes of carmine to outline nostrils, fingers, etc., and half tones of blue and yellow in the flesh spring from from a study of the pictures of Rubens and form an explanation of Greuze's brief mastery of flesh painting, which he was later to lose through overwork, desperation and slipshod execution.

The 1760s also see the climax of the Van Dyck manner, if it may so be called, both in the painting of children's heads and of full scale portraits. Another entry in Wille's diary, this time for 21 February 1762, shows us the sources for this. 'A few days ago my friend M. Greuze came to see us. He found my hundred engravings of Van Dyck portraits . . . and as I saw that he took great pleasure in looking at them I made him a present of them, which pleased him even more.'

In order to characterize this new neo-Flemish manner, it may be easier to examine in detail five works from the years 1763–5. Two of these are portraits, of the *Comte d'Angivillers* (Metz, Salon of 1763) (plate 31) and of *Monseigneur de Valras*, bishop of Mâcon (Mâcon) (plate 32). We have no date for the latter but he died in 1764 and if grounds of style alone could not claim it for Greuze, there is a document in the Archives of Saône-et-Loire commissioning from Greuze a portrait of his successor, Monseigneur Moreau.[20] The Metz picture is, from the point of view of colouring, one of

Greuze's most successful. The background is black, shaded to a dark grey round the head, the coat an unusual clover colour. The only positive colour is in the scarlet ribbon of the decoration and the brilliant waistcoat with its gold embroidery, red roses and green leaves on a white ground. The influence of Rubens becomes more apparent if we compare this portrait with the *Portrait of Babuty* of 1759 or the *Bailli de Crussols* (Phillippe Aubertin collection) which must date from about the same time. The first is dark and Rembrandtesque, the second almost entirely in the La Tour idiom, with a predominance of blue lightened with white, a matt, almost chalky surface, and certain direct imitations, such as the effect of the watered silk ribbon. It is almost as if Greuze were trying to copy a pastel effect in oils. The *Angivillers*, on the other hand, is the work of a painter who has suddenly become interested in glazes. Certain La Tour effects, such as the pronounced blue shadows round chin and jaw, are included, but otherwise the paint is thin, clear and unusually crisp, as can be seen in the cravat, the frogging on the coat, and the curls of the hair. The actual face is painted in a series of transparent glazes, worked up to a sheen on the lip and nose, and the brush strokes are much shorter and more descriptive, notably in the painting of the mouth and nostrils.

Similar qualities can be seen in the painting of the head and hands of *Monseigneur de Valras*, a magnificent and practically unknown portrait which impresses at first sight on account of its size. This must surely be one of the most monumental portraits of the eighteenth century. The pose is taken from Van Dyck: there are many possible sources, the most likely being the portrait of Margaretha de Vos, Frans Snyders' wife, which Greuze may have seen in Wille's album. Van Dyck had been one of Greuze's earliest models in portraiture—the early *Portrait of Pierre Piot* in Tournus already shows his influence—but this is one of the rare instances when he adapts himself to Van Dyck's scale.

Three heads are perhaps even more valuable in this connection than the portraits for, from his earliest days, Greuze had used them as a vehicle for experimenting with the painting of flesh. The ravishing *Jeune fille vue de dos* (engraved title, *La Pudeur agaçante*) at Montpellier (plate 33) is darker in colouring—the background is grey and the hair russet brown—than most works of this period, but technically it is the most brilliant. Here Greuze has concentrated less on glazes, as in the *Portrait of the Comte d'Angivillers*, than on the freshness and subtlety provided by a combination of half tones. This is especially seen in the face with its pink lips and eyelids, bluish transparency round eyelids and bridge of nose, blues and yellows in the flesh, and red brush strokes used to outline nostrils and chin.

The Wallace Collection *Tête de jeune fille* (plate 34) (possibly one of those in the Salon of 1765) and the Edinburgh *Jeune fille qui pleure la mort de son oiseau* (plate III) are typical blonde Greuzes of this period, with the flesh a more sensuous version of that of the ruddy-cheeked bride in *L'Accordée de Village*. The Edinburgh picture is extremely Rococo in colour harmony, everything being reduced to the predominant blue, pink and white, e.g. blue ribbon in hair, pink flower with blue centre, even blue leaves. The influence of Boucher is marked but there is a considerable advance on Boucher in terms of naturalism. The flesh is excellent, warm and white, with blue shadows on eyelid and wrist, pink nostrils, ear, and finger tips, and rosy strokes outlining the fingers of the typical dimpled fleshy hand. The same applies to the Wallace head, which is, however, less carefully painted; *L'Enfant au capucin de bois* (Montauban)—a version of Chardin's *L'Inclination de l'Age*—called 'a little Rubens' by Diderot, and *La Voluptueuse* (Baron E. Rothschild collection) are similar in colour and treatment. The same may apply to the lost portrait of Mme Greuze (Salon of 1763), of which Diderot remarked the '. . . variety of tones . . . reddish brush strokes in the corners of the eyes . . . complexion yellowish on temples and brow . . . luminous transparency' etc.

An interesting transitional picture of 1763 is the Wallace Collection *Miroir Cassé* or *Malheur Imprévu* (plate 26) which marks the end of one type of detailed genre painting and the emergence of another. It is as meticulous in detail as the neo-Teniers production of the late 1750s and the painting of the white satin dress bears witness to a study of a master such as Terborch, but henceforth Greuze was to concentrate on the deliberate ambiguity of the content rather than the pictorial qualities of the subject. The picture best typifies the change of style of the 1760s. In the short plump hands, the disordered dress, and in particular the untidy head with its over-ripe features may be read the future of many Greuze allegories. Otherwise, *L'Enfant Gâté* (1763, Hermitage) and *Les Sevreuses* (1765, Kansas, William Rockhill Nelson Gallery) mark the death of the early manner.

The works of the 1760s which remain to be dealt with are the great *Paralytique soigné par ses enfants, ou le fruit de la bonne éducation* (plate 35), promptly and unanimously christened *La Piété Filiale*,[21] and the drawings of *La Malédiction Paternelle* and *Le Fils Puni* (Lille, Musée Wicar) (plates 38, 39). The first has strong connections with *L'Accordée de Village*. There are clear indications here that Greuze had his public's interest a little too much in mind; an elderly man being cared for by his children is touching enough, but an elderly paralytic would and apparently did send an eighteenth-century audience into convulsions. Grimm saw a woman approach the picture, contemplate it for an instant, and burst into tears. Diderot considered that the feelings of the public would have been spared if Greuze had let it be known that the old man was merely suffering from an attack of gout rather than from a malady which brought overtones of the graveyard too near for comfort. The picture itself appears to be a shabbier affair than *L'Accordée de Village*, with a profusion of dirty linen, and, more worryingly, a certain discrepancy between the ages of the elderly parents and their children. The figures of the parents and of the son and his wife are fundamentally the same as those in *L'Accordée de Village*, a resemblance which gave rise to a discussion of whether or not it were a continuation of the same story.[22] The setting is also the same, although here Greuze's study of Rubens would appear to have orientated him towards a more Baroque type of composition. Nevertheless there is the same feeling that the scene is taking place on a stage at the moment when the curtain is about to fall, and like *L'Accordée de Village* it is a most intricately composed picture. There is the same touch of the bitch feeding her young, '*pour indiquer en quelque sorte l'origine de l'amour filial*'.[23] Above all, the pictures are the same ideologically, that is to say, they are tender, affecting, and fundamentally untragic. Diderot's remark, 'Dr Gatti tells me . . . that the man has a good three years left to live' is an attempt to reassure both himself and his readers that all is for the best in the best of all possible worlds. On the other hand, '. . . woe betide the man who can contemplate it for a moment in cold blood!'

Surprisingly enough, Greuze was left with the picture on his hands until it was sold to Russia in 1766.[24] Mariette implies that Greuze had difficulty in finding a buyer: 'The second picture still awaits a buyer; but to find one Greuze will have to modify his pretensions considerably. He has already turned down a handsome offer and I think he may regret it'.[25] Diderot endorses this in 1765, mentioning the fact that the king, after ordering it to be brought to Versailles, sent it away again. However, the colour, which appeared 'sombre, brownish and rather dull'[26] in 1763, came as a great shock to the Chevalier de Corberon, French chargé d'affaires in Russia, who wrote to the Marquise de Bréhan on 4 February 1776, 'I dined with Count Potemkin; he showed us the Empress's gallery. I noticed . . . with something of a shock Greuze's *Paralytic*; it has lost both its colour and its effect; it amounts to very little now'.[27]

La Malédiction Paternelle and *Le Fils Puni*, of which the preliminary sketches were shown in 1765, are, on the other hand, a different kind of challenge to the conscience. They are uncomfortable; they confront and perhaps affront the spectator. There is no doubt that Greuze considered this to be his real stature as an artist, for the sketches, which are masterly, are executed with infinitely more breadth and conviction than the other large drawings of the period. Not only do the compositions form natural climaxes, with none of the posed overdone character of *L'Accordée de Village* and *Le Paralytique*, the figures have more speed to them, and the wonderful chiaroscuro, never hitherto developed by Greuze with such subtlety, casts a genuine light of horror over the scene. It has been said that the reaction of the public was unfavourable. People resented being jolted from the routine comforts of *sensibilité* by this almost English panorama of curses, ruin and death. The state of contemporary taste may be judged by this remark of Mathon de la Cour's with reference to the *Jeune fille qui pleure la mort de son oiseau*: 'On several occasions I have looked at it for hours on end, delighting in that sweet and tender sadness which is worth more than physical pleasure; and I have come away from it filled with a delicious melancholy',[28] or Diderot's complacent acceptance of the subject of *L'Enfant Gâté*: 'It is his little laundrymaid of four years ago who has got married and whose story he now proposes to tell us'.[29] The reaction to the finished pictures some twelve years later will be discussed in the following chapter. Curiously enough, Greuze was more of a pioneer than has hitherto been recognized. In the history of *sensibilité* his place should be among the first, for his *Lecture de la Bible* preceded the dramas of Diderot; his *Accordée de Village* is contemporary with *La Nouvelle Héloïse*; and his *Malédiction Paternelle* and *Fils Puni* are far ahead of the later, gloomier 'drames bourgeois' of both Mercier and Desforges in the following decade.

As Greuze did not exhibit in 1767, a number of pictures of this period must be dated on grounds of style alone. The more ambitious projects can be connected with the reception picture of 1769. Diderot suggested that Greuze was undecided with regard to a subject, and there exists a small number of paintings and drawings which indicate the models he set himself. It is interesting to note that with the exception of the mythological drawing, all of these works derive from Rubens in subject or style. The closest in both these cases is a drawing, *La Charité Romaine* (Louvre, Inv. 26.983) (plate 36), which is a copy, with slight variations, of the Rubens now in the Hermitage but at the time passing through a variety of French collections.[30] The pictures are *Lot and his Daughters* (Strasbourg, Otto Kauffman collection) and *Queen Thalestris before Alexander*, stated in a sale catalogue of 1912 to be a project for the 1769 picture and described as follows: 'The stricken queen collapses in supplication at the feet of the conqueror; she is supported by an attendant, and behind her her courtiers and people demonstrate the absolute submission she is expressing in their name. Alexander, standing and leaning on his spear, accepts this homage with dignity'. This picture, of which the present writer has only seen a photograph, shows a distinct resemblance to Rubens' *Henri IV receiving the portrait of Marie de Medici* in the Luxembourg Gallery. In addition to these, Greuze tried a religious theme, a *Rest on the Flight into Egypt* (plate 37), for which there is a drawing at Tournus, and a mythological subject, *L'Amour triomphant d'Hercule* (for which there is also a drawing at Tournus). An important drawing entitled *Eponine et Sabine* (Chaumont) shows him attempting a subject from Roman history.[31] These drawings, although not so revealing in style as the finished pictures, can be connected with the same undertaking as they correspond in technique to a dated drawing of 1769, *La Bénédiction Paternelle* (Art Institute of Chicago).

In the end, however, Greuze opted not for Rubens but for Poussin ('*ce tableau . . . prôné par l'artiste lui-même comme un morceau à lutter avec ce que le Poussin avait fait de mieux*'),[32]† and with unfortunate results. Fervent classicists may approve the composition of *Sévère et Caracalla* (plate 41), with its backward glance to Poussin's *Death of Germanicus* (plate 42), but it is almost impossible to appreciate it as a picture. In addition to serious inaccuracies of drawing, it has the dead and paralysed air of something that has been subjected to too much treatment. This is in sharp contrast to the original studies which are grandiose and serious (plate 40). Modest in size and dark in colouring (the prevailing tones are grey, blue, purple and green), the picture impresses solely by the manner in which it was painted. Four years earlier, in 1765, Fragonard could produce his immense fantasy, *Corresus and Callirhoe*, to prove how free the mid-century painter had become from all academic restrictions. Greuze, on the other hand, has made a voluntary return to the manner of Poussin, a manner not due for revival until the 1780s. Despite the jibes of contemporary critics against the painful distortions of the drawing and the weakness of the impact, jibes which are in the main justified, one thing is certain: the date 1769 should be taken as seriously as 1784, that of David's *Oath of the Horatii*, in the story of the evolution of the neo-Poussinist or Neoclassical style in France.

† This painting . . . extolled by the artist himself as a piece to contend with the best that Poussin ever achieved.

Greuze's contribution is historically more remarkable than that of David, for with his unlettered but obstinate intelligence, he seems to have made, quite independently, the discovery that the work of Poussin contained lessons by which mid-eighteenth-century painting could be corrected. In this, David had only to follow Greuze.

One perceptive critic construed the picture's gloomy colouring as analogous to the dark action portrayed: '. . . these masses emphasized by deep shadows lead to an overall darkness in the picture; but few people have seen this as a deliberate ploy on the part of the painter to prepare us for the sombre activities of Caracalla, who in this way, as in the disorder of his appearance, presents the very image of an ungrateful and unnatural son'.[33] (Delacroix used much the same expressionist means of conveying the contrast between the dying Marcus Aurelius and the decadent Commodus in his picture of 1840 at Lyon, a picture which is equally indebted to the Poussin model.) Conceived as a bas relief, the main emphases are everywhere vertical and horizontal, and the two main figures are in very simplified positions. As usual, a great deal of attention was lavished on the heads, all of which were copied after Roman coins or busts. The Caracalla, according to Diderot, was taken from the *Antinous*. The Severus, an unimpressive figure, demonstrates Greuze's deep-seated reluctance to draw from the model, whereas the heads, in particular that of Papinian, show his talent for portraying expression. But it is above all the setting of the room, with its channelled pilasters, its statue of Fortune, and its goat-footed table, that marks the break with current eighteenth-century practice and carries us forward in anticipation to David.

The Salon of 1769 contained a far greater proportion of serious works than hitherto. *La Mère Bien-aimée* (Laborde collection) (plate 43), with its sub-title, *Portrait de Jean-Joseph de Laborde et de sa famille*, had inspired the following tribute from Diderot when it appeared as a sketch in 1765: 'this is excellent both from the point of view of talent and of morality. It preaches population and paints most movingly the happiness and the inestimable worth of domestic peace. It says to every man who has a heart and soul, 'Keep your family in comfort; give your wife children; give her as many as possible; don't give them to anyone else, and be assured of a happy life at home'. He had gone on to add, 'Rubens did not do better in the Luxembourg Gallery', alluding to the latter's *Birth of Louis XIII*. The preparatory study at Besançon is, perhaps, a little more revealing, and by the same token, *Le Tendre Désir* at Chantilly may be a first study for the head.

The effect of the whole is far more exaggerated than anything Greuze had produced so far. As the Marquis de Laborde was an extremely rich financier who, according to Bachaumont, '*ne se montr(ait) jamais qu'avec plus de cent mille francs de diamants et de bijoux sur sa personne*',[34]† Greuze could not logically turn on his usual village accessories and was therefore obliged to rely on the force of the emotion he had unleashed. In any event the picture was commissioned by the mother of Mme de Laborde, Mme de Nettine, which explains her prominent central position. There is a superb and invigorating drawing for this figure in the Louvre (plate 44). Again the picture is a pure tableau vivant: the Marquis enters left and throws up his hands in astonishment at the sight of his wife and six children. Although he has merely returned from shooting, his clothes seem as ready to slip off as do his wife's; a general atmosphere of undress seems to pervade this picture and there is an actual dress discarded in the centre foreground. Given the fact that the Marquis de Laborde was a millionaire banker with several châteaux and estates near Paris, there may be some irony in Greuze's portrayal of his domestic appointments. But Greuze was not a humorous man and it is probable that he relied once again on his own family memories to give shape to what appears to be a very humble living room.

There were, in the same Salon, two drawings of the worst moral implications—*L'Avare et ses Enfants* and *La mort d'un père de famille abandonné par ses enfants* (Tournus)—and four which were more reassuring: *La mort d'un père de famille regretté par ses enfants*, *La Bénédiction Paternelle* (Art Institute of Chicago) (plate 45), *La Consolation de la Vieillesse* (possibly that illustrated by Florisoone[35] under the title *Etude pour une compositione de Paralytique entouré de ses enfants*), and *Le Départ de la Bercelonette, ou la Privation Sensible* (Louvre, Inv. 26.954). This last is the drawing intended to illustrate *La Naissance du ieune Thibault* and succeeding events in Greuze's problematic story, *Bazile et Thibault, ou les deux Educations* (see Appendix). Similarly, *La Bénédiction Paternelle* represents *Le Départ de Bazile*. The *Portrait of Jeaurat* (Louvre) was considered 'a Rembrandt', and the three heads of children, 'two of an exquisite beauty, the third a pastiche of Rubens which should have been given away to a friend and not shown to the public'.[36] Finally, there were the pictures of a girl playing with a dog (England, private collection) (plate 46) and the *Jeune fille qui fait sa prière au pied de l'autel de l'Amour* (London, Wallace Collection) (plate 47).

† Never appeared without over a hundred thousand francs' worth of diamonds and jewels upon his person.

This last is interesting for it shows Greuze indulging in a form of Neoclassicism and applying it to a purely Rococo subject which was to be copied with variations throughout the next twenty-five years. Had Greuze not been so firmly entrenched in his own particular genre, he might have made more experiments in this style, for he was clearly interested and had done a certain amount of studying on the subject. Much archaeological research had gone into the heads in the Caracalla picture. It is equally interesting to note that in 1767 he drew or painted a portrait of Diderot *en camaieu* i.e. like a profile on a medal and very much in the Roman manner. Gavin Hamilton's portrait of *William Hamilton of Bangour* (Edinburgh, Scottish National Portrait Gallery) is almost exactly the same in style and suggests a common source.

Greuze, however, preferred a public he knew to one of whose reactions he was not quite sure, and his *Jeune fille qui fait sa prière au pied de l'autel de l'Amour* remains a compromise. Although he was the first to give the subject this particular form, he was not the first to treat it, for in 1761, Michael van Loo had shown a *Première Offrande à l'Amour*, with two girls in draperies and a classical setting, and in 1763, Vien had shown a *Sacrifice sur l'autel de l'Amour*. Reynolds, in France in 1763, took the idea back with him to England and in the following year painted *Lady Sarah Bunbury sacrificing to the Graces*. Sacrifices, however, were fairly common; Greuze wanted something more original and more touching and used complicated methods in order to acquire it. The winged figure of Cupid on a pedestal proffering a garland of flowers is taken from Mariette's *Traité des Pierres gravées*, engraved by Bouchardon. (Greuze admired Bouchardon and occasionally copied him; four academies by Bouchardon are included in an inventory of Greuze's possessions made soon after his divorce.) The bare-breasted girl in classical draperies seems to have been inspired by Vien's *Offrande à Cérès* (1763) and the idea of the landscape setting has been adopted from Michael van Loo. The sacrificial scene on the bronze ewer and the smoking altar both bear witness to a certain amount of archaeological study, but in spirit the picture belongs to the Rococo Neoclassicism of Vien or the Boucher of pictures like *L'Attention dangereuse*, a Neoclassicism adopted merely for its piquancy and with no overtones of social or moral significance whatsoever.

The fact was that although Neoclassicism was already in existence as a movement and was even enjoying a certain amount of success as a fashion,[37] it had as yet no validity as an aesthetic. And above all, there was no public demand for it or understanding of it. This criticism reflects the spirit in

III. *Girl with dead bird*

which the pictures exhibited by Vien in the Salon of 1763 were received: 'the works of M. Vien are distinguished in the Salon by a rigorous imitation of the antique . . . great simplicity in the positions of the figures which are almost upright and without movement, very few draperies, and those very thin and as it were clinging to the body; a severe sobriety in the accessories, all these features being well known attributes of the antique. If such austerity can sometimes, even in sculpture, appear cold and insipid, how can it constitute a merit and a necessary means of perfecting our school in painting? . . . It would be wrong to suppose . . . that none of the works exhibited by M. Vien is pleasing to the public. On the contrary; no one could fail to enjoy the agreeable sentiment inspired by the touching and naive expression of a young girl about to present an offering to the Temple of Venus. The touching graces of an affair of the heart are wedded to a timid modesty . . .', etc.[38]

In fact, there was more response to the sentimental content of the Vien than to its pictorial expression, and Greuze, who realized this, exploited it in his own picture. Prayers, oaths, and sacrifices to love then followed with monotonous frequency. In 1773 came Vien's *Deux jeunes grecques qui font serment sur l'autel de l'amour de ne jamais aimer*; in 1777, Mlle Vallayer's *Jeune personne montrant à son amie la statue de l'amour*, and in the same year, Ollivier's *Sacrifice à l'amour*. Also from this period are Fragonard's *Serment d'Amour* (Orléans), and Theaulon's *Sacrifice à l'Amour* (Angers). In 1783, Roslin painted his lovely *Jeune fille qui s'apprête à orner de fleurs la statue de l'Amour* (Louvre), and in 1786 Trinquesse produced a *Serment à l'Amour* and an *Offrande à Vénus* (Dijon). In the 1790s Le Barbier transformed the main figure, crowned it with a Roman helmet, and called it *Le Retour du Guerrier*, while as late as 1809 Mme Chaudet exhibited a *Jeune fille à genoux devant la statue de Minerve qui fait le sacrifice des dons de l'amour*. These are only a few examples, without taking into account the parallel treatment of the theme in England, where the original Reynolds treatment had been supplemented by Angelika Kauffman in the 1780s. In England, however, it generally remained confined to the mythological portrait.

Greuze did not emerge from the Salon of 1769 in a settled temper. He had failed to please, and his public had expressed its disappointment in a wealth of sharp and detailed technical criticism. Moreover, faced with such serious exercises, certain critics expressed a marked nostalgia for the sweeter, less challenging manner of 1761 and a desire to be indulged further in their hunger for tender and pious sentiment. Nobody wanted Greuze to be a

113

history painter except Greuze himself. This note is well sounded by the author of *Sentiments sur les tableaux exposés au Salon de 1769* in his criticism of the Caracalla picture: 'Certain uneducated people have taken this unhappy scene to be some domestic quarrel in the life of his Paralytic, especially as several fine sketches indicate an interesting series of episodes in the life of that infirm creature up to his death'. Greuze had indulged his public so far that he was now to a certain extent its victim.

The 1760s had been a prolific period. They had begun by Greuze's breaking new ground in various genres. From about 1763 date Greuze's unique exercises in the realm of book illustration. He prepared three drawings to be engraved by Moreau le Jeune, one for an edition of Ariosto (canto 29, strophe 5), one for *La Rosière, ou la Fête de Salency* by Billardon de Sauvigny (*Cruels, c'est votre loi qui le fait mourir, reprenez votre couronne*), and the last (*Madame, vous la voyez!*), for *Sophronie, ou la leçon prétendue* by Mme Benôit.[39] These are very close to and are probably based on the style of book illustration made popular by Gravelot. In addition to this, Greuze had made contact with Russia (two unnamed portraits, the *Paralytique*, and the Tchernitchev portraits) and through no fault of his own had broken it again.

Reviewing his position from the standpoint of 1769, we find that this style has settled into fairly recognizable lines. He is the painter of family pictures, and there are indications that he has a leaning towards moral pictures in the English melodramatic style. He is not, in the opinion of the Académie, a history painter. He has painted only three or four fallen innocents but on the other hand a great many heads of children in various moods: usually wistful (*La petite soeur, Le petit frère*, Chantilly), or serious (*La petite Nanette*, Montpellier; the so-called *Pierre-Alexandre Wille*, Strasbourg). He has renounced Rembrandt in favour of Rubens and will soon give up Rubens and rely on his own experience, much as Boucher boasted of never drawing from the model after the age of thirty. He has given up the fine genre drawings, such as *La Poupée Dansante* (Vienna, Albertina) (plate 48), and from 1770 onwards his drawing will decline in quality. The 1769 fiasco will affect him in two ways. Firstly, he will need to pander to the public to retain its favour and its purchasing power: more portraits and more insinuating allegory. Secondly, his large pictures, with the exception of *Le Gâteau des Rois*, will all be designed to vindicate his thwarted ambitions for the title of history painter. His purpose will receive posthumous recognition from Watelet: 'Paint therefore with pleasure, with interest, with sentiment, the image of an old man who inspires a just respect as an excellent father; of a young child who will give you a fine idea of the grace of infancy; of a woman recognizable by the truth of the form rather than the smallest details of her features and the exaggeration of her accessories. Paint animals, landscapes and flowers, and if you have a secret pride, inspired by your most cherished preoccupations, paint them in such a way that they announce that they were executed by an artist superior to what is generally understood by the term genre painter.

'Genre painters, it is your turn to have the noble ambition to explore territories which formerly seemed forbidden to you. Portraiture is your field; that much is clear. Now study the nude and the antique, as if you were destined to paint gods and heroes. Such works are rare today, I agree, but you do not know the destiny that awaits you . . .'[40]

Greuze's Development as an Artist from 1769 onwards

We have only a handful of dated works from the 1770s, although the period contains some of Greuze's most famous productions. *La Cruche Cassée* (Louvre) (plate 49), not exhibited until 1777, was finished and engraved by Molès in 1773. With this, or perhaps a little anterior to it, may be grouped: *La Vertu Chancelante* (Sammlung der Bayerischen Hypotheken- und Wechsel-Bank, Alte Pinakothek, Munich) (plate 50) in which a girl is seen sitting in a garret pondering over the sinister gift of a gold watch; an impressive Neoclassical head of a girl (ex-Wildenstein), the *Portrait of Mme de Porcin* (Angers) (plate 53), and *Mlle Clairon en Roxane* (formerly in the Pasadena, Calif., Museum of Fine Arts). The companion pictures of a little boy with a dog and a girl in a gauze scarf (London, Wallace Collection) (plates 51, 52) may also be dated *c.* 1770. The fixed points of portraiture are *La Marquise de Champcenetz* (dated 1770), *Benjamin Franklin* (1778, Mr and Mrs Lamont du Pont Copeland collection), *Paul Stroganov* (1778, Leningrad, Hermitage) (plate 54), the Schuvalov portraits (before 1781, Leningrad, Hermitage) (plate 55), and the Saint-Morys portraits (1778, Nantes) (plate 56). The *Portrait d'un jeune garçon* in the Musée Cognac-Jay, Paris, is near to the *Stroganov* in style and may be placed in the late 1770s. The most significant production of these years, however, consists of no less than seven large moralities: *Le Gâteau des Rois* (1774, Montpellier), *La Dame de Charité* (for dating see below, Lyon), *La Malédiction Paternelle* (1777, Louvre), *Le Fils Puni* (1778, Louvre), *Le Donneur de Chapelets* (New Jersey, Montclair Art Museum) which Edgar Munhall has dated 1780, and *Le Retour de l'Ivrogne* (Oregon, Portland Art Museum), which can be dated before 1785, when it passed through the sale of the Marquis de Véry, and after 1781, for it shows the revivifying influence of David's *Belisarius*, exhibited in the Salon of that year. There are in addition the engravings of *La Belle-Mère* (1781), *Le Testament Déchiré*, which Flipart was engaged on in 1782, and the picture of *La Veuve et son Curé* (Leningrad, Hermitage), which the Grand-Duke Petrovitch bought for his mother during his visit to Paris in 1782. Thus in the twelve years 1774–86 Greuze can be said to have painted some of his most important works, although with the exception of *La Malédiction Paternelle* and *Le Fils Puni*, they are less well-known than those of his earlier period.

La Cruche Cassée (Louvre) (plate 49) takes up the note so eloquently sounded in the *Jeune fille qui pleure la mort de son oiseau* of 1765, but treats it with far greater sophistication. It was all too obvious to the spectator that this was another allegory of lost innocence, but it appeared, to Mme Roland, among others, a remarkably decent work. It is certainly, for a subject of this type, a very painterly one. The luscious tender flesh, still painted with Rubens shadows of grey and blue, is now on the verge of decadence; the plump hands are becoming mannered. The dress, roughly painted with stiff loaded brush-strokes, sets off the melting Greuzian softness of the head, and the colours of the accessories (pink roses, green leaves, dark grey-blue sky) overflatter the tender passages. Yet in spite of all this, the girl seems to have been painted as a study, i.e. objectively, and the stillness of the figure, a quality rare in Greuze, almost triumphs over the *double entendre*. Greuze must have realized this, for when he painted a later version he greatly increased the action.[1]

La Vertu Chancelante (plate 50) prefigures in a curious way Holman Hunt's *Awakening Conscience*, thus underlining the fact that *sensibilité* comes very close at times to the nineteenth-century phenomenon that Baudelaire castigated as 'bourgeois hypocrisy'. Both pictures are concerned with the conflict between an invitation to high living and memories of former innocence. Yet *La Vertu Chancelante* has an additional significance: the classical, or more properly speaking Neoclassical regularity of the girl's features, albeit summarily painted. The impulse at this date can only have come from Vien, but this example of Greuze's efforts towards the real Neoclassical movement shows him to have anticipated, in however small a way, the advent of David in the following decade.

The *Portrait of Mme de Porcin* (Angers) (plate 53), less richly painted than *La Cruche Cassée*, has the same roughly executed white négligé and gauze scarf, the same Rubens flesh with its pink fingers and breast and blue shadows round the mouth and throat. With its grey background and neatly painted garland of flowers, it is a charmingly subdued portrait, and in comparison with contemporary Rococo productions, must have seemed an extremely naturalistic one. The significance of Greuze in this connection is not that he invariably painted women with their clothes falling off, but that he preferred to paint them in their *déshabillé du matin*, easily identifiable from contemporary fashion prints, and before the paint and powder had disguised the natural qualities of their skin. This particular motif of crowning a lapdog with a garland of flowers became widely popular, especially with Russian patrons, and was continued by Mme Vigée-Lebrun during her stay in Saint Petersburg.

As to the other portraits of the 1770s, the *Stroganov* (Leningrad, Hermitage) (plate 54), of which there is a drab and woolly copy in Besançon, has a tender charm that is on the verge of becoming routine. The *Portrait of the Comte de Saint-Morys* (Nantes) (plate 56) is interesting in that it is painted on panel and is remarkably forceful in colouring. Its pendant, the portrait of the Count's young son, bears a faint resemblance to *La Cruche Cassée* and is notable for the excellent painting of the white satin jacket and the pink and white carnation. Otherwise it appears to have been mutilated about the eyes, eyebrows, and nose, by being thickly scored with the wrong end of the brush. The little boy with a dog[2] and the girl with a gauze scarf (plates 51, 52), with their bright colours and enamel surface, are polished but routine productions which do not repay long contemplation.

We come now to the large family pictures which in this decade run the whole gamut of the emotions. *Le Gâteau des Rois* (1774) (plate 57) was a private commission for the Duc de Cossé-Brissac and is therefore less original than the other independently painted works, It shows a family assembled around a table, the father offering to the youngest son a choice of pieces of the *galette des rois* or Twelfth Night cake, one of which will contain the lucky favour that will make him king of the feast. There is, despite the child's exaggerated recoil, no drama in the subject; the setting is the familiar Lyonnais interior, and in fact this seems a determinedly nostalgic regional picture. It is a family piece in the style of *L'Accordée de Village*, tender and muggy in sentiment and undistinguished in execution. The colour is an almost exact continuation of that of *L'Accordée de Village*, with notes of grey-white, blue, yellow and sepia predominating. There is one point of interest about the composition. Like all other large pictures of this decade, with the partial exception of *La Malédiction Paternelle*, it is horizontal and frieze-like, as against the shallow semi-circular emphasis of *L'Accordée de Village* and *Le Paralytique*. This seems to indicate that Greuze resented the slurs made by the *Avant-Coureur* on his studies of Poussin and concentrated on a markedly Poussinesque type of composition. This will be more apparent in *La Dame de Charité*, *Le Fils Puni*, *Le Retour de l'Ivrogne* and *La Belle-Mère*, while the early pictures of David, in particular the first version of *Andromache weeping over Hector's body* in the Hermitage, are painted according to the same convention and follow the examples established by the Greuze.

The picture painted for the Duc de Cossé-Brissac did not contain the figure of the sulking child on the extreme right. A second version—the one now in Montpellier—painted for M. Duclos-Dufresnoy, contained this 'boudeuse', and Cossé-Brissac, who saw it, asked Greuze to include this figure in his own version. This was done by means of an additional strip of canvas. The picture was engraved in 1778 with the following inscription:

> *Que le hasard ici donne la royauté*
> *O père, O fils, O mère, O fille,*
> *Tout au sein de cette famille*
> *Va retentir les chants de l'aimable gaité.*
> *Mais autour d'une table abondamment garnie*
> *Où règne les ennuis et la cérémonie,*
> *Souvent sous les lambris d'un magnifique toit,*
> *On articule à peine en baillant 'Le roi boit'.*†

There is a large finished oil sketch for the head of the mother in the museum at Nimes.

In contrast to this, *La Dame de Charité* (Lyon) (plate 59) is a picture which challenges the consciences but in the name of all the public virtues. There is some dispute over the dating of this picture. Edgar Munhall ('Greuze and the Protestant Spirit', *Art Quarterly*, Vol. XXVII, 1964) states that it was painted in 1772 and this date is accepted and quoted by Jean Seznec in his article '*Diderot et l'Affaire Greuze*', *Gazette des Beaux-Arts*, May 1966. Jean Martin, in his catalogue of Greuze's works, states that the picture passed through the Paillet sale in 1774. This conflicts with Louis Hautecoeur's statement that Greuze exhibited the work in his studio in 1775. The evidence for this last fact is slight but convincing and is to be found in the letters written by Mme Roland, then Mlle Phlipon, to her

---

† Chance here bestows the royal favour—father, son, mother, daughter. All in the bosom of this family echo the songs of happy cheer. But around a table weighed down with plenty, where boredom and ceremony reign, often under the ornate vaulting of a magnificent roof one barely articulates for yawning 'the king drinks'.

friends Sophie and Henriette Cannet. In the late summer of 1775 Sophie Cannet paid a visit to Mlle Phlipon in Paris and together they went to Greuze's studio. This visit is recalled by Mlle Phlipon on the occasion of another visit to Greuze's studio two years later in 1777: '*Je me suis rappelé avec attendrissement, jeudi dernier, le plaisir que nous goûtâmes ensemble, Sophie, en allant chez M. Greuze il y a deux ans*'.† The picture that they saw in 1775 is not named but apparently it compares favourably with *La Malédiction Paternelle* which Mlle Phlipon saw in 1777: '*. . . l'ensemble de l'ouvrage ne produit pas l'impression touchante que nous ressentîmes toutes deux en considérant l'autre*'.†† This 'touching' picture might have been *Le Gâteau des Rois* or *La Dame de Charité*. That it was probably *La Dame de Charité* is implied in an earlier letter of Mlle Phlipon to Mlle Cannet, dated 31 October 1775, in which she remarks, quite out of context, '*. . . je dirais de lui ce que j'ai dit à M. Greuze de son tableau: si je n'aimais pas la vertu, il m'en donnerait le goût*'.†‡§ *Le Gâteau des Rois* is virtuous enough in that it shows a happy family united in some unexceptional but peaceable exercise. *La Dame de Charité*, on the other hand, strikes a blow for good works and proclaims the concept virtue to the most negligent observer. Moreover, the advanced form of the composition, which is considerably more interesting than that of *Le Gâteau des Rois*, would support this later dating.

There can be no doubt whatever over the interpretation of *La Dame de Charité*. A little girl is being given her first lesson in *bienfaisance*, which consists of presenting a purse to a poor old man and his wife who now have nothing left but a sword, mark of their original station in life. We have thus moved up a class, although there is an additional source for the motif of the sword hanging at the head of the bed, namely David's *Antiochus and Stratonice*, exhibited at the Salon of 1774 (plate 60). It is curious to reflect that the same setting and poses of the figures were used by both artists, and it is at this point that the connection between Greuze and David becomes meaningful. Greuze borrows from David in *La Dame de Charité* and *Le Retour de l'Ivrogne*, David from Greuze in the idea of the *Belisarius* (copied back from that same *Dame de Charité*) and more closely in the first version of *Andromache* described on page 148.

† I recalled with emotion, last Thursday, the pleasure which we experienced together, Sophie, when we went to M. Greuze's studio two years ago.

†‡ As a whole the work does not produce the same 'touching' sensation which we both felt when looking at the other.

†‡§ I would say of him what I said to M. Greuze of his painting: if I didn't already love virtue, he would give me the taste for it.

Greuze's picture belongs firmly to an earlier age in its contrast between the sour-faced nun of the order of St Vincent de Paul in the background and the compassionate lay virtue of the little girl's mother, thus making the once revolutionary distinction between religion and morality. In accordance with the status of the protagonists, the treatment is somewhat more heroic in style. There is less picturesque clutter, a classless but vaguely historical drapery has been added, and a great deal of the action is concentrated in the hands, which provide the focal as well as the emotional climax of the story. The colours are low in tone: the draperies a dull greenish-yellow, the the little boy on the left in a reddish jacket with blue sleeves. As usual, the linen is painted with a heavily loaded brush which contrasts with the smooth even treatment of the heads. The colours have now darkened very badly and it is possible that if the picture were cleaned, the group of the mother and child would be far more melting and subtle in colour harmony. An important feature of the picture is its planimetric emphasis, the rigid verticals and horizontals of the door-frame on the right and the picture on the left, the position of the bed, and the tendency of the protagonists to present themselves nearly in profile, all of which gives the lie to Mauclair's statement, 'Le talent de Greuze n'a jamais varié'. The lesson of Poussin, perhaps of that same Death of Germanicus which inspired Severus and Caracalla, or, more probably, a conflation of the Death of Germanicus with the same master's Testament of Eudamidas is producing results, for with its closed dull ground and the box-like structure of the room, it must be admitted that this is a more Poussinesque composition than David's Antiochus and Stratonice.

As important as the finished picture is the superb study for the head of the old man in the Musée Fabre in Montpellier (plate 58). Broad in treatment and very thickly impasted, it has the force of a Géricault. There is great feeling for the planes of the head, the light on the gaunt bones of the face, the shadows of the cavernous neck. As a painting of an invalid, it is Romantic rather than sentimental. All of this is completely lost on the large canvas, where the effect given is that of a touching but nevertheless slightly caricatured old man.

It will be remembered that La Malédiction Paternelle (plate 61) and Le Fils Puni (plate 62) were found disturbing when they appeared in the form of drawings in 1765. When worked up into finished pictures and shown in Greuze's studio in 1777 and 1778, their success was almost overwhelming. This is because sensibilité, now approaching its decadence and craving stronger stimulants, was turning to the glooms and passions of English pre-Romanticism. It is the epoch not only of Mercier but of Loaisel de Tréogate[3] and an appetite for strong, sometimes murderous or suicidal passions is now in order. The pictures, however, have changed as well. The drawings showed a modest cottage interior with a rough wooden door and lattice windows. The son was ragged and obviously villainous, the women wore shapeless clothes and caps, and the father had apparently died with the full benefits of his religion. Now the local colour has been completely cleared away. The status of the people involved seems altogether more comfortable, although they are no longer easily recognizable types. The heads are more noble in style, they express more elevated passions, and significantly enough, the women's dresses all have the character of draperies. Even their hair is plaited *à la grecque*. Thus Greuze, denying himself the easy popularity of the quaint and rustic, is concentrating the attention of the spectator on to the emotional and moral crisis portrayed. He is in fact painting classical pictures.

Both pictures have a dark setting; in fact a weakness of the compositions is that the same door apparently opens into two different rooms, the familiar cluttered and disordered ground floor interior in *La Malédiction Paternelle* and the mortuary bedroom in *Le Fils Puni*. In the first picture the father's curse has just been uttered, to the horror of the family and especially of the renegade son about to disappear with the recruiting sergeant. A fine pyramid of action is composed by the father, the mother and the son, whose eloquent hands tell as much of the story as do their expressions. Colours are, as usual in Greuze's moral pictures, subdued. The setting is a dark olive grey shading darker to the left. The son is in white, with a blue coat and pink kerchief; the mother, a conspicuously Roman figure, wears a white drapery over a blue dress; the father a brown coat, blue trousers and white stockings. The only positive colour is provided by the small boy's red jacket and trousers in the foreground. The strokes are thick and heavy, the action weighty, and it may not be too fanciful to see the uplifted spotlit hand of the son as a forerunner of the hand of the elder Horatius in David's *Oath of the Horatii*.

In *Le Fils Puni*, to judge from the age of the renegade son, several years have passed and the father has died either of rancour or overwork. The same dingy colouring is lightened by the extreme subtlety of the painting of the whites and creams of the bed linen. Despite the exaggerations of the story, there is a feeling of genuine tragedy. The slow classic theatrical gestures gain an additional heaviness from the greater thickness of the brush strokes. The excited dog of the Lille drawing is now frozen into immobility. It will by now be unnecessary to emphasize the classical planimetric disposition of the two works. There is even a feeling, in *La Malédiction Paternelle*, that Greuze has been looking more intently at reproductions of classical sculpture, even perhaps at the *Laocoon*. And the figure of the mourning girl in *Le Fils Puni* in a certain sense passed back into sculpture for it appears to have influenced the figure on the left of Houdon's beautiful tomb of the Comte d'Ennery (Louvre), which is signed and dated 1781. Again, as can be seen in the Louvre drawing of the kneeling boy (plate 63), there is a sharp contrast between the freshness of the original drawings and the comparative rigidity of the finished pictures.

Above all, and this should never be forgotten in an evaluation of Greuze's works, *La Malédiction Paternelle* and *Le Fils Puni* are pictures built not only around a story but also an idea. They represent didactic moral painting before the advent of David, who learned so much from Greuze, and deserved their high reputation in an era given over largely to immaculate futilities. Greuze's incorrigible seriousness, muted as it was to suit the less exacting demands of his public, sought to convey that life does contain elements of conflict and disaster. His own tragedy was that his comparative lack of training, his ferocious pride and his unhappy financial position obliged him to cater for the tastes of contemporary collectors rather than to follow the development of this innovation in eighteenth-century French painting with which his name should be inextricably connected.

Strangely different and vastly inferior to the works just discussed is *Le Donneur de Chapelets* (plate 64) which can be dated about 1780. The subject of this painting is puzzling. A venerable monk, assisted by a younger bare-foot man in a more conventional monk's habit, is seen handing out rosaries to a congregation of young women. The action takes place in a kind of open air stockade or grotto, which has led Edgar Munhall to the conclusion that this is a '*prêche au désert*', the kind of stratagem to which Protestants were driven in France by the Revocation of the Edict of Nantes.[4] Munhall sees this as a further argument to support Greuze's supposed Protestantism; as against this, it must be pointed out that the rosary is an essentially Catholic institution. More disquieting than this problem, in the present writer's view, is the appearance of a new kind of mannerism: an untidy slapdash looseness of drawing and characterization, an obsessional love of girls, a caricatured observation of the contrast between extreme youth and extreme age, and a disappearance of the sculptural sense that animated the two previous works. This must surely have been a private commission. The picture is neither engraved nor mentioned in any contemporary account; it has none of the developing sense of tragedy that is Greuze's most marked characteristic in these years and which reaches its climax in *Le Retour de l'Ivrogne* (plate 65).

This picture can be assigned to the early 1780s. As has been stated, it passed through the sale of the Marquis de Véry in 1785. In the Salon of 1781 there appeared a work which inaugurated the new dark manner of the young David, the *Belisarius begging for alms* (Lille, Musée Wicar) (plate 66). Prominent in the *Belisarius* are a Roman matron who offers alms and a young boy with outstretched hands who assists Belisarius. It is not too fanciful to see echoes of these two figures in Greuze's more homely morality. A drunken father is confronted by his wife and two shoeless children in a dark bare interior. The significant reduction in the number of figures is also Davidian in inspiration, but Greuze retains his thickness of impasto and his deliberate regional naturalism, as if persisting in his desire to prove that tragedy is not confined to Roman history but is frequent in the lives of common people. This was basically the conviction that under- lined the '*drame bourgeois*', but Greuze has taken it several steps further. The complete absence of décor, the stark frieze-like treatment, the important part played by the hands, and the heavy insistent profiles mark an advance even on the innovations of *La Malédiction Paternelle* and *Le Fils Puni*. With this picture may be briefly considered the engraving called *La Belle-Mère* (plate 67), announced in a letter from Greuze to the *Journal de Paris* of 13 April 1781 and quoted above. Greuze had overheard a conversation on the Pont-Neuf and had created a whole scenario from it. The inscription on the engraving reads, '*Oui, elle lui donne du pain mais elle brise les dents avec le pain qu'elle lui donne*'.† This subject was prepared specifically as an engraving but can be considered in the same context as the preceding works because of the frieze-like treatment and the almost Poussinesque effect obtained by the interlocking arms.

Greuze's attempts to elevate his genre were not unnoticed, and indeed with the exception of the hostile Bachaumont, reactions to the pictures of this period are a good deal more unanimous than hitherto. Comparisons are no longer made with Rembrandt, Rubens, Teniers and Ostade, but with the

---

† Yes, she gives the child bread but she breaks her teeth with the bread which she gives her.

great masters of the classical school, Raphael, Poussin and Le Sueur. 'A second Raphael', pronounced Lebrun,[5] and the cautious La Harpe stated, 'Poussin was known as the painter of the intellectuals; we dare to tell M. Greuze that we consider him the painter of sensitive souls'.[6] One critic said of *La Malédiction Paternelle*, 'Raphael has not done better',[7] while La Harpe continued his burden, 'M. Greuze, it is said, is not in the category of history painters, but is not the history of the passions as valuable as that of Greece and Rome?'[8] Most precious of all is this statement added by one writer as an appendix to his review of the Salon of 1777: '... this is the ability to move at its most sublime (he was speaking of *La Malédiction Paternelle*) ... all the figures are purely and nobly drawn ... If they were given other costumes, although their own are very good as they are, if they were given heroic draperies, we should have one of the finest of history pictures ... Finally, this picture is a masterpiece from every point of view and to be compared with the greatest masters of expression ... Poussin, Le Sueur, Raphael himself would not have disowned it'.[9]

Bachaumont's criticism of the same picture, although justifiable, strikes us as mistimed and short-sighted. 'M. Greuze, who hopes to treat in this manner a series of similar moral subjects, always chooses characters from the lower classes, no doubt because he hopes to preach virtue with greater success in this way, but also because his manner is closer to this genre. His brush is dull, his draperies mean; but he has a prodigious understanding of light and shade'.[10]

As a postscript to this period of intense intellectual activity, the *Innocence entraînée par les Amours et suivie du Repentir* (Louvre) (plate 68), painted for the Comte d'Artois and given by him to Catherine of Russia, is a return to an earlier type of allegory but now treated in Neoclassical guise. This curious picture, an allegory of Greuze's temptations and repressions, is remarkable mainly on account of its landscape setting and its palace architecture (possibly by another hand). There may again be a reference to David's *Belisarius* in the veiled figure of Repentance, and, more specifically, in the raised arms of the girl releasing a dove. This subject was also treated by Prud'hon (collection of Duchesse de la Rochefoucauld-Bisaccia) but whether this is because both used a common source or because Prud'hon, in deference to his mentor, copied Greuze, has yet to be proved. The Prud'hon was not painted until 1810 but there are sketches dating from twenty years earlier.

At the same time that Greuze was painting the most serious of his family moralities, parallel developments were taking place at the other end of the scale. In 1779 Greuze sent to his friend Abraham Fontanel of Montpellier, for an exhibition organized by the *Société des Beaux-Arts* of that town, a 'head of a young girl expressing admiration and desire' (Montpellier, Musée Fabre) (plate 69). This, at first sight, would appear to be the epitome of every voluptuous Greuze bust ever painted. What it is, in fact, is a more intense version of the head of the girl praying to love which had been exhibited in the Salon of 1769. This goes some way to explaining the origin of this particular genre. Greuze, as has been noted, was in the habit of painting life-size studies for all the characters in his large family pictures. When he was forced either to abandon the latter because of lack of public interest, or to make money very quickly, he continued with these heads, which took little time to execute, giving them the pornographic twist which he knew was popular. It has been pointed out that the head at Chantilly known as *Le Tendre Désir* was ultimately connected with *La Mère Bien-aimée*, as was the Montpellier head with *La Prière à l'Amour*. The same connection can be traced between *La Prière du Matin* (Montpellier, Musée Fabre) (plate 70) and the endless heads derived from it. Thus although the '*tête de jeune fille*' had been in existence for almost twenty years, it did not emerge as an independent genre until 1779, and in so doing took on those overtones of provocation and corruption that were the delight of nineteenth-century collectors and are the despair of twentieth-century historians.

The 1780s are even less rich in dated works than the 1770s. The fixed points are a drawing connected with a picture which Métra saw in 1780, *A young girl opening her bodice to shelter a bird* (Besançon); *Le Donneur de Chapelets*, *Le Retour de l'Ivrogne*, *La Veuve et son Curé*, and *L'Innocence entraînée par les Amours* which have already been discussed; The Wallace Collection *Psyche* of 1786, and *La Colombe Retrouvée* (Moscow) painted for Yussupov in 1789. The portraits of *Mme Mercier* (Montreal, Mrs Van Horne collection), *Sophie Arnould* (London, Wallace Collection), *Princess Beloselskaya-Beloserskaya* and *Varvara Nikolaevna Gagarin* (present owners unknown; reproduced in L. Réau, '*Greuze et la Russie*', *L'Art et les Artistes*, 1919) can be dated 1786 or thereabouts on grounds of costume. Similarly, the portrait of a boy known as *Espièglerie* (London, Wallace Collection) can be dated around 1782. *La Laitière* (Paris, Louvre) (plate 71), of which the engraving was announced in the *Mercure de France* in 1783, and *La Petite Fille au Panier* (Montpellier, Musée Fabre), alike in style and in their bright colouring and thin paint, may be tentatively placed around 1780, since certain conventions of the former, e.g. the hands and the painting of the sleeve, spring from the stock of *La Cruche Cassée*. The Wallace Collection *Fidelity* is a barely altered copy of *La Colombe Retrouvée*, and *La Prière du Matin*[11] (Montpellier, Musée Fabre) is a recognizable version of it although it doubtless precedes it in date. The heads based on this last picture (Montpellier, Edinburgh, Berlin, Lord Bearsted collection) may be included among the productions of the 1780s. All exhibit a full-blown mannerism which will reach its apogee in the 1790s and which is already apparent in *Le Petit Mathématicien*[12] (Montpellier, Musée Fabre) (plate 72) of the preceding decade.

The only superior productions of these years are the three portraits, *Mme Mercier*, *Sophie Arnould* (plate 73), and *Varvara Nikolaevna Gagarin*. Mme Mercier is wearing the multiple garment known as '*négligé avec robe en chemise*', as shown in the *Cabinet des Modes* of February 1786, and has her hair '*en pouf avec boucles à l'Américaine*'. Sophie Arnould, on the other hand, with her large-brimmed felt hat and short curls, is dressed very much in the English manner, and it should be remembered that the taste for English fashions was very strong at this time. Varvara Nikolaevna wears a dress with a round frilled collar and is placing a garland around the neck of a little dog. A convenient résumé of all three portraits is provided by a plate prepared by Watteau le fils for the *Gallerie des Modes et Costumes Français* of 1785. It shows a girl wearing a large-brimmed felt hat crowning a spaniel with a garland, and the inscription reads, '*Jeune bourgeoise assise dans une promenade publique contrefaisant la Dame de Qualité en minaudant avec son chien; elle est en grand chapeau en colettes et grandes boucles à l'Américaine*'. Both the *Mme Mercier* and the *Princess Gagarin* appear to be thinly painted. The *Sophie Arnould*, with its melting outlines and soft colour harmonies, as if seen through a light veil of gauze, is one of the most notable portraits from Greuze's hand.

All the other pictures of this period, however, with the exception of *Le Retour de l'Ivrogne*, show a quite obvious decline. *La Veuve et son Curé* (plate 74), in which a venerable old man rebukes a young girl in the presence of her mother and brother, presumably for the usual fault—a picture prefigured some thirty years earlier in *La Mère en Courroux*—is unctuous and silly. The engraving, which appeared in 1786, was dedicated to '*Mm. les Curés*', with these words: '*C'est à vous, conservateurs de la Religion et des Moeurs, Pères spirituels de tous ordres de citoyens, c'est à vous que je dois l'idée de ce tableau: daignez en agréer la dédicace avec l'hommage de mon respect'*.[13]† *La Prière du Matin* (Montpellier, copy in Musée Cognac-Jay), with its glaring faults of drawing and anatomy, shows how Greuze had forgotten his powers as a draughtsman. Equally revealing are the subject heads based on this picture (Edinburgh, Montpellier, Lord Bearsted collection), with their dirty white linen purposely coarsened to enhance the *sfumato* effects, distended and impotent-looking hands, immense shoulders, swimming eyes, and ruddy, unsubtle complexions. *Le Petit Mathématicien* (Montpellier, Musée Fabre) (plate 72), with its unpleasant crowding of the figure on to the front plane of the picture, belongs to full mannerism, as do the three horrific heads of *Psyche* (London, Wallace Collection) (plate 75), *La Colombe Retrouvée* (Moscow, Pushkin Museum), (plate 76) and *Fidelity* (London, Wallace Collection). These voluptuous tear-drenched figures are basically repentant Magdalens, but the typical Greuze mouth and oval eyes are now awash with humidity. All have a wealth of heavy and complicated hair, immensely thick necks and shoulders, and tiny fat hands. In the true mannerist tradition, they are painted in completely unreal colours, shiny cosmetic tones of mauve, pink and yellow. Greuze's mastery of flesh painting has now become less than a clever trick, spoiled through mechanical over-production, over-emphasis, and slipshod execution.

The Greuze girl, therefore, seems to have reached her peak in the late 1780s, for the three heads mentioned above are more extreme than any other of this genre. The Wallace Collection *Innocence* (plate 77), painted in chocolate box colours and with a china surface, went through the Duclos-Dufresnoy sale in 1795 and belongs in technique to the 1790s. It is calm and static, and with its drapery may even have pretensions to strict Neoclassicism. The *Girl with Doves* (London, Wallace Collection) (plate 78) is signed and dated 1802 and is traditionally accepted as a repetition of *L'Innocence tenant deux pigeons* exhibited in the Salon of 1800. *La Surprise* (Chantilly), alike in dress, colour, and features, and the two blonde heads in the Albertina in Vienna may be dated *c*. 1800. Also exhibited in the Salon of 1800 was the last *Jeune fille qui pleure la mort de son oiseau* (Louvre) (plate 79) which is now not so much a study in double meaning as a fascinating piece of mannerism. The heavy hair has acquired a serpentine life of its own and twines in and out of the knotted drapery. The hands are boneless and affected, the head very large in proportion to the body. The effect is

† It is to you, preservers of Religion and Morals, spiritual fathers of all classes of citizens, it is to you that I owe the idea of this picture; I beg you to accept this dedication with the homage of my respect.

IV. *Portrait of E.-F. Bertin*

increased by the tired soiled colours, for in the last five years of his life Greuze's palette had become irretrievably dim and muddy. The *Letter-Writer* (London, Wallace Collection) (plate 81), for which there is a study in the same gallery, is perhaps the *Jeune fille se disposant à écrire une lettre d'amour*, the companion piece to the *Jeune fille qui pleure la mort de son oiseau* of 1800, although a drawing formerly in the Wildenstein collection would appear to be an alternative and larger project for the same subject. The girl in Directoire dress in the Musée Cognac-Jay, Paris, must be dated fairly late on grounds of costume. *Ariadne* (London, Wallace Collection) is probably the *Ariane dans l'Ile de Naxos* exhibited in the Salon of 1804. Bacchantes had made an early appearance; one had passed through the sale of Vassal de Saint-Hubert in 1774, and several were painted in the 1790s (e.g. the picture at Metz wrongly attributed to Regnault) but the subject was one treated with very great frequency in the last years, and the Wallace picture is certainly very late. Last of all would seem to be the girl in the blue dress (Wallace Collection) called *L'Espagnole* or *L'Ingénuité* (plate 82), a weak fumbling piece of work, made all the more pathetic by its miserable attempt at gaiety.

That Greuze could still occasionally treat the study of a young girl with charm and with restraint is attested by the portrait of *Countess Mollien* with an armful of puppies, dating from 1791, in the Baltimore Museum of Art (plate 80). Certainly the head is huge, the eyelashes drawn in with considerable lack of subtlety, the puppies scarcely recognizable as such, but the expression is reserved and dignified, and one of Greuze's peculiar gifts to eighteenth-century portraiture—a melting softness of paint—is very much in evidence. That he still occasionally had David in mind is shown in a drawing in the collection of Lord Clark, a *Lamentation over the dead Christ* (plate 83), in which only Christ's legs and feet are visible, as in David's *The Lictors bringing back to Brutus the bodies of his sons* of 1789. This desperate, haggard and impressive drawing should also be dated early in the 1790s.

In 1790 Greuze was visited by Romney. Hayley, in his *Life of Romney*, states, 'The living painters of France who chiefly engaged his notice were David and Greuze. Each of these artists favoured us with his company to dinner and David attended us in our visit to the Luxembourg Gallery'. Although this was a passing visit, not fraught with consequence for either artist, Greuze showed some of his old vitality and produced a markedly Romneyesque portrait and at least two drawings in his manner. The portrait is that of a girl with a gauze drapery over her head in the National Gallery, London, which can be compared with various portraits by Romney, notably that of Lady Hamilton with her hands clasped together under her chin in the National Portrait Gallery, London. The most Romneyesque of the drawings are the study at Tournus for the picture known as *La Peur de l'Orage*, with its thick bistre wash over a pen and ink foundation, and *La Vigilance endormie* (exhibited Cailleux Gallery, Paris, 1951).

Greuze now made another effort in the direction of Neoclassicism, based in the first instance on the rather spurious version popularized by Angelika Kauffmann, who would appear to be the inspiration behind the two portraits of his wife (dated 1785) and *Elizabeth Alexandrovna Demidov*, both as vestal virgins. David's successes in recent Salons seem to have had a supplementary influence on his style, and from the early 1790s we have a number of drawings, Neoclassical in style but Rococo in sentiment, which seem to occupy a place midway between the movements in France and England at the end of the eighteenth century, e.g. *L'Amour parmi les jeunes filles* (Dijon, Musée des Beaux-Arts) (plate 84) and *La Diseuse de Bonne Aventure* (Chalon-sur-Saône). In addition there is a handful of large canvasses: a half-finished *Paris and Helen* (Vigny-Chatou sale, Frankfurt, present owner unknown), based on the David of 1788, a *Prière à l'Amour* (Ferris-Thompson collection), and a melancholy *Psyche crowning Love*, overflowing with Neoclassical bric-à-brac, at Lille (plate 85). Here the scene takes place in a fully Davidian interior, with drapery, columns, statues in niches, and couch, and the inspiration behind it is surely David's *Paris and Helen* of 1788 (plate 86). Yet there is a sad contrast between the rigour of the setting and the mournful creatures who people it. A nearly nude vestal virgin watches tragically over the ceremony of love, while the protagonists, barely distinguishable from each other, are completely devoid of that chaste but powerful sexuality that is the keynote of David's picture.

The only painterly productions of the 1790s are a series of portraits of personalities of the revolutionary régime and the Directoire. The various portraits painted of Napoleon are now largely untraceable, but two of the most important are still in France, the full-length at Versailles (plate 87) and the portrait in the collection of Prince Napoleon, as well as the so-called 'Talleyrand' at Saint-Omer. The Versailles portrait is traditionally known as *Napoléon Premier Consul*, but there are two reasons against an acceptance of this title. Firstly, there exists an engraving of a bust portrait by Greuze, totally different from the portrait at Versailles, inscribed '*Napoléon Premier Consul*'. Secondly, the portrait at Versailles shows a man in his early twenties wearing a sword. A sketch for this portrait shows the same figure standing in the open air, with a portion of columniated architecture on the right (as in the finished picture) but with an *échappé* on the left on to a rather generalized battle scene. Therefore the intention seems to have been to portray him as a successful soldier, that is to say, before the *coup d'état* of 1799 by which he became First Consul.

Similar iconographical considerations have led to a revaluation of the large portrait at Saint-Omer traditionally known as '*Talleyrand*' (plate 91). The title of this portrait continues to be in doubt. M. Lacour-Gayet[14] has pointed out that the sitter bears no resemblance to the likenesses of Talleyrand by David, Prud'hon and Isabey, but that the portrait was found in the collection of Anna Greuze after her death, together with a sketch for a portrait of Talleyrand. He suggests that the titles got mixed and goes on to prove that the Saint-Omer picture is an official portrait illustrating an important point in the career of Napoleon. The subject of the picture is seen seated in a room, his sword slung around the pedestal of a statue, and surrounded by books and manuscripts. One of the most prominent objects in the room is the statue of the Belvedere *Hermes* or *Antinous*, which was brought from Italy to the Louvre in 1798 and returned to the Vatican in 1816. After the conclusion of Napoleon's Italian campaign, a peace treaty of purely Napoleonic inspiration was drawn up between France and Italy. The eighth article of the treaty read as follows: '*Le Pape livrera à la République Française cent tableaux, bustes, vases ou statues, au choix des commissaires qui seront envoyés a Rome ... et cinq cent manuscrits au choix des memes commissaires*'.†
Bearing the spoils of his victory, Napoleon then made a triumphal entry into Paris on 9 and 10 Thermidor An VI (27 and 28 July, 1798). M. Lacour-Gayet suggests that this is an official portrait of Napoleon as patron of the arts and was almost certainly painted in 1798. An argument which supports this is the fact that Napoleon is seen wearing civilian costume, which he preferred to do when in Paris. Modern scholars are sceptical about the identification of the soigné model of this portrait with Napoleon and the present writer is of the opinion that the sitter is one of those '*commissaires*' who took part in the Italian campaign and went on to choose the booty. The particular conjunction of the sword and the statue would tend to support this. Be that as it may, this ultra-sophisticated portrait of a connoisseur is as unexpected as was the earlier portrait of Mgr de Valras and is almost

† The Pope will deliver to the French Republic one hundred paintings, busts, vases or statues according to the choice of the *commissaires* who will be sent to Rome ... and five hundred manuscripts according to the choice of the same *commissaires*.

without precedent in Greuze's work. It is tempting to compare it with Ingres' *M. Rivière* of 1805 (plate 90) and to advance the theory that there may be some connection between the two works.

With the partial exception of the Versailles portrait, the revolutionary portraits, which include the *Fabre d'Eglantine* and the *Gensonné* (plate 88) in the Louvre, the *Cambacérès* (plate 89) at Chartres, the *Citizen Dubard* (plate 92) in the California Palace of the Legion of Honour, and an *Unknown Man* in Marseilles, all are painted in a distinctive and recognizable manner. All are dark but not drab in colouring, with a great deal of plain black and white, and neutral backgrounds, while the painting of the heads returns in a certain measure to the style of La Tour. The flesh is ruddy and highly coloured with pronounced blue shadows round the chin and jaw, and the surfaces are thick and chalky. The rapid, austere and unaffected likeness of *Cambacérès* and the portrait of an unknown man in Marseilles best typify this stern republican manner, the only manner in which Greuze renounces his Rococo colouring and joins his contemporaries on an equal footing. Of the Versailles portrait, which is in a different category, one need only remark that it is a meek attempt at the European style of state portraiture, a tradition which goes back ultimately to Titian's portraits of Charles V and which was renovated in Greuze's lifetime by Pompeo Batoni and Reynolds.

It is just possible that Greuze, inspired by Romney's visit, had been studying English engravings, for in the Salon of An VIII (1800) appeared a notably English drawing, *Le Depart pour la Chasse* (Louvre, R. F. 1870, 2058) (plate 94). Charming, windblown, and rapidly executed, this is a portrait of sitters who are only known by the initial 'C'. It is, however, an isolated example, for the pictures of the last five years are all traditional in style. Few pictures painted by Greuze in the nineteenth century survive or at least can be traced, and it is possible that of the known ones only a few are by his hand. Of the exhibits in the Salon of 1800, three have already been discussed: *Un enfant hésitant de toucher un oiseau dans la crainte qu'il ne soit mort* (Paris, Louvre), *Une jeune fille se disposant à écrire une lettre d'amour* (London, Wallace Collection), and *L'Innocence tenant deux pigeons*, of which the Wallace Collection picture is a signed and dated copy. There were two male portraits and a portrait of Mme Lefevre disguised as a *Jeune fille préludant sur un forte-piano* (once in the Goncourt collection). There were three '*têtes de différents caractères*': *La Crainte et le Désir*, *Le Sommeil*, and '*La Peur de L'Orage*'. This last must be *L'Effroi* in the Louvre (plate 93), painted as a detailed study for the large picture which was exhibited at the Leger Gallery, London, in 1946. There was also a *Jeune fille se bouchant les oreilles pour ne pas entendre ce qu'on lui dit.*

The Salon of An IX (1801) contained two male portraits, a portrait of a child (undoubtedly the gem-like *Edouard-François Bertin* in the Louvre (plate IV), *Le Repentir de Sainte Marie l'Egyptienne dans le désert* (possibly painted some years earlier), and a large patriarchal piece entitled *Le Premier Sillon, ou un cultivateur remettant la charrue à son fils en présence de sa famille* (Moscow, Pushkin Museum) (plate 95), for which there are full-scale drawings at Tournus and in the collection of M. Cailleux, Paris. This picture has a certain topographical interest, for according to Mme de Valory, Greuze painted it with an actual scene in mind: 'He had painted practically no landscapes and in order to recapture memories of his childhood he took as the setting for this picture one of the richest sites of the borders of the Saône, his home territory'.[15] However that may be, *Le Premier Sillon* differs in style from the other large pictures, not only in its landscape content but in the traditional procession-like form of its composition. All the types are familiar, but the straggling figures and haggard expressions show how weak and nerveless his hand had become. In sharp contrast, the exquisite *Bertin*, with its lightly rubbed background reminiscent of a David portrait of the 1790s and its intimations of a liquid tearfulness, reminds us that as a portraitist Greuze was still to be counted among the most important of the eighteenth century.

The Salon of An XII (1804) saw the reappearance of *Le Repentir de Sainte-Marie l'Egyptienne*, the Wallace Collection *Ariadne*, a female portrait, two '*têtes de jeune fille*' (*La Timidité* and *La Gaieté*), and as a fitting gesture after so long and dramatic a life, the magnificent *Self-portrait* now in Marseilles (plate 96). Greuze has painted himself in exactly the same position as in the very early work in Tournus; the colour is low, the execution rapid, but for sheer quality of expression the portrait deserves to rank among the finest productions of the entire period.

In 1805, while painting *La Veuve et son Seigneur*, a pendant to *Le Premier Sillon*, Greuze died. In the same year David was painting *Le Sacré* and entering upon his own mannerist phase. It may now seem to us, separated as we are from Greuze and David by the Romantic movement in painting, that the two artists have a certain similarity, since the mannerism of the late eighteenth century takes the two traditional forms: distortion of form expressing a distortion of idea (Greuze) and extreme formal austerity (David). Yet to the minds of contemporaries, the Jacobin David succeeded

Greuze, the '*homme sensible*', with the inevitability of one historical period succeeding another, although the two artists had roughly the same output and in some cases painted for the same patrons. The Neoclassical movement did not destroy Greuze as an artist in the sense that it put him out of work. It was his own obstinacy in refusing to recognize his faults, such as drawing from memory, and to a certain extent his own complacent acceptance of these faults that identified him with the period against which David and his school were reacting. As late as the 1790s he was pontificating to Nitot-Dufresne on the subject of drawing from the model: 'M. Greuze was telling me that too great a study of anatomy could be harmful to the art of drawing . . .'[16]

Curiously enough, Greuze's posterity was longer-lived than that of David. His temporary eclipse was not due to the character of his subject matter but to his refusal, or inability, to recognize the official style of academic drawing. When this too became recognized as a reactionary movement, the pendulum swung back again, and in the nineteenth century he achieved a sort of posthumous recognition in both academic and sentimental painting in France and England.

Greuze's acceptance by his contemporaries varied considerably throughout his lifetime. To the public of the 1760s he appeared very much as a man of genius in the style of Jean-Jacques Rousseau, striding about, speaking always '*avec chaleur*', abnormally proud, and working with intensity but with complete independence. 'We have three painters who are competent, fertile, and studious observers of nature, who do not begin or finish anything without frequent recourse to the model. They are La Grenée, Greuze, and Vernet. The second practises his art everywhere, in crowds, churches, markets, public gatherings, houses and streets; he goes everywhere in his quest for action, passion, character and expression. Chardin and he speak very well of their art; Chardin judiciously and calmly, Greuze with warmth and enthusiasm.'[17] 'He (Greuze) makes endless studies, always observing nature in the streets, thoroughfares and public gatherings. If he has a subject in mind, he is obsessed by it; it follows him everywhere. Even his character is affected by it and takes on that of his picture; he is brusque, gentle, persuasive, caustic, gallant, sad, gay, cold, warm, serious or light-hearted, according to the project he has in mind.'[18] At this period Greuze is so completely master of the scene that he is rarely criticized on technical or compositional grounds. Diderot on occasion gives a detailed appreciation of his pictures; other critics of the 1760s content themselves with an off-hand comparison with Rembrandt, Rubens, or Van Dyck.

This situation continues to a certain extent throughout the 1770s except that the standards of comparison are now Raphael and Poussin. The 'enthusiasm' which was his outstanding characteristic in the previous decade is replaced by a solemnity and a sort of martyr's prestige. This, together with the increasing gravity of his pictures, leads to a different conception of his character as an artist; he is now accepted as a master on two different levels, as sterling in morality as he is accomplished in expressing it. He corresponds to the ideal painter of Hagedorn[19] or Laugier: 'If the poet should be a painter in execution, the painter should be a poet in invention . . . The first duty of any intelligent man who composes for the public is leave no doubt surrounding his subject. A painter should not even need a title for his work. The work should imply the title straight away.'[20]

The reaction, which dates from the 1780s, is not apparent until much later, as Greuze is so much eclipsed by the new austere and tightly-drawn style that he receives very little public attention, and with the one or two exceptions quoted above, is not mentioned in writing at all at the time. The source of the reaction is the cooling of fervour on his behalf and the switch of interest to David; thus a fatal detachment sets in, and in this spirit Greuze is re-examined as an artist and all his faults of drawing made apparent. Thus late criticism of Greuze is in the main technical, as can be seen in the two posthumous appreciations of Taillasson[21] and Gault de Saint-Germain.[22]

Taillasson begins in no uncertain manner. 'Greuze is without doubt one of the most talented French painters since the age of Louis XIV.' Yet he condemns without hesitation his 'too uniform brush strokes', his 'violet tones', and states, 'the most justified reproach one can make about Greuze is his negligence in the manner of draperies. He even elevates this defect into a principle; he neglects them on purpose in order to emphasize the flesh. If one paints a girl wearing a chemise, the chemise should look like linen, not linen purposely dirtied to add to the effect'. In much the same spirit, Gault de Saint-Germain gives as his distinctive characteristics, 'scenic compositions and lay-outs, profound knowledge of the anatomy of the head, firm drawing, planes strongly indicated, tremendous passions, common characters, working-class attitudes, delicate flesh painting, dirty draperies, irregular touch, draperies in bad taste, feeble light and shade, sentimental execution'.

Both however unite in admiration of his originality and of the volume of

sentiment which his work carries. Taillasson considers the revival of painting at the end of the eighteenth century to be partly due to Greuze for these
very reasons: 'To the agreeable and picturesque type of composition common to his time and usually appealing only to the eyes, he joined reason and
nature and all in order to express touching and decent ideas'. He says of
Greuze's '*têtes de caractère*', '. . . although they are not in a traditional style,
they have a sort of nobility, a grace, and much expression; one has no
hesitation in stating them to be one of the causes of the French school's
return to naturalism'.

Gault de Saint-Germain goes on to say: 'Greuze, who must be considered
as the painter of the passions of the soul, is unique in the French school. He
is without precedent or follower. His touching dramas have earned him the
title of "La Chaussée of painting"; the energy of his characters, "the French
Hogarth" '. This parallel with Hogarth seems to have been taken very
lightly. It is in fact less apparent in Greuze's finished works than in the big
series which he planned and failed to execute, probably through lack of time.
The text of his '*roman en tableau*', *Bazile et Thibault, ou les deux éducations*,
is printed in the Appendix; here it is only necessary to note its striking
similarity to Hogarth's *Industry and Idleness* of 1747. The idea is perhaps
common enough, and Greuze only differs from Hogarth in starting his story
earlier and including a good many scenes of childhood morality, with the
usual points made about maternal breast-feeding and its opposite vice,
wet-nursing. The professional lives of the four characters, however, have
much in common. Both Thibault and the idle apprentice consort with
women of low life; both extort money from their mothers (though in
different ways); both die appalling deaths, the idle apprentice being executed
at Tyburn and Thibault committing suicide in his prison cell. In the same
way, Bazile and the industrious apprentice follow a parallel road to success:
the industrious apprentice becomes sheriff and Lord Mayor of London,
while Bazile enters the service of a prince and is made '*lieutenant criminel des
plus considérables villes de province*'. Granted the social differences between the
two countries, the lapse of some twenty years between the two stories and
the subsequent modifications in public taste, one can safely say that *Bazile et
Thibault* is nearer to Hogarth than anything else in late-eighteenth-century
French art.

That it was foreign to French taste is proved by the fact that many found
Greuze's isolated moralities slightly repellent, especially *La Malédiction
Paternelle* and *Le Fils Puni*, with their undertone of retribution. Mme de

Valory, in her polemic, foresees and wards off anything resembling a comparison with Hogarth, whom she considers a very low-class artist. On the other hand, Greuze's compromise with *sensibilité* was regarded as cowardly and hypocritical by the pseudo-English author of *Lettres d'un voyageur à Paris à son ami Sir Charles Lovers demeurant à Londres*. 'Learn, Charles, that our Hogarth is still the only artist to compose series of engravings with a moral purpose and which have been likened to novels by some because they have a beginning, a middle and an end. The French artist, M. Greuze, from whom one might have expected similar silent novels, has so far limited himself to presenting us with a few genre scenes, taken from the middle range of society without troubling himself too much about accuracy of costume . . .'

There is yet another reason for Greuze's temporary eclipse and for his posthumous importance. No appreciation of this artist would be complete without an assessment of the influence he had on his contemporaries and pupils, many of whom rose up to copy him and thus to contribute to his financial downfall.

8

Greuze's Influence and Posterity

Greuze had the unfortunate distinction of being plagiarized both in his lifetime and after his death, by his contemporaries and by his pupils. Although serious competition did not make itself felt until the mid 1770s, there were indications that his genre was not to be exclusive as early as 1767, when his pupil, Wille the younger, produced *La Mère Mécontente*, a close copy of the figures of the mother and daughter in *L'Accordée de Village*, and Lépicié a family morality entitled simply *Tableau de famille*. The first is a completely unoriginal and deservedly forgotten artist, the second, an important figure in the history of eighteenth-century genre painting, yet despite their inequalities they gave parallel competition to the Greuze monopoly and together contributed to the first stage of his decline.

Pierre-Alexandre Wille was born in Paris in 1748 and died there in 1821. He entered the studio of Greuze in 1761 and three years later passed on into that of Vien. The latter artist, however, had little influence on his work; he attempted few pictures in the Neoclassical vein and those that he did seem to have been unpopular for they are mentioned only in later sales catalogues and not in contemporary accounts. His one claim to artistic merit is his ability to paint textures, especially the beautiful bouffant satin dresses of the late 1770s and 1780s, which he owed to his father's preoccupation with Dutch masters such as Terborch and Metsu. Apart from this, however, his work is wholly and utterly Greuzian, the only difference being that he relies less on single figures and almost always portrays groups, and that with a few exceptions he comes to be regarded as the painter of blazing and unadulterated virtue unshadowed by warning or reflection.

In 1775 Wille showed a *Danse Villageoise* and a *Retour à la Vertu,* but it was not until 1777 that his strength became apparent. The Salon of that year saw a *Fête des Bonnes Gens, ou Récompense de la Sagesse et de la Vertu,* a *Repas Villageois, Deux Joueurs de Cartes, Une Dame qui reçoit une lettre qui l'afflige,* and three moralities whose titles require a certain amount of attention. The first, *L'Aumône,* appears to be a mixture of Greuze's *La Pauvre Famille* and *La*

Dame de Charité: 'a farmer's family, husband, wife, and five children, one still at the breast, victims of an accident which has ruined them, homeless, and having been able to save only one small chest, are succoured by a virtuous man who encounters them while out walking with his wife and daughter, whose face the mother searches for some sign that she is moved by the spectacle of their indigence'. The second and third, *Le Devoir Filial* and *Le Repos du Bon Père*, have similar associations with *Le Paralytique*. The description of the first reads, '. . . an old man is taking the air, upheld by his daughter and son who have laid aside their work in order to help him to walk. A small boy tries to sweep their path. Two others, slightly stronger, carry a large armchair, and the mother, who can be glimpsed in the background, thanks heaven for having given her such good children'. As to the third, 'A convalescent is resting. His elder daughter motions her younger sister to take away some soup she was bringing, as a sleep will be more beneficial to him'.

Being a more derivative artist, and relying more on the tastes of the public than on his own predilections, Wille stood a considerable chance of rapid success. He takes his themes from literature (*Les Etrennes de Julie*, 1781), from the pastimes of polite society (*Des dames de la ville allant boire du lait à la campagne*, 1779), even from incidents in the newspapers (*Le Maréchal des Logis*, 1785). An examination of the list of his exhibits in the Salons (his pictures seem to be totally lost) shows how closely he followed the ruling dictates of the day. Thus in the 1770s, his pictures are overpoweringly sentimental. In the 1780s, he follows the sterner trend inaugurated by Greuze but takes the precaution of choosing uplifting or affecting subjects with no underlying feelings of horror or retribution. In this category are his *Double Récompense du Mérite* of 1781 (plate 105), which shows a young officer receiving the hand of his future bride and the Croix de Saint-Louis simultaneously, *Les derniers moments d'une épouse chérie* (Cambrai Museum, 1785), and the sensationally successful *Maréchal des Logis* of the same year, the year, it may be remembered, in which David exhibited his *Oath of the Horatii* in Paris. This picture of Wille's illustrates an act of bravery which had caused a great stir in society. Louis Gillet, *'maréchal des logis'* or battery sergeant-major for the regiment of the Comte d'Artois, was travelling one night from Nevers to Autun when he heard sounds of a struggle. He turned aside into the forest and there saw a young girl being tied to a tree by three ruffians. Drawing his sword, he defended himself and the girl against all three and eventually put them to flight. Wille's picture, when it appeared, shared some of the moral glory of the incident itself: 'How sublime! What a choice of subject! How well the soldier is drawn! and the young girl, opening her mouth in an expression of terror! Someone less skilful than M. Wille, your Greuze, for example, would have made her faint at this horrible scene. But M. Wille . . .'. With similar aplomb, Wille made a gesture towards the rise of history painting which took place at the end of the century by producing a *Death of Duke Leopold of Brunswick* in 1787, and in 1794, when nationalist and republican feeling were rife, he rose to heights of patriotism and *sensibilité* with *Liberté, Egalité, Fraternité*, a picture of extraordinary public appeal, showing an aristocrat dancing with a peasant on the village green, an aged couple enthroned under a banner reading '*Respect à la Vieillesse*', vestal virgins decorating a bust of liberty, families reconciled etc.

Wille's successes in the Salons were due partly to the fact that he was willing to provide the public with what it wanted and partly to the even simpler fact that Greuze was no longer available and Wille was. ('We are compensated for the absence of M. Greuze by other painters who have followed his manner'.)[1] Moreover, he was able to profit from Greuze's mistakes, as is obvious from the reception of *La Double Récompense du Mérite*: 'this picture is really very attractive. The white satin shimmers in a way which dazzles and deceives. Moreover, in his choice of subjects, M. Wille will always please the majority of the public. Sensitive and decent souls are deliciously affected by such touching scenes whereas they are revolted by the sight of a father cursing his son because he has joined the army or a stepmother breaking a child's teeth with a crust of dry bread. If such people exist, why paint their atrocious actions?'[2]

Wille's success, however, although overwhelming, was short-lived. He exhibited nothing after 1787, and with the exception of the 1794 picture nothing more is known of him until his death in 1821.

Lépicié, admitted to the Académie in 1764, makes his first appearance as a painter of *sensibilité* in 1767 with his *Tableau de Famille*, of which we have no details. A curiously complex character, he began his career as an engraver and turned to painting because of his failing eyesight. Like La Tour he became intensely neurotic, ending his days in such a fervour of devotional ecstasy that he always worked in a monk's habit. His work falls naturally into the two main divisions of history painting and genre; this last, with which we are concerned, is gentle, restrained and rather bookish, low in tone and always very near to Teniers. In the 1770s, however, Lépicié's work, like that of every other contemporary French genre painter, underwent a crisis of soulfulness and he produced a number of figure studies relying very closely for their effects on subjects already made popular by Greuze. This was apparent in the enchanting *Lever de Fanchon* (Saint-Omer, Hôtel Sandelin) (plate 98) and *L'Elève Curieux* (Paris, Louvre) (plate 97)—a sad and faithful reminder of Greuze's *Jeunesse Studieuse*—of 1773; in the *Devoir Maternel* of 1774, and *L'Atelier du Menuisier* of 1775; and rose to a climax in the years 1775–7, with *L'Union Paisible*, *La Solitude Laborieuse*, *Le Repos*, and two versions of *L'Accordée de Village*, entitled *Les Accords* (present owner unknown—most of the works already cited are untraceable) and *La Réponse Désirée* (France, private collection) (plate 99). The difference between *L'Accordée de Village*, and *La Réponse Désirée* is illuminating. The first had a phenomenally sudden success; it corresponded to a quite ephemeral phase of public taste so that once the associations disappeared, the picture itself lost a good deal of its value. It had little interest from the technical point of view and the paint had lost its original freshness. Lépicié's picture, on the other hand, is the work of a painter and also of a man of deep feeling. Its composition and colour harmonies owe a great deal to Teniers, but its restraint and timelessness are isolated and original qualities in French painting of the latter half of the eighteenth century. Lépicié is therefore an interesting example of an artist belonging in spirit to the atelier of Chardin but chained by circumstances to the popularity of Greuze.

This dualism with Greuze is less apparent to us than it was to their contemporaries who were deeply interested in the situation and considered themselves called upon to take sides. In 1783 this gave rise to an argument of some force in which the pro-Lépicié author of *Le Véridique au Salon* challenged the pro-Greuze author of the *Réponse aux critiques des tableaux du Salon de 1783*. The impartiality of the argument was more damaging to Greuze than the most virulent attack. 'M. Lépicié, considered as a painter of *bambochades*, gives a yellowish tone to everything and is a little monotonous. It is true that he compensates for this defect by the lightness of his touch, his way with draperies, and the variety of his heads which are those of the lower classes. He does not seem to be interested in subjects which express passions. His pictures are a little cold. We concede that M. Greuze, *his rival in this genre*, would seem to exhaust the possibilities of this manner by the energy of his heads and the choice of his subjects. M. Greuze's colour, although as little true as that of M. Lépicié, has nevertheless the advantage of being more rich and varied and consequently more interesting. But the latter is better at painting textures and his drawing is more correct; such at least is the opinion of connoisseurs who view their talents impartially and reflectively. To sum up, M. Greuze, who is an *homme d'esprit*, makes better pictures and M. Lépicié is the better painter.'

After the climax of 1777 Lépicié reverted to the straight unliterary type of genre painting for which he seemed best fitted, yet among his undated works there are several *'boudeuses'*, *'dévideuses'*, and *'savoyardes'* (Périgueux, Orléans etc.) and a corpus of detailed drawings at Le Havre and Orléans which throw light on his hesitation between the style of Chardin and the style of Greuze.

A runner-up of Wille and Lépicié, and possibly the best genre painter of the period, is the short-lived Etienne Aubry, who was born in 1745 and died at the age of thirty-six. He studied under Sylvestre and Vien and remained uninfluenced by either. Apart from his two history paintings, and the works based on Marmontel, including the lovely *Bergère des Alpes* (Detroit Institute of Arts) (plate 100), his genre paintings fall into two recognizable categories, the maternal and the melodramatic. Only in the former is he original, by virtue of his simplicity and a naive pleasure in the painting of décor and costumes, which are always treated in impeccable detail. *Les Amants Curieux* (Heim Gallery) and its pendant, *L'Horoscope Réalisée* (Berne), *La Bonté Maternelle, L'Occupation du Ménage, L'Amour Paternel* (Birmingham, Barber Institute) (plate 101), *La Correction Maternelle*, and above all, *La Première Leçon d'Amitié Fraternelle* (Kansas, William Rockhill Nelson Art Gallery) (plate 102), and *Les Adieux d'un villageois et de sa femme au nourrisson que le père et mère leur retirent* (Williamstown, Mass., Clark Institute), with its elegant figure of the young mother in a country setting, are the most pleasing illustrations of this strain of *sensibilité* to be found in the painting of the entire period.

When, however, he paints in the serious vein, he reverts to stock characters and situations, e.g. *La Malédiction Paternelle* and *Fils repentant de retour à la maison paternelle*, and produces the worst kind of neo-Greuze melodrama. Here, for example, is the subject of his picture *Le Mariage Rompu*, as given in the catalogue of the Salon of 1777. 'A young man and a young woman are ready to receive the nuptial blessing. While the curé is writing out the contract, a woman, accompanied by a bailiff, arrives and presents the curé with a protest and a proposal of marriage which she had received. This woman throws herself at the young man's feet and tries to move him by showing him two children, the fruits of their secret passion. The future husband, seeing his bride fall into a swoon in her mother's arms, flies to her side and begs her pardon for his perfidy. The young man's father, touched by the sight of the unfortunate offspring, turns his son's gaze towards them. The son, feeling his heart break at the sight, gives in, and paternal love triumphs.'

This scenario of Aubry's leads us on to an indirect result of Greuze's popularity, the increasing rapprochement between painting and literature. Pictures were coming to be regarded as 'so many situations, gay or touching, taken from our modern dramas, and painters of this kind could legitimately call themselves the Sedaines, the Favarts, and the Marmontels of painting, while the latter are pleased to describe themselves as the Greuzes, the Aubrys, the Théaulons, and the Willes of dramatic poetry'.[3] The mechanics of *sensibilité* entailed the maximum response to an approved stimulus; artists had only to confine themselves to a few stock themes to be sure of provoking the expected effect. Just as Marmontel, Florian, and Baculard d'Arnaud have stories entitled *La Douleur Maternelle*, *La Tendresse Conjugale*, *Le Respect Filial*, *La Bonne Mère* etc., so we find these themes doubled in painting, in *L'Accord Parfait*, *Le Vrai Bonheur*, *Les Délices de la Maternité* of Moreau le Jeune, the *Tendresse Maternelle* of Bounieu, the *Gaité Conjugale* and *Complaisance Maternelle* of Freudeberg, the *Premiers pas de l'Enfance* of Schenau and so on. Similarly, there was a growing unity between painting and the 'drame bourgeois'. In the late 1770s pictures no longer have to be looked at but read and to simplify this the spectator is provided with a résumé of the plot. Wille's *Derniers Moments d'une Epouse Chérie*, Aubry's *Le Mariage Rompu*, Théaulon's *La Mère Sévère* ('a coquettish girl has received a bouquet from a young man. Her mother has torn the bouquet to pieces and to humiliate her daughter has made her put on on her clogs in the presence of the local girls and of the young man who brought her the flowers, while the father is teaching another younger child about decent conduct and a contempt for coquetry') are but a few examples of this trend which was continued in the next generation by Hilaire Ledru and Mme Chaudet.

It is important to realize that Greuze's notoriety and the discussions which it aroused promoted a more general interest in genre painting as a whole, and in the 1770s and 1780s the increase in the number of genre pictures is almost overwhelming. 1777 may be taken as the high water mark inside the Académie. In the Salon of that year, in addition to eight pictures from Wille, four from Lépicié, and three from Aubry, Huet and Le Prince showed a number of sentimental farmyard scenes; Ollivier a *Sacrifice à l'Amour*; Mlle Vallayer, *Une jeune fille qui vient de reçevoir une lettre* and *Une jeune personne montrant à son amie la statue de l'amour*; Bounieu a '*boudeuse*', a *Patisserie bourgeoise*, a *Petite fille à sa toilette*, a *Jeune femme lisant, son fils reposant sur ses genoux*, a *Buveur de bière*, *L'Après-diner*, *La correction du savetier* and numerous *petites filles* engaged in various occupations; Martin, *L'Education d'une petite fille par sa mère*; and Théaulon, *La Mère Sévère, Une Blanchisseuse, Une femme faisant de la bouillie pour son enfant*, and '*plusieurs têtes d'étude*'.

Outside the Salon Greuze's influence was felt in popular paintings and engravings such as Daniel Chodowiecki's heavily domestic series *Der Lebenslauf*, showing married felicity through the years. Here, not surprisingly, it was the scurrilous and pornographic element that received the most attention. It was in this spirit that Wille painted his *Mère Indulgente* and *La Prévoyance aux Plaisirs*; Schenau, *L'Aventure Fréquente* and *Le Miroir Cassé* (faithful reflections of Greuze's *Les Oeufs Cassés* and *Le Malheur Imprévu*) (plates 103, 104); Freudeberg, his *Gaité Conjugale* etc. Debucourt, who is perhaps too Rococo an artist to carry a weighty pornographic insinuation, started the whole cycle of Greuze themes off again in the 1780s with two versions of *La Cruche Cassée* (1781 and 1787), *L'Oiseau Ranimé* (1787), *Jouis, Tendre Mère* (1789), and *La Bénédiction Paternelle ou le Depart de la Mariée* and *Grandpapa, ou les Plaisirs Paternels* (1785).

It is also important to realize the extent and continuity of this plagiarism which reached its height when Greuze was still in mid-career. The habit of returning again and again to themes which had proved successful was guaranteed by the ostentatiously advertised likes and dislikes of the people for whom the pictures were painted. The later painting of *sensibilité* was thus a vicious circle, and no one was more liable to suffer than the unfortunate and now eclipsed originator of the themes. How could Greuze find comfort in his last years if Théaulon in 1775 produced an *Offre Déshonnête* and an *Heureux Ménage*, versions of *La Vertu Chancelante* and *Le Bonheur Conjugal*; Jean Haver, *Un Vieillard reçevant des secours d'une famille charitable*; Perier, *Un Contrat de Mariage dans un intérieur rustique*, while in 1787 Bilcoq produced *L'Instruction Villageois*, which follows Greuze's *Lecture de la Bible* down to the detail of the inattentive child playing with an animal?

This leads us on to the true copyists of Greuze's style, his pupils. The only surviving male pupil, and the only artist of any personality, however deplorable, was Wille. Of his numerous and largely unidentifiable female pupils, the most important are his daughter Anna, Philiberte Ledoux, Geneviève Brossard de Beaulieu, Constance Mayer, Geneviève Bourliar, and in a somewhat different category, Mme Vigèe-Lebrun.

Anna (Anne-Geneviève) Greuze's personality and work are so completely merged with those of her father that it is almost impossible to extract any information regarding her as an individual. Born in 1762, she lived like her father to the age of eighty. After Greuze's death her situation was extremely painful; she had no money, tried with little success to sell one or two pictures she had been left, and was finally reduced to giving drawing lessons. One of her pupils apparently was George Sand. She must have started painting with her father when she was quite young, for some of her pictures passed through the Duclos-Dufresnoy sale in 1795 under the heading:

'La Citoyenne A.-G. Greuze:

85) Two pictures, one of a child near a chiffonnière, her hands holding a doll, the other a half length view of a girl in a white dress embroidered with gold and a lilac girdle, her head supported by her left hand and her elbow leaning on a table.

86) Half-length figure of a girl, her hair floating loose, wearing a black bodice and gauze fichu, her eyes gazing upwards, leaning against a table on which are placed several letters. A picture full of feeling which does honour to this young artist.'

The first of these is *L'Enfant à la Poupée* in the Louvre, which has always been accepted as a Greuze; the last appears to be of the stock of *La Prière du Matin* with different accessories. There are no other authentic pictures by Anna Greuze, but the example in the Louvre shows that many of the inferior productions assigned to Greuze may well be from the hand of his daughter.

Even less is known of Philiberte Ledoux, who was born in 1767 and died in 1840. She was already in Greuze's studio when Constance Mayer arrived in 1795, and the M. Ledoux who saved Greuze from assault at the hands of his wife may be her father. She put in a timid appearance at the Salon of 1795 when she showed *Le Repos de la Peinture*, *Petites Filles à une Croisée*, and *L'Amour Caché*, but was apparently discouraged for she did not exhibit again after that date. Her works are no doubt numerous; the *Jeune Fille* in Budapest and the two heads in Nancy are sufficiently near to Greuze to pass as his and sufficiently bad to earn him a great deal of opprobrium.

Geneviéve Brossard de Beaulieu is more original. Marie-Renée-Geneviève Brossard de Beaulieu was born in La Rochelle in 1755; her father was a painter who exhibited in the Salon of Pahin Champlain de la Blancherie in 1783 and his daughter, who accompanied him to Paris, must have entered Greuze's studio at about this time. As her father's lessons had already made her technically proficient, her progress was rapid. Her Académie reception piece, *Niobe* (Rome, Academy of St Luke) was until 1947 attributed to Greuze. In 1785 she painted her major work, *La Muse de la Poésie livrée aux regrets que lui laisse la mort de Voltaire* (Poitiers) (plate 110), which in style resembles Greuze's *Jeune fille qui pleure la mort de son oiseau* crossed with a Guido Reni *Magdalen*. The picture was bought by Catherine of Russia, and among her other foreign patrons were Prince Poniatowski, who bought an *Atlanta*, and Princess Lubomirska who commissioned a portrait. She removed to Lille where she conducted a school of free instruction in drawing for young people until 1793 when she was forced to close it. To the Salons of 1806 and 1810 she contributed several '*têtes d'expression*', as yet untraced. She painted little after this date although she continued to work on engravings. The date of her death is not known.

Constance Mayer was sufficiently impregnated with the style of Suvée, in whose studio she had served an apprenticeship, to have been able to resist the temptation of becoming a mere copyist when she entered Greuze's studio in 1795. According to her contemporary, Mme Amable Tastu, '. . . she copied Greuze . . . several heads now on the market thought to be by Greuze are in fact by her'. The most recognizably Greuzian of her works are *Une petite fille en prière*, *Une jeune personne surprise par un coup de vent*, and *L'Enfant tenant une colombe* of 1799, *Une mère et ses enfants au tombeau de leur père* (1802), *L'Heureuse Mère* and *La Mère infortunée* (1810, Louvre), *Le Rêve du Bonheur, ou deux jeunes époux dans une barque avec leur enfant sont conduits sur la fleuve de la vie par l'Amour et la Fortune* (1819, Louvre), and the posthumous *Famille Malheureuse ou l'Ouvrier Mourant* (collection Iacobi), which was finished by Prud'hon.

It was apparently in the studio of Greuze that Constance Mayer met Prud'hon. The latter came to Paris for the second time in his life in 1796 and was received with notable lack of interest by most of the reigning artists of the day, but not by Greuze. 'Prud'hon paid a few visits on his arrival in Paris; David and Girodet did not receive him kindly. The only famous artist to give him a decent welcome was Greuze. With his usual abruptness he asked him, 'Have you got talent?' 'Yes', replied Prud'hon. 'So much the worse', said Greuze. 'With talent and a family to support you should end in the gutter. What does talent mean today, now that there is neither God nor the Devil, no King, no court, no rich and no poor? You know I am as good a painter as any, yet look at my cuffs.' And with these words he showed him the torn lace. But Greuze recognized Prud'hon's talent. He is credited with the saying: 'That one will go farther than I have; he will span the two centuries with his seven-league boots" '[4]. There exists a precious drawing entitled *Visite au tombeau de Greuze*, showing Prud'hon and Constance Mayer bringing flowers to his grave.[5]

There is no documentary evidence for Geneviève Bouliar or Bourliar who passed through the studios of Duplessis, Greuze and Doyen, apart from the lists of her exhibits in the Salons of 1791, 1795, 1797 and 1798. These were invariably female portraits, *'têtes de femme'*, and variations on the theme of *Aspasie*. There is a *'tête de jeune fille'* by her hand in the museum at Lyon.

Mme Vigée-Lebrun was never actually a pupil of Greuze although she modelled her style on his and was brought into close contact with him when she married one of his closest friends, Jean-Baptiste-Pierre Lebrun. Mme Vigée-Lebrun was essentially a self-taught artist, and in her *Souvenirs* she tells us how she borrowed from various artists. 'In addition, to strengthen my technique, I copied some pictures by Rubens, a few heads by Rembrandt and Van Dyck, and several heads of girls by Greuze because these last taught me about the half-tones in a delicate complexion; Van Dyck also teaches this but more subtly.' And in her *Conseils pour la peinture du portrait*, she says, 'Look at Greuze's heads and observe the hair very closely, for this adds to the resemblance and the truth'. The most clearly derived of her works are the portrait of the Comtesse de Montessan wearing a peasant costume and an intense expression and *La Vertu Irrésolue* (engraved by Dennel), a version of Greuze's *La Vertu Chancelante*.

Greuze had a great affection for Mme Vigée-Lebrun, signed a petition for her to be allowed back to France, and was the first to visit her when she returned to Paris after her exile in 1802. It is just possible that Greuze may have recommended her to his Russian patrons, for although she got on well with the younger set, headed by the Grand-Duchess Elizabeth Alexeevna, Catherine had taken an instant and fearsome dislike to her. So many of the great families for whom she painted—Stroganov, Narychkin, Yussupov, Demidov, Kourakin, Orlov, Besborodko, and Beloselski-Beloserski—had originally been patrons of Greuze that the connection cannot be entirely fortuitous. Moreover, many of her Russian portraits are painted not in the manner of Greuze, for she inherited only his sentimentality and none of his sensuality, but with Greuze accessories, e.g. *Comtesse Yussupov tenant une couronne de roses*,[6] *Comtesse Potocka qui presse une colombe contre son sein* (private collection, Buenos Aires).

Greuze's contribution to the Neoclassical movement was both stylistic and psychological. The importance of his own movement towards the expression of passions, moral truths and crises was swallowed up in the general evolution of painting in the last quarter of the century. David, however, had paid careful attention both to the expressions of the heads and the undecorated frieze-like compositions of the 1770s, as had been pointed out in preceding chapters. The most Greuzian of David's pictures is the first version, in the Hermitage, of *Andromache weeping over Hector's body*, of which the group of Andromache and Astyanax should be compared with the daughter and the little boy at the head of the bed in *Le Fils Puni*. Similarly, the three figures in the *Belisarius* could never be wholly original after *La Dame de Charité*. Also important in this connection is a note made by Métra on 7 October 1783: 'I must tell you that M. David's picture, originally announced as a *Paralytic*, although the subject turns out to be Andromache weeping over Hector's body, has won him admission to the Academy of Painting'. It is just possible that this 'Paralytic' was a Pool of Bethesda subject, but in view of David's known reliance on Greuze, it is also possible that his project was a version or a variant on the theme of Greuze's famous picture of 1763.

Another, more abstract, example of Greuzian expression merging into Neoclassical form is Gerard's *Joseph reconnu par ses frères* (Angers), but apart from these few instances, Greuze's influence on individual artists at this time was confined to men who attempted to make a compromise between the grand style of historical painting and the painting of anecdote or sentiment, e.g. Charles Muller, *Appel des dernières victimes de la Terreur* (Versailles), or Le Barbier, *Antigone, ou la Piété Fraternelle*.

The spirit of Greuze survived the Revolution, and the Salons of 1801, 1806 and 1808 contained much that was reminiscent of him, e.g. *A young girl singing in order to distract her blind old father*, by Mme Benôit, who was a pupil of David and who also produced a picture entitled *La Lecture de la Bible* (Louviers); *A young woman, unable to nurse her child, watches him being suckled by a goat and abandons herself to the thoughts this situation inspires*, by M. Lorimier, pupil of M. Regnault; Mme Charpentier, *A convalescent mother cared for by her children*. Hilaire Ledru, whose allegiance to Greuze is proved by his picture of *L'Accordée de Village au tombeau de Greuze* (Douai), also produced *Indigence and Honour* ('A young person rejects the seductive offers that a jockey is making on behalf of his master. Surrounded by her sick father and mother whose situation requires her tenderness, her work and her care, by her two brothers, the elder of whom would be her protector if he were strong enough, she enjoys, with her good parents, the most outstanding benefit, her honour, of which unfortunate circumstances have not been able to deprive her'). Also in Greuzian vein, Mme Chaudet produced *Une jeune fille pleure un pigeon qu'elle chérissait*, *Une jeune fille à genoux devant la statue de Minerve lui fait le sacrifice des dons de l'amour*, etc.

Boilly is a convenient example of the way in which Greuze's influence was perpetuated in the nineteenth century. Boilly no doubt met Greuze when they were both members of the *Société des Amis des Arts* in the 1790s, and he certainly copied him, as is witnessed by a note in the catalogue of the Le Barbier sale of 1826: '*27bis*, several paintings by Boilly, Bonaventure, Bernard, copies after Greuze and others'. On the strength of a number of rather scurrilous paintings and engravings, Boilly was cited for immorality before the *Société Républicaine des Arts* in 1793, and after that date his innuendoes become a good deal more veiled. He therefore really marks the transition from the Greuzian morality of the later eighteenth century to Baudelaire's 'bourgeois hypocrisy' in the mid-nineteenth. He was a painter whose eye was taken by crowds and families and he produced some excellent straight genre such as *L'Arrivée d'une Diligence* (Louvre), *Intérieur d'un Café* (Chantilly), and on a smaller scale, *Les Amateurs d'Estampes* (Louvre). At times he seems to belong to one period, as in the licentious *Leçon d'Amour Conjugal*, in which an extremely dishevelled couple on a sofa are seen to be watching with some amusement a pair of doves kissing, as well as in purely sentimental productions such as *La Visite chez le Grandpère* (Budapest) or *La Bienfaitrice* (Norway, private collection) (plate 106), which has the same elegant woman relieving an indigent family and the same nun of the order of St Vincent de Paul as Greuze's *Dame de Charité*. Yet at other times he seems to belong more fully to the nineteenth century: there is the picture known as *Les Epoux Heureux*, with its Victorian paraphernalia of dogs and work-baskets; there is above all his *Receuil de Sujets Moraux* of 1827, which includes things like, *Monsieur, c'est-y ça que vous cherchez?* (honest beggar boy holding out lost wallet to gent), *Il y a plus malheureux que moi* (beggar woman giving money to blind man), and best of all, *Je te donne ma malédiction* (mother to disgraced girl seen leaving the parental home in a yellow plume-decked bonnet and pink dress with frills on) (plate 107). It is interesting to note the continuity of the *Malédiction Paternelle* theme and the modifications made by succeeding generations. Generally speaking, whereas the ungrateful son was the stock figure of the eighteenth century, the nineteenth preferred the fallen girl who eventually became embellished with an illegitimate child and a blinding snowstorm outside the window. Boilly is perhaps the first to make the change. Redgrave's *The Outcast* (London, Diploma Gallery, Royal Academy) is a good example of the parallel in England.

The quality that makes of Boilly an artist in spite of himself is his objectivity. He is much more of an illustrator in the modern sense; he feels no need for a plot, an incident will suffice. Drawings such as the exquisite piece in the collection of the late Vicomtesse de Noailles—a boy offering a flower—have a quality of honest description not to be found in many eighteenth-century draughtsmen. Also, and this is more significant, he has a sense of humour. His political cartoons, and engravings such as *Le Spectacle Gratuit* and *L'Effet du Mélodrame* are caricatures which to a certain extent prepare the way for Daumier.

Greuze's relations with England are extremely problematic. We have a few beguiling scraps of information in this connection such as Mme de Valory's statement, 'See how the Englishman and the rich inhabitants of the North, charmed by your works, come to France to try to take them away'; Wille's description of a dinner party which took place on 27 March 1771 and consisted of 'M. Sandeau, the Prussian envoy, an English lord, M. Louther-bourg and Greuze'; the Herbert portraits; and the statement in the obituary article in the *Journal des Débats*, 'The celebrated Raynolds, whose admiration for Greuze was such that he wished to come to France in order to make his acquaintance . . .'. We have one concrete example of an early connection: Greuze's *La Maman*, a drawing from the Damery collection, used to illustrate a Chelsea porcelain vase of about 1770 (London, Victoria and Albert Museum). Yet apart from this we have very few pictures, although a considerable strain of Greuzian feeling runs through English sensibility. Reynolds, despite his admiration, seems only to have approached Greuze in his *Infant Samuel* (original burnt in 1816, versions in the Tate Gallery and at Montpellier); this was painted for Catherine of Russia and may therefore possibly have been a conscious exercise in style. Reynolds also approaches Greuze in the numerous portraits he painted on the theme of Lesbia or the dead sparrow, e.g. *Girl with Dead Bird* in Lord Glenconner's collection, although the Greuzian insinuations are missing, as they are in John Russell's portrait of his daughter (plate 108). In the same way, John Hoppner could draw and engrave *The Broken Pitcher*, a version of *La Cruche Cassée* which is robustly and manifestly innocent in intention (plate 109). In the 1790s, Opie drew for Boydell's Shakespeare Gallery a scene from Act IV of *Romeo and Juliet* which is far nearer in feeling to the finished *Fils Puni* than anything in Shakespeare's play. The Greuze strain in Romney, which one might have

150

expected to be prolific, seems to be confined to portraits of *Lady Hamilton at Prayer* (London, Kenwood) (plate 111) and *Lady Hamilton as a Nun praying* (Tankerville Chamberlayne collection).

In Wheatley, Morland and Northcote, however, there is evidence of a knowledge of the conventions of *sensibilité*. Francis Wheatley was nearer in spirit to Greuze than to Hogarth and seems to have studied the former fairly thoroughly; indeed, as an obituary notice in the *Gentleman's Magazine* stated, 'he frequently dresses our English peasants in French frippery'. He was born in 1747, was a pupil of Richard Wilson, and attended the Royal Academy school. During the 1760s and 1770s he exhibited a number of landscapes and portraits at the Society of Artists. In 1779 he went to Ireland and stayed there for five years painting views of country seats. He returned to London in 1784 and his story pictures date from the Royal Academy exhibition of 1785. From that date nearly every year contained a picture with a moral, usually that of charity or married felicity. He was obviously attracted by French literature and fashions for in 1786 he drew and etched two illustrations to Rousseau's *La Nouvelle Héloïse* (now in the British Museum) and in 1787–8 produced two illustrations to a story by Marmontel. That he had looked at Greuze can be seen from his picture of *John Howard relieving prisoners* (Earl of Harrowby collection) (plate 112), which is clearly based on elements from the *Paralytic* and *La Dame de Charité*. He treated the completely French theme of filial piety in a pair of drawings now in the Victoria and Albert Museum, *The Relentless Father* and *The Forgiving Father*. The moral behind these is quite shocking: the young couple have been turned out once for having an illegitimate child but are welcomed back once armed with a marriage licence. These date from 1786. In 1792 he made his contribution to the serial story in painting with his *Life of a Country Girl* (England, private collection). This consists of four episodes, Maidenhood, Courtship, Marriage, and Married Life. *Maidenhood* (plate 113) is undoubtedly indebted to *L'Accordée de Village*, while *Married Life* reflects something of that tidal wave of family happiness which Greuze expressed so ruthlessly in *La Mère Bien-aimée*. (In this connection it is important to remember that many of Greuze's pictures were known in England by engravings: *Le Bonheur Conjugal* became known as *Domestic Bliss*, *L'Accordée de Village* as *The Nuptial Blessing*, *La Mère Bien-aimée* as *Nuptial Felicity* etc.). The *Morning Herald* said of the *Life of a Country Girl*, '...he has with singular felicity employed his pencil in delineating the progress and manners of humble life, pursuing and attaining happiness through the channels of prudence and industry. If we knew a man whose mind, soured and contracted by the presence of undeserved calamity, was verging to misanthropy, we should place this picture before him and we think his social affections would revive'.

George Morland is a more complicated example for fundamentally he springs from Hogarth, whose pupil he proves himself in several over-loaded moralities. He visited France in 1785 but never went to Paris. Much of his youth, however, was spent in copying engravings, of which a number were certainly French. In 1786 he produced a serial story in six episodes called *Laetitia*, which is in effect a *Harlot's Progress* redeemed from a ghastly end by the power of *sensibilité*. The first scene, called *Domestic Happiness* (plate 114) shows Laetitia before she has been corrupted sitting at home with her parents, and brings to mind the almost inevitable comparison with *La Lecture de la Bible*. The next scene is *The Elopement*, or Laetitia seduced under promise of marriage. Then comes a very French scene, *The Virtuous Parent*, in which Laetitia endeavours in vain by presents to reconcile her parents, followed by the best-known of the series, *Dressing for the Masquerade*: Laetitia flies from reflection to public entertainments. Then comes *The Tavern Door*: Laetitia, deserted by her seducer, is thrown upon the town, and the series ends with a reconciliation scene called *The Fair Penitent*: Laetitia in penitence finds relief and protection with her parents, which brings the wheel full circle back to Greuze.

The Greuze strain in Morland appears only with regard to virtue. There is, for example, a *Happy Family* (engraved by Dean in 1787), with full cast of mother, father, grandmother, child and dog. His vice, on the other hand, is all Hogarth. In particular, his puritan streak comes out in pictures painted on the theme of Industry and Idleness, for example, *The Comforts of Industry* and *The Miseries of Idleness* (Edinburgh, National Gallery of Scotland). He returned to the theme several times: *The Fruits of early Industry and Economy, The Effects of Youthful Extravagance and Idleness, The Idle and Industrious Mechanic, The Idle Laundress and the Industrious Cottager*, etc.

Actually the theme was surprisingly long-lived. It took on a new moral twist in Northcote's *Diligence and Dissipation*, painted in 1796 and engraved in the same year. This was a series of ten canvasses comparing the lives of a good daughter who marries above her and a bad daughter whose career follows the same lines as Hogarth's Harlot or Morland's Laetitia. Northcote's spiritual father would appear to be Samuel Richardson, and his story is a good deal more horrific and sanctimonious than Morland's, although it has distinct overtones of Greuze's *Malédiction Paternelle* and *Fils Puni*. In the first scene the modest girl and the wanton are fellow servants in a gentleman's house. The second scene shows the housekeeper giving the good girl some barely needed advice. Scene three shows the wanton in her bedchamber, in the pose of the Capitoline *Ariadne*; significantly enough, she is reading a French novel, Crébillon's *Le Sopha*. Immediately after this, we see the modest girl saying a prayer in her bedchamber (plate 115). Then comes the wanton turned out of doors for misconduct. Next, the modest girl rejects the illicit advances of her master, just as Richardson's Pamela rejected the advances of Mr. B. Then comes the wanton revelling with her companions; and immediately after, the good girl receives the honourable addresses of her master. The wanton dies of poverty and neglect in a garret and the good girl turns up with a purse full of money like Greuze's *Dame de Charité*. The last scene, in the nature of an apotheosis, shows the good girl married to her master, with, in the background, the wanton laid in her grave.

With the exception of Redgrave's *Outcast*, previously mentioned, and its numerous Victorian progeny, the last outcome of the Greuze strain in English painting would appear to be a pair of pictures by Julius Caesar Ibbetson, painted in 1800 and now in the Tate Gallery. They are called *The Married Sailor's Return* and *The Unmarried Sailor's Return* (plates 116, 117) and strike the familiar note, made popular by both Greuze and Hogarth, of family happiness and unmarried dissipation and neglect.

Conclusion

Greuze's pictures have an immediate appeal—to the sentimental and untutored, of whom, fortunately, there are still many. They reserve a deeper satisfaction for the connoisseur who delights in the drawings and the portraits; ignores, probably with justification, the heads of adolescent girls on the verge of orgasm; and can even find time to admire the family pieces for their submerged passion and their occasional painterly forthrightness. We should regard Greuze seriously and discard the spoofing approach which comes all too readily to the contemporary metropolitan mind. Greuze is an idealist, and seen in this context, appears as a curiously tragic figure possessed of a desire for fame and a pride not inferior to those of Rousseau himself. It is generally true to say that those pictures which we now consider to be his worst are the ones which brought him his greatest popularity, and for these it would be shortsighted to blame him. Greuze is *sensible*, his faults are those of *sensibilité*, and therefore belong to the wider domains of morals and taste. Even those who refuse to see him in the more general context must be impressed by one of his least acknowledged gifts: an emotional equipment which responded to all the basic drives of the age in which he lived and which contained many that had shrivelled through misuse or neglect. This outsider tried, clumsily, but with a marked if brief success, to reintroduce into the heartless dexterity of mid-eighteenth-century French painting concepts of a nostalgic regard for his own simple background and a desire to harness this nostalgia to more abstract intellectual ideas. In many ways Greuze was baffled by the shifting loyalties and tides of taste in which he was engulfed in Paris. The weathercock friendship of Diderot, the self-regarding witticisms of the critics, the hostility or patronizing attention of many of his colleagues left him permanently scarred. But he was sufficiently sane and persistent to realize that the reaction to all that was theoretically 'above' him—the hegemony of Boucher—was bound to come, and he was sufficiently infected by the growing mania for a return to classic moral statements to pioneer a new way of presenting these statements in a manner that would be immediately intelligible both to those who desired only to see an improving image and those who desired to see a reconsecration of the lessons of the greatest genius of seventeenth-century French painting, Nicolas Poussin. It is no accident that the equally great Jacques-Louis David, in his own struggle to free himself from the Rococo sympathies of his youth and evolve a bitingly simple language of shock, thrill and aspiration, should have leaned so heavily on Greuze. In comparison with David, Greuze seems suddenly a little shabby, a little muddled; he seems to shrink back into the company of his literary contemporaries Nivelle de la Chaussée and Louis-Sébastien Mercier. But although his work was uneven and his life tormented, he has his moments of triumphant simplicity. The painter who could respond so openly to the civilized charm of the Marquise de Bezons (plate 24), who could remember the exact stance of a bashful country girl (plate 30), who could paint Wille (plate 28) and Sophie Arnould (plate 73) and the luminous infant Bertin (plate IV) is one who deserves a permanent place not only in histories of art but in the affections of those who try, with a seriousness equal to Greuze's own, to understand the evolution of his century.

Appendix

BAZILE ET THIBAULT, OU LES DEUX EDUCATIONS

This manuscript, originally in the possession of Caroline de Valory, was noted in the *Journal de l'Empire*, II Frimaire An XIV, and published by Philippe de Chennevières under the title *Un Roman de Greuze* in the *Annuaire des Artistes* for 1861. Only the sixth episode (episode f), *Le Jeune Thibault commence à montrer son mauvais naturel*, is in Greuze's handwriting; the rest was apparently dictated.

a) NAISSANCE DU JEUNE BAZILE
Bazile est auprès de sa femme qui depuis peu d'heures est accouchée; elle tient son petit enfant dans ses bras; elle a la tête appuyée contre sa main et un peu renversée; elle le regarde d'une manière tendre et tient une de ses mains; l'autre est passée par-dessus l'épaule, et dans cette attitude, il semble la consoler des douleurs qu'elle vient d'éprouver. La mère de la jeune femme, assise au pied du lit, appuyée les deux mains l'une sur l'autre regarde avec plaisir l'union qui règne entre ses enfants et le premier sentiment de la paternité. Debout, devant la cheminée, est une garde, à qui une jeune servante parle à l'oreille en riant.

b) NAISSANCE DE JEUNE THIBAULT
Le jeune Thibault part pour aller en nourrice; c'est le moment où il quitte l'appartement de sa mère. La nourrice en est chargée et va le mettre sur le cheval qui est à la porte; la mère, qui est dans son lit, tient un bouillon que sa garde vient de lui donner; son mari est à côté d'elle, lui tient la main et paraît fort peu occupé de son fils. Sa grand'mère tient les mains du nourricier et semble l'engager d'une manière très pathétique à prendre soin de son petit-fils. (*Le Départ de la Nourrice, ou la Privation Sensible*, drawing, Louvre, Inv. 26.954.)

c) BAZILE À L'AGE DE QUATRE ANS
Le jeune Bazile entre son père et sa mère debout leur prend la main et semble vouloir les réunir parce qu'ils s'étaient brouillés. La mère paraît faire une faible résistance en regardant tendrement son mari, qui passe son bras à son cou pour l'embrasser. Une domestique, à la porte, prête à sortir de l'appartement, les regarde en riant.

d) THIBAULT DE RETOUR DE NOURRICE

Le jeune Thibault revient de nourrice avec tous ses bagages; sa nourrice le présente à sa mère qui s'empresse à le recevoir; alors le petit enfant se rejette avec effroi dans les bras de la mère qu'il connaît, et, par cette action, fait des reproches à sa mère pour son indifférence. (Les Préjugés de l'Enfance, ou le Retour de Nourrice, engraving, Hubert, 1767.)

e) BAZILE À L'AGE DE SIX ANS

Le jeune Bazile aperçoit un pauvre avec un petit garçon qui demande l'aumône; la scène se passe dans une grande cour au bas d'un escalier, d'où il a l'air de descendre avec précaution. Comme il n'a rien à donner que son déjeuner qui est un morceau de pain et deux pommes, il en fait volontiers le sacrifice en se cachant le mieux qu'il peut; il regarde avec un air inquiet à une fenêtre qui est au-dessus de sa tête pour savoir s'il n'est pas aperçu. Le père et la mère sont au haut de perron, qui, le voyant sans en être vus, s'embrassent et semblent s'applaudir de voir dans leur enfant un aussi bon coeur et un aussi bon naturel.

f) LE JEUNE THIBAULT COMMENCE À MONTRER SON MAUVAIS NATUREL

Il est dans la chambre de sa mère et tient un oiseau par les pattes et le plume tout en vie. Sa grand'mère qui est présente à cette action barbare semble s'y opposer fortement; elle est repoussée par la mère de l'enfant qui fait un grand éclat de rire. Une jeune domestique qui est debout derrière la grand'mère pleure, voyant que le petit oiseau sera la proie d'un chat qui va le dévorer et qui est devant le petit garçon; le père, assis dans l'embrasure d'une fenêtre et écrivant sur une petite table semble ne faire aucune attention à ce qui se passe.

g) BAZILE À L'AGE DE ONZE ANS

Le jeune Bazile remporte le premier prix de la classe qui consiste en deux volumes in-quarto qu'il rapporte dur sa tête, et une couronne passée dans son bras; il est suivi de quatre ou cinq de ses amis. Sa mère qui le voit venir court audevant de lui pour l'embrasser; son père est sur la porte avec plusieurs personnes qui semblent le féliciter d'avoir un fils aussi bien né.

h) SUITE DU MAUVAIS NATUREL DE THIBAULT

Le jeune Thibault fait l'école buissonnière avec quatre ou cinq petits garçons à peu près de son age. Il est chassé, ainsi que ses camarades, de la vigne d'un pauvre homme qu'ils dévastaient et sont poursuivis par un gros chien. Deux paysans vont pour le barrer le passage et leur cause le plus grand effroi; ils se sauvent à la faveur d'un ruisseau.

i) BAZILE À L'AGE DE TREIZE ANS

Le jeune Bazile est surpris dans le milieu de la nuit par sa mère et son père à travailler au lieu de prendre du repos. Ils lui ôtent sa lumière en lui faisant les plus tendres reproches; le père lui indique son lit d'une main et tient une petite lampe de l'autre; le jeune homme, encore assis devant sa table, se tourne vers sa mère et semble la prier de vouloir bien lui permettre de continuer son travail.

j) FAIBLESSE DANGEREUSE DE LA MÈRE DE THIBAULT
La mère du jeune Thibault le fait dejeuner dans son lit après dix heures du matin, ce qui est indiqué par un rayon de soleil qui marque sa hauteur et qui donne dans la chambre. Sa mère est assise auprès de son lit, tenant un pot de confitures avec lesquelles elle le fait dejeuner. La grand'mère aussi auprès du lit, d'une colère furieuse, fait des reproches à sa fille de la faiblesse qu'elle a pour son petit-fils et semble lui prédire toutes sortes de malheurs. Le petit garçon a la tête baissée avec un sourire moqueur.

k) EXEMPLE SENSIBLE POUR LE JEUNE BAZILE, ALORS AGÉ DE QUINZE ANS
Le jeune Bazile est conduit par son père chez un chirurgien, où il voit plusieurs malades défigurés par différents ulcères qui leur dévorent le visage, restes de leurs débauches. Il est saisi d'horreur et veut se retirer mais son père le retient par le bras et lui dit, 'Il est bon que je vous instruise parce que nous allons nous quitter; sachez que dans la vie il y a des précipices affreux qui sont couverts de fleurs'.

l) CONDUITE DE THIBAULT À L'AGE DE QUINZE ANS
Le jeune Thibault insulte une jeune domestique de son age; le père et la mère arrivent à ses cris. La scène se passe dans une espèce de grange à la campagne. Un paysan et une vieille paysanne accourent et regardent avec douleur l'indifférence et l'adulation du père et de la mère du jeune homme. La jeune fille est debout, toute échevelée, la gorge découverte et baignée de larmes; vainement elle se plaint de l'insulte qu'elle vient de recevoir; le père, d'un air goguenard, en lui passant la main sous le menton, semble lui dire, 'Mon enfant, vous n'en mourrez pas'.

m) DÉPART DE BAZILE
Le jeune Bazile quitte la maison paternelle et reçoit la bénédiction de son père. La scène se passe dans un salon par bas. Le père est assis dans un fauteuil près de la fenêtre; son fils arrive en habit de voyage; il tombe aux pieds de son père, un genou en terre; père lui met la main gauche sur l'épaule en lui disant, 'Va, prospère! Ton père te bénit'. La mère, debout, les mains levées vers le ciel, semble dire, 'Grand Dieu, protégez sa jeunesse'. Sa soeur cadette, appuyée sur une cheminée, la tête dans sa main, pleure le moment qui va le séparer de son frère. La porte entr'ouverte laisse voir le cheval qui doit le transporter à sa destination. (La Bénédiction Paternelle, drawing, Salon of 1769, Art Institute of Chicago.)

n) THIBAULT ET BAZILE VONT DEMEURER ENSEMBLE CHEZ UN PROCUREUR DANS UN LIEU PRÈS DU RIVAGE DE LA MER
Le jeune Thibault quitte la maison paternelle. La scène se passe au bord d'une rivière, sur

laquelle est un coche prêt à partir; différents voyageurs se pressent à entrer dedans; deux récollets, un capucin, deux ou trois femmes et quelques autres personnages sont spectateurs de la scène que je vais retracer. Le jeune Thibault tient sa mère par la main et est prêt à l'embrasser, lorsqu'une femme du peuple arrive avec sa fille qui lui fait des reproches, en pleurant de ce qu'il l'a abusée. Il est debout et a l'air de plaisanter. Le père la repousse par le bras d'une manière aussi dure que sévère; mais la grand'mère, sensible au malheur de cette jeune personne, lui remet en cachette une bourse pour la dédommager de sa disgrace.

o)   BELLE ACTION DU JEUNE BAZILE À DIX-HUIT ANS

Les Anglais font une descente sur la côte et viennent piller la ville; le jeune Bazile se mêle parmi les volontaires, se bat avec tant de bravoure et de prudence qu'il est regardé comme l'auteur de la destruction des Anglais. Il rentre dans la ville tout couvert de blessures et y est complimenté par le maire et les principaux citoyens.

p)   SUITE DE L'INCONDUITE DE THIBAULT

Le jeune Thibault profite du trouble qui se passe dans la ville et de la terreur qui est répandue pour enlever la fille du procureur chez lequel il demeure. Cette fille emporte tout ce qu'elle a pu voler en argent et en bijoux. Enfin ils sont arrêtés à deux heures de la ville, le père, accablé de la plus vive douleur, baissant la tête et n'osant regarder personne, ramène sa fille par la main. Thibault, lié, garotté, et attaché sur des chevaux de la maréchaussée, rentre en cet état dans la ville et est suivi par une populace dont les gestes et les cris montrent l'indignation.

q)   BAZILE PARVENU À L'AGE DE DIX-NEUF ANS

Le jeune Bazile est chargé de complimenter un prince qui passe par la ville où il demeure; il s'en acquitte si bien qu'il est admiré de tout le monde et particulièrement par le prince qui lui demande ce qu'il fait et quel est son état. Satisfait de ses réponses, il lui demande s'il veut le suivre en qualité de son premier secrétaire. Le jeune Bazile accepte la proposition.

r)   TARDIFS REPROCHES DES PARENTS DE THIBAULT SUR SON INCONDUITE

Le jeune Thibault reste un an en prison et y est visité par son père et sa mère qui lui font des reproches sur sa mauvaise conduite et sur les malheurs qu'il a attiré sur la famille. Il est assis sur une mauvaise escarbelle de bois, la tête appuyée contre le mur sur une de ses mains, dans le contenance d'un homme insensible; sur la gauche on voit, sous une espèce de petite voûte, un mauvais grabat, une cruche d'eau et une mauvaise table. Sa chambre est eclairée par une petite fenêtre carrée garnie de barreaux de fer.

s)   RETOUR DE BAZILE

Le jeune Bazile, avant d'arriver chez ses parents, passe chez Manon Bastier, fille d'un riche laboureur, qui demeure à deux heures de chez son père. Dès sa plus tendre enfance il a aimé cette jeune personne chez laquelle il est resté deux jours. Comme il est prêt à la quitter, il obtient du père et de la mère leur consentement. La jeune fille baisse la tête, les yeux, en faisant la volonté de sa mère. Le père est à côté du jeune homme, a la main appuyée sur son épaule, et dans cette attitude, regarde en souriant cette scène innocente qui se passe en présence de plusiers domestiques et de quelques voisins. On voit, dans le fond de la cour, des animaux et divers instruments d'agriculture.

t) THIBAULT, PROTEGÉ PAR BAZILE, RETOURNE DANS SA PATRIE

Le jeune Thibault sort de prison par la protection de Bazile et retourne dans sa patrie qui est à toute extrémité du chagrin que lui a causé la perte de plus de la moitié de son bien pour sauver la vie de son fils. Sa mère est dans son lit, assise sur son séant; son mari la soutient; elle a la tête penchée sur sa poitrine, comme quelqu'on qui touche à son dernier moment. Elle parle à ce fils d'une voix mourante et semble encore lui reprocher sa mauvais conduite. Il est debout au pied du lit, la tête baissée, les bras croisés et a l'air ennuyé du sermon de sa mère: ce qu'il exprime en regardant de coté d'un air farouche. Sa grand'mère qui soutient aussi sa fille à la ruelle du lit et paraît être déchirée de la plus vive douleur.

u) ARRIVÉE DE BAZILE CHEZ SON PÈRE

Le jeune Bazile arrive à la maison de son père et est reçu de la famille qui l'accable de caresses. Le jeune Thibault vient lui remercier d'avoir obtenu sa grâce; il est à la porte et, d'un air timide, qui annonce plus de jalousie que de repentir, il se cache à moitié derrière son père parce que la vertu offusque toujours les coupables.

v) THIBAULT PERSISTE TOUJOURS DANS SON INCONDUITE

Le jeune Thibault, après avoir exigé de son père, et de la manière la plus malhonnête, ce que lui revient du bien de sa mère, se livre à toute la fureur des passions et va perdre le peu d'argent qui lui restait dans un billard dont il est chassé par des fripons qui l'assomment à coups de billes. La scène se passe au milieu de la nuit; les voisins y accourent avec des flambeaux, ce qui éclaire cette scène de la manière la plus terrible.

w) BIENFAIT DU PRINCE ENVERS BAZILE

Bazile retourne chez le prince au service duquel il est. Il est chargé d'une commission très importante pour les pays étrangers; il s'en acquitte avec la plus grande distinction. Le prince, pour le récompenser, lui fait obtenir à son tour la place de lieutenant criminel des plus considerables villes de province. Bazile, ayant obtenu cette charge, prend congé de son bienfaiteur qui paraît très affecté du départ de son protégé. La scène se passe en présence de la princesse et de quelques personnes de sa suite.

x) CRIME HORRIBLE DE THIBAULT

Thibault se livre avec des femmes de mauvaise vie chez lesquelles il assassine un jeune homme pour le voler. Il est arrêté, traîné en prison avec ses complices et jeté dans les cachots. Après *avoir subi plusieurs interrogatoires, Thibault paraît assis sur la sellette avant Bazile pour lors lieutenant criminel de l'endroit. Bazile est pénétré de la plus vive douleur, ne peut résister à la vue d'un de ses anciens camarades, sur lequel il est obligé de prononcer la peine de mort; il détourne les yeux. Deux autres juges sont à ses côtés; le greffier est assis devant une petite table sur laquelle il écrit, et à la porte sont le guichetier, deux soldats et un gros chien. La salle est décorée avec quelques instruments qui servent à la question.*

y) MARIAGE DE BAZILE

Bazile épouse Manon Bastier. Tendres adieux de Manon à sa mère, la scène se passe en présence de plusiers filles du village, de ses amies. Les unes pleurent, les autres rient et chacune à sa manière exprime la peine ou le plaisir. La mère, debout près du cheval sur lequel sa fille est montée, vêtue en habit d'amazone, lui tient la main et détourne la tête pour cacher les larmes qui la suffoquent, son père lui semble souhaiter toute sorte de bonheur. La fille, dans ce moment, saisit la main de son père pour la baiser. Bazile, à cheval près de son épouse, attend avec impatience la fin de tous ces compliments.

z) FIN TRAGIQUE DE THIBAULT AGÉ ALORS DE TRENTE ANS

Thibault est visité dans son cachot par son père et sa grand'mère. Le géôlier reste à la porte; il tient le gros chien par sa chaîne et un trousseau; de l'autre main il tient un flambeau qui éclaire toute la scène. La grand'mère a le pied sur la dernière marche de l'escalier par lequel on descend dans ce cachot; elle est courbée par l'age et par ses malheurs. Le père, déjà près de son fils, lui addresse ce discours: 'Lève la tête et regarde-moi; vois ton père pour la dernière fois. Le glaive de la justice ne frappe point les pères coupables du désordre de leurs enfants. Je t'ai précipité dans l'abîme affreux où je te vois, en ne réprimant pas, dès ton enfance, tes funestes penchants. Tu vas servir d'example aux pères inconsidérés, et moi, pour apprendre à la postérité quel fut mon désespoir, c'est à tes yeux que je viens me donner la mort'. Il se frappe et tombe dans les bras de sa mère, qui tombe quelques minutes après. Le géôlier tourne la tête avec effroi et semble appeler du secours.

BAZILE AND THIBAULT, OR TWO EDUCATIONS

a) BIRTH OF YOUNG BAZILE

Bazile is sitting with his wife who has just given birth to a son; she holds the child in her arms; her head is propped on her hand and slightly thrown back; she looks at Bazile tenderly and holds one of his hands; his other hand is placed round her shoulders and in this attitude he appears to be consoling her for the pains she has so recently suffered. The young woman's mother, seated at the foot of the bed, with hands placed one upon the other, watches with pleasure the union between her two children and the first stirrings of paternal feeling. Standing by the fire is a nurse to whom a young servant girl speaks laughingly.

b) BIRTH OF YOUNG THIBAULT

Young Thibault is put out to a wet-nurse; this is the moment when he is leaving his mother's home. The nurse has him in her arms and is about to mount the horse which is at the door; the mother, who is in bed, holds a bowl of bouillon that the nurse has just given her; her husband is by her side, holds her hand, and does not appear concerned for his son. The grandmother holds the nurse's hands and seem to urge her tearfully to take good care of the child.

c)   BAZILE AT THE AGE OF FOUR

Young Bazile stands between his father and mother, takes their hands, and seems to want to join them because they have quarrelled. The mother puts up a weak resistance while looking tenderly at her husband, who places his arm round her neck in order to kiss her. A servant girl, near the door and about to leave the room, watches them with a smile.

d)   THIBAULT RETURNS FROM THE WET-NURSE

Young Thibault returns from the wet-nurse with all his luggage; the nurse presents him to his mother who runs forward to welcome him; the child draws back fearfully into the arms of the only mother he has known, and in this way reproaches his real mother for her indifference.

e)   BAZILE AT THE AGE OF SIX

Young Bazile notices a beggar with a little boy asking for alms; the scene takes place in a large courtyard at the foot of a staircase which he seems to have descended carefully. As he has nothing to give but his breakfast, which consists of a piece of bread and two apples, he gives them up willingly whilst hiding himself as best he can; he casts worried looks at a window above his head in case he has been seen. His father and mother are, unknown to him, at the top of the staircase; they kiss and seem to rejoice in the fact that their son has such a good heart and disposition.

f)   YOUNG THIBAULT BEGINS TO REVEAL HIS BAD DISPOSITION

In his mother's room he holds a live bird by the claws and tears its feathers off. His grandmother who is present at this barbarous scene seems to object strongly; she is pushed out of the way by the child's mother who roars with laughter. A young servant girl standing behind the grandmother weeps, seeing that the bird will soon be eaten by a cat near the little boy; the father, seated by a window and writing at a small table, seems to be paying no attention to the scene.

g)   BAZILE AT THE AGE OF ELEVEN

Young Bazile has carried off the first prize for his class: two quarto volumes which he is carrying on his head, and a laurel wreath round his arm; he is followed by four or five of his friends. His mother, who sees him coming, rushes to kiss him; his father is at the door with several people who seem to be congratulating him on having such a good son.

h)   THIBAULT'S BAD DISPOSITION

Young Thibault is playing truant with four or five little boys the same age as himself. They are being chased from a poor man's vineyard which they were ravaging and are pursued by a large dog. Two peasants bar their path and give them a great fright; they escape by means of a stream.

i)   BAZILE AT THE AGE OF THIRTEEN

Bazile's father and mother find him in the middle of the night studying instead of asleep. They take his light away while remonstrating with him most tenderly; his father points to the bed with one hand and holds a small lamp with the other; the youth, still seated at his table, turns to his mother and seems to beg her to allow him to continue with his work.

j)   THE DANGEROUS WEAKNESS OF THIBAULT'S MOTHER

Thibault's mother gives him breakfast in bed after ten o'clock in the morning, as is indicated by a ray of sunlight shining high into the room. The mother sits by the bed holding a pot of jam which she is giving him for breakfast. The grandmother, also seated by the bed, is furious, reproaches her daughter for her weakness, and seems to foretell all sorts of misfortunes. The boy lowers his head with a mocking smile.

k)   AN IMPROVING EXAMPLE FOR YOUNG BAZILE, AGED FIFTEEN

Bazile is taken by his father to a surgeon's where he sees several sick people disfigured by facial ulcers, the legacy of their debauches. He is seized with horror and tries to leave but his father holds him by the arm and says, 'This is something you must know about for we are soon to part; learn that in life there are terrible pitfalls which are covered with flowers'.

l)   THIBAULT'S CONDUCT AT THE AGE OF FIFTEEN

Thibault insults a young servant girl of his own age; the father and mother are summoned by her screams. The scene takes place in a sort of barn in the country. A peasant and his elderly wife watch with distress the indifference and adulation of the young man's parents. The girl is dishevelled, bathed in tears, her breast bare; she complains in vain of the insult she has just received; the father, with a roguish look, chucks her under the chin and seems to be saying, 'There, there, you won't die of it'.

m) BAZILE'S DEPARTURE
Bazile is leaving the family home and receives his father's blessing. The scene takes place in a sitting room. The father is seated in an armchair by the window; his son appears in travelling dress; he falls at his father's feet, one knee on the ground; the father puts his left hand on his shoulder, saying, 'Go forth and prosper. You have your father's blessing'. The mother, standing, raises her hands to heaven and seems to say, 'God protect his youth'. The younger sister, leaning on the chimneypiece, her head in her hands, bewails the moment which will separate her from her brother. Through the half-open door can be seen the horse which will take him to his destination.

n) THIBAULT AND BAZILE GO TO LIVE WITH A GOVERNMENT OFFICIAL AT A PLACE NEAR THE SEA
Young Thibault leaves the family home. The scene takes place on the banks of a river, near which a coach is ready to depart; various travellers hurry to get in: two monks, a friar, two or three women and several other people are witnesses of the scene I am about to describe. Young Thibault holds his mother's hand and is about to kiss her when a peasant woman arrives with her daughter, in tears and reproaching Thibault for having abused her. He is standing and has a jocular manner. His father pushes the girl aside in a manner both cruel and severe; but the grandmother, moved by the girl's plight, unobtrusively gives her a purse of money to compensate for her disgrace.

o) WORTHY ACTION OF BAZILE, AGED EIGHTEEN
The English land on the coast and proceed to pillage the town; young Bazile joins the volunteers and fights with such bravery and prudence that he is regarded as being responsible for the failure of the English raid. He returns to the town covered with wounds and is congratulated by the mayor and the principal citizens.

p) THIBAULT'S CONTINUED MISCONDUCT
Thibault takes advantage of the upheaval in the town to elope with the daughter of the government official with whom he is lodging. The girl takes with her all she has been able to steal in money and jewellery. They are finally arrested at two hours distance from the town; the father, quite overcome with grief, lowers his head, not daring to look at anyone and leads his daughter back by the hand. Thibault, trussed up and on horseback, returns to the town in this manner and is followed by the populace whose exclamations and gestures show their indignation.

q) BAZILE AT THE AGE OF NINETEEN
Young Bazile is given the task of addressing a prince who is passing through the town; he acquits himself so well that he is admired by everyone and particularly by the prince who asks him what his profession is. Satisfied by his answers he asks him if he would like to become his first secretary. Young Bazile accepts the offer.

r) TARDY REPROACHES BY THIBAULT'S PARENTS ON THE MATTER OF HIS MISCONDUCT
Young Thibault spends a year in prison and is visited there by his father and mother who reproach him for his bad behaviour and for the misfortunes he has brought on the family. He is seated on a rough wooden bench, his head propped on one of his hands and leaning against the wall with a passive expression on his face; on the left can be seen a rough bed, a jug of water and a crude table, under a sort of little vault. His room is lit by a small square barred window.

s) BAZILE'S RETURN
Bazile, before going to his parents' house, visits Manon Bastier, the daughter of a rich farmer who lives two hours away from his father. Since childhood he has loved this girl, with whom he now stays two days. As he is about to leave he obtains the father's and mother's consent. The girl bows her head and obeys her mother's wishes. The father is beside the young man, his hand on his shoulder, and in this attitude he watches with a smile the innocent scene which takes place in the presence of various servants and neighbours. In the background can be seen animals and agricultural implements.

t) THIBAULT, UNDER BAZILE'S PROTECTION, RETURNS HOME
Thibault leaves prison through the intercession of Bazile and returns home which is in an extremity of grief, having lost half its possessions in order to buy back the son's life. His mother is sitting up in bed, supported by her husband; she has her head bowed forward on her chest like someone who has reached her last

moments. She speaks to her son in a weak voice and seems to reproach him yet again for his bad behaviour. He stands at the foot of her bed, his head bent, his arms crossed, and with an expression of boredom on his face which is indicated by a fierce sideways glance. His grandmother, who is also at the bedside supporting her daughter, appears to be in the grip of a terrible grief.

u) BAZILE ARRIVES AT HIS FATHER'S HOUSE
Bazile arrives at his father's house and is welcomed by his family who cover him with kisses. Thibault comes to thank him for having obtained his pardon; he stands by the door, half-hiding behind his father, with an air of embarrassment which is motivated more by jealous anger than by repentance because virtue always offends the guilty.

v) THIBAULT CONTINUES TO BEHAVE BADLY
Thibault, having extorted from his father in the most dishonourable manner the money due to him from his mother's estate, gives way to the full force of his passions and loses the rest of his money in a billiard saloon from which he is chased by ruffians who knock him out by striking him with billiard balls. The scene takes place in the middle of the night: the neighbours rush in with torches and illuminate the scene in the most terrifying manner.

w) THE PRINCE REWARDS BAZILE
Bazile returns to the prince, his employer. He is entrusted with an important commission for a foreign land; he acquits himself with the greatest distinction. As a reward the prince obtains for him the position of legal superintendent of all the more important provincial cities. Bazile takes leave of his benefactor who appears moved by the departure of his protégé. The scene takes place in the presence of the princess and various members of her entourage.

x) THIBAULT'S HORRIBLE CRIME
Thibault squanders his existence with women of low repute and one day kills a young man in order to rob him. He is arrested, dragged to prison with his accomplices and thrown into the dungeons. After several interrogations, Thibault appears in the dock before Bazile in his capacity of legal superintendent of the district. Bazile is deeply moved and cannot look his former friend, on whom he is obliged to pronounce the death sentence, in the face; he turns his eyes away. Two other judges are beside him; the clerk of the court is seated at a small table on which he is writing, and at the door are the turnkey, two soldiers and a large dog. The room contains several pieces of evidence.

y) BAZILE MARRIES
Bazile marries Manon Bastier. Tender farewells from Manon to her mother, the scene takes place in the presence of several girls from the village. Some weep, others laugh, each expresses pain or pleasure in her own way. The mother, standing by the horse on which her daughter, dressed in a riding habit, is mounted, holds her hand and turns her head away to hide her tears, her father seems to be wishing her happiness. The daughter seizes her father's hand and kisses it. Bazile, on horseback beside his bride, impatiently awaits the end of all these congratulations.

z) THIBAULT'S TRAGIC END AT THE AGE OF THIRTY
Thibault is visited in gaol by his father and grandmother. The gaoler stands by the door; he holds a large dog by a chain and a set of keys; in the other hand he holds a torch which illuminates the scene. The grandmother stands on the bottom step of the staircase leading down into the dungeon; she is bent by age and misfortune. The father, standing by his son, addresses him thus: 'Lift your head and look at me; see your father for the last time. The sword of justice does not strike fathers guilty of their children's misdemeanours. I cast you into the terrible abyss in which I now see you by not reproving your wretched instincts when you were a child. You will serve as an example to thoughtless fathers, and as for me, to show posterity the extent of my despair, I shall kill myself before your eyes'. He kills himself and falls into the arms of his mother who succumbs a few minutes afterwards. The gaoler turns his head away in terror and appears to be crying for help.

Notes

CHAPTER ONE

1. Paul Hazard, *Crise de la conscience européenne* (Paris, 1935).
2. Bernadin de Saint-Pierre, *Paul et Virginie*, Préambule.
3. Thémiseul de Saint-Hyacinthe, *Pensées secrètes et observations critiques* (London, 1735).
4. Marquis d'Argens, *La Philosophie du Bon Sens, ou Réflexions philosophiques sur l'incertitude des connaissances humaines, à l'usage des cavaliers et du beau sexe* (London, 1737).
5. Marquis de Lassay, *Receuil de différentes choses* (Lausanne, 1756).
6. G.-Jean Soret, *Essai sur les Moeurs* (Brussels, 1756).
7. Baron d'Holbach, *Le Christianisme dévoilé* (London, 1756).
8. Baron d'Holbach, *Essai sur les Préjugés* (London, 1770).
9. Abbé J.-B. F. Hennebert, *Du Plaisir, ou du moyen de se rendre heureux* (Lille, 1764).
10. Père Lacombe, *Lettre d'un serviteur de Dieu contenant une brève instruction pour tendre plus surement à la perfection chrétienne* (Paris, 1686).
11. *Pensées de la Bienheureuse Marguerite-Marie Alacoque* (Paris, 1880).
12. Published by P. M. Masson, *Fénelon et Mme Guyon, documents nouveaux et inédits* (Paris, 1907).
13. Père Caussade, *L'Abandon à la Providence Divine, envisagé comme le moyen le plus facile de sanctification* (Paris, 1861).
14. Masson, op. cit.
15. Quoted by E. Seillière, *Du Quiétisme au Socialisme romantique* (Paris, 1919).
16. Fénelon, *Les Délices d'un homme de bien* (Lille, 1923),
17. Ibid.
18. *Rêveries d'un Promeneur Solitaire.*
19. Quoted by P. M. Masson, *La Religion de Jean Jacques Rousseau* (Paris, 1916).
20. *Les Confessions*, Book 9.
21. Rigoley de Juvigny, *De la Décadence des Lettres et des Moeurs depuis les Grecs et les Romains jusqu'à nos jours* (Paris, 1787).

CHAPTER TWO

1. *Le Spectateur Francais*, 1722–3.
2. *Sara Th . . ., Journal Encyclopédique*, 1.11.1965.
3. Laclos, *De l'Education des Femmes*, (Paris, 1903).
4. *De la sensibilité par rapport aux drames, aux romans et à l'éducation*, (1777).
5. *Le Bon Mari, Théâtre*, An II.
6. Paul Grigaut, 'Marmontel's *Shepherdess of the Alps* in Eighteenth-Century Art' (*Art Quarterly 1949*).
7. 'Les Vrais Plaisirs', in *Délassements de l'Homme sensible*, (1783–7).
8. *Le Pouvoir de la Pitié*, ibid.
9. Florian, *Théâtre, avant-propos*.
10. Preface to *Le Glorieux*, (1732).
11. *Epitre à M. Zulichem*, preface to *Don Sanche*.
12. *Réflexions critiques sur la poésie et la peinture* (Paris, 1719).
13. *L'Ecole de la Jeunesse*, Act IV, Scene 2.
14. *Correspondance littéraire, philosophique et critique, adressée à un souverain d'Allemagne* (Paris, 1813).
15. *Entretien sur le Fils Naturel* (1758).

16. *Essai sur la Poésie dramatique* (1758).
17. *Troisième entretien sur le Fils Naturel* (1758).
18. First performed at Fontainebleau, 20.10.1769.
19. *La Peinture* (Paris, 1769).
20. Diderot to Grimm, December 1765.
21. *Essai sur le genre dramatique sérieux* (1767).
22. *Nouvel examen de la tragédie française* (1778).
23. *Essai sur l'art dramatique* (1773).
24. Ibid.
25. Preface to *Jenneval*.
26. Ibid.
27. Ibid.
28. To the Empress of Russia, *Correspondance Littéraire . . .*, 1774–89, Letter 22.
29. Grimm, *Correspondance Littéraire . . .* (Paris, 1813).

CHAPTER THREE

1. De Piles, quoted by André Michel, *Histoire de l'Art* (Paris, 1923).
2. Oudry, quoted by Louis Hourticq, *De Poussin à Watteau* (Paris, 1921).
3. Voltaire, *Le Siècle de Louis XIV* (Berlin, 1751).
4. Marquis d'Argens, *Réflexions critiques sur les différentes écoles de peinture* (Berlin, 1752).
5. Le Mierre, *La Peinture* (Paris, 1769).
6. Gougenot, *Lettre sur la peinture, la sculpture et l'architecture* (Paris, 1748).
7. Mariette, *Abecedario*, published by Ph. de Chennevières and A. de Montaiglon in *Nouvelles Archives de l'Art Français* (1857–8).
8. Milton Brown, *Painting of the French Revolution*, Critics Group (New York, 1938).
9. La Font de Saint Yenne, *Réflexions sur quelques causes de l'état présent de la peinture en France* (Paris, 1746).
10. D'Alembert, 'Réflexions sur l'usage et sur l'abus de la philosophie dans la manière du gout' *Oeuvres* (Berlin, 1821).
11. Bastide, *Le Temple des Arts, ou le Cabinet de M. Braamcamp* (Amsterdam, 1766),

CHAPTER FOUR

1. A Guillaume Greuze was seigneur of Joncy-la-Guiche in 1700 (Archives de Saône-et-Loire F.323)
2. Parish registers of Saint-André, Tournus.
3. Attached to his marriage lines in the register of Saint-Martin, Paris. Quoted by Piot, *Etat-Civil de quelques artistes français* (Paris, 1873).
4. Marius Audin and Eugene Vial, *Dictionnaire des artistes et ouvriers d'art du Lyonnais* (Paris, 1918), Vol. I.
5. Mme de Valory, op. cit.
6. Grétry, *Mémoires, ou Essai sur la Musique*, Pluviose, An V.
7. Mme de Valory, op. cit.
8. '. . . il l'exposa chez lui aux yeux de tout ce qu'il y avait d'artistes et d'amateurs à Paris; il encouragea le jeune auteur en lui commandant de nouveaux ouvrages.' (Notice sur Greuze, peintre de l'Ecole Française. Lu dans la séance de la Société Libre d'Emulation de Rouen . . . le premier Floréal, An XIII, par C. Lecarpentier.)
9. 'Notice sur l'abbé Gougenot par son petit-neveu le chevalier Gougenot de Mousseaux' (*Revue Universelle des Arts*, 1853).
10. The full title is *Voyage d'un Français en Italie fait dans les années 1765 et 1766* (Venice and Paris, 1769).
11. Archives Nationales, O^i 1940.
12. Natoire to Marigny, 25.5.1756. Archives Nationales O^i 1940. *Bulletin de la Société de l'Histoire de l'Art Francais*, 1877–1901.
13. *Répertoire biographique et bibliographique* (Paris, 1930). His evidence for this is no doubt based on Molès' engraving of the head of the girl in *La Prière a l'Amour* (1774), the plate of which was dedicated to *Mme la Princesse de Pignatelli*. It might equally be the picture which Réau, describes as being in the Yussupov collection, dated 1755, and entitled *L'Embarras d'une Couronne* (L. Réau, 'Greuze et la Russie' in *L'Art et les Artistes*, 1919; Réau had not seen the picture). It could also be the tiny panel at Amiens of a girl at an altar surrounded by cupids in a vague columnar setting.
14. E. Michea, *Quelques détails inédits sur le voyage de Greuze et de Gougenot en Italie*. (Etudes Italiennes, 1934).

15. Archives Nationales, O^i 1940.
16. Ibid.
17. Gougenot de Mousseaux, op. cit.
18. *Caractères de peintres français actuellement vivans*, 1759.
19. *Lettres critiques à un ami sur les ouvrages de messieurs de l'Académie, exposés au Salon du Louvre*, 1769.
20. Published in *Archives de l'Art Français*, 1852-3
21. Salon, 1765.
22. Register of Saint-Benoît. Quoted by Piot, op. cit. The child died eight months later at her grandfather's house in the rue Saint-Jacques.
23. Diderot to Sophie Volland, 30.9. 1760: '*Cela me rappelle un mot plaisant du peintre Greuze contre Mme Geoffrin qui l'avait bien contristé. "Mort-Dieu", disait-il, "si elle me fâche, qu'elle y prenne garde, je la peindrai". Moi, je dis le contraire de Greuze. "Mort-Dieu, si elle me fâche encore, qu'elle y prenne garde, je ne le peindrai plus." '*
24. Mariette, *Abecedario*, tells a story of Greuze being summoned to Versailles to paint the royal portraits and refusing to paint the Dauphine because she wore so much rouge: '*je ne sais pas peindre de pareilles têtes*'. This incident must have taken place *c*.1760 as the portrait of the Dauphin appeared in the Salon of 1761. Floding repeats the story with variations in a letter of 23.11.1761, adding that Greuze was introduced at court by La Live de Jully. ('*Le graveur suédois Pierre Floding à Paris, 1755–64*', by Gunnar Lundberg in *Archives de l'Art Francais*, tome XVII, 1931–2).
25. A drawing entitled *Le Fermier incendié* which corresponds in every detail to Diderot's description (Salon, 1761) is in the Musée Condé at Chantilly, but signed and dated 1763.
26. Commissioned by Randon de Boisset.
27. Lundberg, op. cit.
28. '*Observations d'une société d'amateurs sur les tableaux exposés au Salon cette année 1761.*' (*Observateur Litteraire*, Abbé de la Porte.)
29. Ibid.
30. Quoted Jal, *Dictionnaire critique de biographie et d'histoire* (Paris 1872).
31. Wille, *Journal*, 21.2.1762.
32. *Lettre à Mme X sur les Peintures, les Sculptures et les Gravures exposées dans le Salon du Louvre en 1763.*
33. Mariette: '*c'est, j'ose le dire, un chef d'oeuvre; Rubens ni Van Dyck ne l'auraient désavoué*'.
34. *Lettres à Mme. X . . .* etc.
35. Ibid.
36. *Description des tableaux exposés au Salon du Louvre avec des remarques par une société d'amateurs.*
37. *Lettres sur le Salon de MDCCLXIII.*
38. *Journal de Wille*, 11.11.1763 (Greuze had painted a portrait of the Russian financier, Bacharach.) *M. Greuze était animé par la raison de fair honneur à ma recommendation et aussi qu'on pût voir à Saint-Petersbourg le talent supérieur qu'il possède.* In 1766 Greuze painted portraits of the daughters of Pyotr Grigorievitch Tchernitchev.
39. Also exhibited as an afterthought was *La Voluptueuse* (Baron E. de Rothschild collection), a gift from Mme de Grammont to her brother the Duc de Choiseul.
40. Cf. another writer on the portrait of Mme Greuze: '*Plusiers personnes ont parus inquiets de savoir dans quel état elle est représentée*' etc. (*Critique des Peintures et des Sculptures de Mm. de l'Académie Royale, 1765*.)
41. *Lettres à M. X sur les Peintures, les Sculptures et les Gravures exposées au Salon du Louvre, 1765.*
42. Diderot, *Salon*, 1765.
43. Diderot, *Salon*, 1769.
44. '*Cochin n'aime pas Greuze et celui-ci le lui rend bien.*' Diderot to Falconet, 15 August 1767.
45. Ibid.
46. Ibid.
47. Diderot, *L'Année Littéraire, Lettre sur le Salon de Peinture de 1769, Sentiments sur les tableaux exposés au Salon, 1769.*
48. *Lettre de M. Raphael à M. Jérôme*, 1769.
49. Bachaumont, '*Sur les peintures, sculptures, et gravures de Messieurs de l'Académie Royale exposées au Salon du Louvre le 25 août, 1769*'. *Memoires secrets . . .*, ed. Pidansat de Mairobert, 1777–87.
50. *Lettre de M. Raphael à M. Jérome. Réponse de M. Jérôme, rapeur de tabac, à M. Raphael, peintre de l'Académie de Saint-Luc, 1769.*
51. Bachaumont, op. cit.
52. Archives Nationales O 1926/8. F. 17a. 1064.
53. Diderot, *Salon*, 1769.
54. Jean Seznec, '*Diderot et l'Affaire Greuze*', *Gazette des Beaux-Arts*, May 1966.
55. Diderot, *Salon*, 1769.

56. 'Plainte de Greuze contre sa femme', Bulletin de la Société de l'Histoire de l'Art Français, 1875–8.
57. Diderot to Sophie Volland, 1.10.1769.
58. Diderot, Salon, 1769.
59. Sentiments sur les tableaux exposés au Salon, 1769.
60. Bachaumont, op. cit.
61. M. Raphael, op. cit.
62. Goncourts, L'Art du dix-huitième siècle, 1859–75.
63. Archives Nationales O 1076. 52.
64. Archives Nationales O 1069. 553.
65. Archives Nationales O 1069. 392.
66. Archives Nationales O 1076. 52.
67. Archives Nationales O L069. 431. O L069. 432.
68. Announcement of engraving of Les Sevreuses in Avant-Coureur: 'Greuze . . . qui la distribue chez lui, rue Pavée, la première porte cochère à droite en entrant par la rue Saint-André-des-Arts'.
69. Procès-verbaux d'expertises d'oeuvres d'art extraits du fond du Châtelet aux Archives Nationales (Y. 1904), quoted Wildenstein, Rapports d'experts, 1712–91. Greuze and La Tour were involved on an expertise concerning a portrait of Mlle Coste by Renou. Their addresses are given as 'Maurice-Quentin de la Tour . . . demeurant aux galleries du Louvre. Jean-Baptiste Greuze . . . demeurant rue Thibotodé'.
70. Archives Nationales O 1147, Fol. 130.

CHAPTER FIVE

1. Le Bas, notes to the 1789 edition of his engravings.
2. Ibid.
3. Bachaumont, Mémoires secrets . . ., 31.7.1777.
4. Mme de Valory, op. cit.
5. Dialogues sur la Peinture, 1774.
6. La Harpe, Journal de Politique et de Litterature, 25.9.1775.
7. Ibid.
8. Almanach historique et raisonné des architectes, peintres, sculpteurs, graveurs et ciseleurs; contenant des notions sur les cabinets des curieux du Royaume, sur les Marchands de Tableaux, sur les Maîtres à dessiner de Paris et autres renseignements utiles relativement au dessin, (Paris, 1776). Cf. also 'Epitre à M. Greuze sur son tableau de la Dame de Charité par M. Doigni', Almanach des Muses, 1776.
9. Lettres inédites de Mme Roland aux demoiselles Cannet, de 1772 à 1780, (Paris, 1841); Letter of 19.9.1777.
10. Bachaumont, op. cit., 17.6.1777.
11. Bachaumont, op. cit., 9.9.1777.
12. Feutry, quoted by Métra, Correspondance secrète, politique et littéraire, ou mémoires pour servir à l'histoire des cours, des sociétés, et de la littérature en France depuis la mort de Louis XV, (London, 1787); Entry for 11.10.1777.
13. Métra, op. cit., 31.5.1777.
14. Journal de Paris, 3.10.1777.
15. Bachaumont, op. cit., 28.11.1779.
16. Métra, op. cit.
17. Greuze's fame was not confined to France. In December 1779, Dr Thomas Eyre, writing to Lord Herbert who was making the Grand Tour, on behalf of his father, tells him, 'Lord Pembroke desires to know for whom you set for the picture at Rome, and begs when you go to Paris . . . that you will set to Greuze . . .' For the picture, now in the collection of Sir Alec Douglas-Home, Greuze charged 1,200 louis d'or. Lord Herbert, Henry, Elizabeth and George (London, 1939).
18. Bachaumont, op. cit., 9.9.1777.
19. Métra, op. cit., 26.9.1780. There is a drawing for this picture in Besançon.
20. Pahin-Champlain de la Blancherie, Essai d'un tableau historique des peintres de l'école français (Paris, 1783).
21. Journal intime de l'abbé Mulot (Paris, 1777–82).
22. Journal de Paris, 13.4.1781.
23. Salon des Arts de Lyon, 1786. Catalogue.
24. Bachaumont, op. cit., 3.12.1786.
25. Archives de la Seine, 4 AZ. 828.
26. A contract with Flipart, Gaillard, Massard and Levasseur was also in operation.
27. This account is based on documents printed in the Bulletin de la Société d'Emulation d'Abbeville, 1910.

28. *Mémoire de Greuze contre sa femme* (*Archives de l'Art Français*, 1852–3).
29. Louis Réau, '*Greuze et la Russie*' (*L'Art et les Artistes*, 1919).
30. Grimm, *Correspondance littéraire, philosophique et critique adressée à un souverain d'Allemagne*, 1813.
31. Mme de Valory, op. cit. This did not happen immediately; Greuze's own engraving of the picture appeared in 1786. The Grand-Duke may also have bought the considerable number of Greuze drawings now in the Hermitage.
32. Grimm to Catherine, 12.10.1782. Published by Louis Réau in *Archives de l'Art Français*, 1931–2.
33. *Correspondance littéraire, philosophique et critique par Grimm, Diderot, Raynal et Meister*, Ed. Tourneux (Paris, 1879).
34. Kotzebue, (*L'Année la plus remarquable de ma vie*, Paris, 1802) mentions that the apartments of the Empress at Michaelovitch contained three Greuzes and a Gérard, Cf. Fortia de Piles, (*Voyage de deux Français, 1790–2*, Paris, 1796) who saw a *Tête de jeune fille* in the Royal Palace at Warsaw and two others at Lagenki.
35. Mme de Ségur was the wife of Louis-Philippe, Comte de Ségur, a Russian contact in Paris. In 1784 he had been sent as minister plenipotentiary to St Petersburg where he became friendly with Catherine and wrote comedies for her theatre. In January 1787 he concluded with her a commercial treaty containing terms advantageous to France. He returned to Paris in 1789.
36. Hayley, *Life of Romney* (London, 1809). Romney left for Paris on 31 July 1790.
37. '*Procès-verbal d'apposition des scellés chez Greuze après son divorce*' (*Bulletin de la Société de l'Histoire l'Ile de France*, 1896.)
38. *Nouvelles Archives de l'Ecole Français*, 1874–5.
39. *Procès-verbaux de la Commune Generale des Arts*, etc. Edited by Henry Lapauze (Paris, 1903).
40. *Journal des Debats*, 27.3.1805.
41. Paul Ratouis de Limay, '*Un Chanteur de l'Opéra, graveur et collectionneur au début du dix-neuvième siècle.*' (*Bulletin de la Société de l'Histoire de l'Art Français*, 1949.)
42. Mme Greuze *mère* had in fact left her all her personal effects on condition that she stayed on as housekeeper to Jacques. (*Bulletin de la Société des Amis des Arts et des Sciences de Tournus*, 1909.)
43. Archives of the Tupinier family, published by Baraude (Baron Tupinier), '*Histoire d'un portrait*', extrait des annales de l'*Académie de Mâcon*, 1935.
44. Delort, *Mes Voyages autour de Paris* (Paris, 1821).
45. *Mercure de France*, premier Frimaire, An IX (22.11.1800); seizième Frimaire, An IX (2.12.1800).
46. Ibid.
47. *Mercure de France*, 16 Nivôse, An X.
48. *Souvenirs de Mme Vigée-Lebrun* (Paris, 1854).
49. Mme de Valory, op. cit.
50. *Archives de la Seine* (*Série d'état-civil reconstitué après les incendies de 1871*).
51. *Journal des Débats*, 27 March 1805.
52. Mme de Valory, op. cit.
53. *Journal des Débats*, 27 March 1805.
54. *Journal des Débats*, 2 December 1805.
55. Possibly the society of which he was made an honourary member in 1766. (*Revue des Documents Historiques*, 1873.)

CHAPTER SIX

1. Reproduced in Edgar Munhall, '*Quelques découvertes sur l'oeuvre de Greuze*', *La Revue du Louvre et des Musées de France*, 16e. annee; 1966, I.
2. Mme de Valory, op. cit.
3. G. Renouvier, *Histoire de l'Art pendant la Révolution* (Paris, 1863).
4. The whole argument can be read in Munhall, 'Greuze and the Protestant Spirit', *Art Quarterly*, Vol. XXVII, 1964.
5. *Sentiments sur plusiers des tableaux exposés cette année 1755 dans le Grand Salon du Louvre.*
6. *Lettre à un partisan de bon goût sur l'Exposition faite dans le grand salon du Louvre le 28 août, 1755.*
7. *Lettre sur le Salon de 1755 adressée à tous ceux qui la liront.*
8. *Sentiments sur plusieurs des tableaux . . .* , etc.
9. *Lettre à un partisan de bon gout . . .* etc.
10. *Sentiment sur plusieurs des tableaux . . .* , etc.
11. L. Hautecoeur, *Greuze* (Paris, 1913).

12. Gautier d'Agoty, *Observations periodiques sur la physique*, 1757, tome III, '*Lettre à l'auteur sur l'exposition de cette année.*

13. Mariette, *Abecedario*: '*Il a fait aussi nombre de dessins qui dans le commencement lui ont été payés prodigieusement par quelques curieux*'.

14. Nothing is known of Damery who possessed an apparently unlimited number of drawings. Wille speaks of him as a '*très grand officier et grand amateur des beaux-arts*' (16.4.1760), and engraved pictures, including a Schalken, a Terborch and a Netscher from his collection. He was godfather to Greuze's second child and the two families appear to have been on friendly terms. According to Wille, he suffered a considerable reversal of fortune: '*M. le chevalier de Damery, avec lequel j'étais très lié autrefois, me vint voir, me proposant un tableau pour s'acquitter des cent vingt livres que je luy ay prêtées il y a une dizaine d'annees. Il me l'envoya le lendemain, mais je le renvoyai. Ce bon M. de Damery a eu bien des malheurs, sans cela il m'aurait payé depuis longtemps; il est très honnête homme*'. (12.12.1788).

15. T. Kamenskaya, '*Greuze et Mme Geoffrin*', *Gazette des Beaux-Arts*, 1934.

16. Described as '*un morceau de Boucher*' (Diderot, *Salon of 1761*).

17. Diderot, ibid.

18. The same drawing with minor alterations (Louvre, Inv. 26.978) was used for *Annette*, which, with its companion piece, *Lubin*, was engraved by Binet in 1769.

19. Munhall, *Art Quarterly*, op. cit.

20. Archives de Saône-et-Loire, C.493, fol. 104-5.

21. i.e. by Diderot and the authors of the *Lettres à Mme X sur les Peintures, les Sculptures, et les Gravures dans le Salon du Louvre, 1763*; *Description des tableaux exposés au Salon du Louvre avec des remarques par une Société d'Amateurs*; *Lettres sur le Salon de MDCCLXIII*.

22. Diderot: *On dit . . . que cet artiste est sans fécondité et que toutes les têtes de cette scène sont les mêmes que celles de son tableau des Fiançailles et celles de ses Fiançailles les mêmes que son Paysan qui fait la lecture à ses enfants . . . D'accord, mais si le peintre l'a voulu ainsi? s'il a suivie l'histoire de la même famille?* (Salon, 1763).

23. Ibid.

24. Grimm, Correspondance . . . , 1767.

25. Mariette, *Abecedario*.

26. *Lettre sur le Salon de MDCCLXIII*.

27. *Journal intime de Chevalier de Corberon, chargé d'affaires en Russie* (Un Diplomate français à la cour de Catherine II, 1775-80), H. Labaude (Paris, 1900). It is interesting to compare this with a remark made by Pierre (quoted by the Goncourts) when *L'Accordée de Village* was sold with the rest of the Marigny pictures in 1782: '*Tous les glacis dont M. Greuze a fait usage sont évaporés en sorte qu'il règne une crudité qui n'existait pas. Les tableaux peints à pleines couleurs gagnent avec les années; ceux dont l'harmonie est fictive se perdent. Tous les artistes ont été frappés du fait actuel*' . Thus, although the colours of *L'Accordée de Village* have barely darkened, it is now impossible to get any idea of the original surface of the pictures.

28. Mathon de la Cour, *Lettres à Mme X sur les peintures, les sculptures, et les gravures exposées au Salon du Louvre en 1765*.

29. Diderot, *Salon of 1765*.

30. Jullienne, Robit.

31. Munhall, '*Les Dessins de Greuze pour Septime Severe*', *L'Oeuil*, 124, April 1965.

32. Diderot, *Salon of 1769*.

33. *Sentiments sur plusiers tableaux exposés au Salon, 1769*.

34. Bachaumont, op. cit.

35. M. Florisoone, *Le Dix-huitième siècle* (Paris, 1948).

36. Diderot.

37. '*Depuis quelques années on a recherché les ornements et les formes antiques; le goût y a gagné considérablement et la mode en est devenue si générale que tout se fait aujourd'hui à la grecque. La décoration extérieure et intérieure des bâtiments, les meubles, les étoffes, les bijoux de toute espèce, tout est à Paris a la grecque.*' (Diderot to Grimm, 1763.)

38. *Description des tableaux . . . avec des remarques par une société d'amateurs*.

39. The Ariosto appeared in 1773, the other two were engraved in 1768. The original drawing for *Sophronie* is now in the Fogg Museum, Harvard, Conn.

40. Watelet, *Dictionnaire des Arts de Peintures, Sculpture et Gravure* (Paris, 1786).

CHAPTER SEVEN

1. There were at least three versions of this picture, including a signed copy in the possession of Mme du Barry at the time of the '*saisie de Louveciennes*'

(22 Pluviôse, An II) and the one which passed through the Véry sale in 1785: '*on connaît au cabinet de Mme du Barry le pareil sujet dont celui-ci est une réplique par l'auteur avec quelques légers changements*'. There is also an oil sketch in Edinburgh.

2. Engraved by Schultz in 1779.
3. Loaisel de Tréogate, *Aux ames Sensibles*, Elegie, 1780.
   '*Mon oeuil est fatigué de ce jour homicide* . . .
   Descendons sous ce bois où la tristesse habite;
   C'est parmi les rochers que le sage médite.
   Je marche dans la vie à travers des orages . . .
             Je pleure avant l'aurore;
   Dans mes larmes noyé la nuit me trouve encore;
   Je revois mes plaisirs, mais de poignards armés,
   Simulacres affreux, serpents envenimés,
   Se disputant un coeur abreuvé d'amertume
   Et toujours embrasé du feu qui le consume', etc.
4. Munhall, 'Greuze and the Protestant Spirit', *Art Quarterly*, Vol. XXVII, 1964.
5. Lebrun, *Almanach historique et raisonné des architects, peintres sculpteurs, graveurs et ciseleurs; contenant des notices sur les cabinets des curieux du Royaume, sur les marchands de tableaux, sur les maîtres à dessiner de Paris et autres renseignements utiles relativement au dessin* (Paris, 1776–7).
6. *Journal de Politique et de Littérature*, 25.9.1775.
7. *La Prêtresse, ou nouvelle manière de prédire ce qui est arrivé*, 1777.
8. *Journal de Politique et de Littérature*, 26.11.1778.
9. *Lettres pittoresques à l'occasion des tableaux exposés au Salon de 1777.*
10. Bachaumont, *Mémoires secrets* . . ., 9.9.1777.
11. Duclos-Dufresnoy sale, An III (1795).
12. Ibid.
13. *Journal de Paris*, 5.12.1786.
14. G. Lacour-Gayet, '*Un prétendu portrait de Talleyrand par Greuze*', *Gazette des Beaux-Arts*, November 1927.
15. Mme de Valory, op. cit.
16. Paul Ratouis de Limay, '*Un chanteur de l'Opera, graveur et collectionneur au début du dix-neuvième siècle*', *Bulletin de la Société de l'Histoire de l'art Français*, 1949.
17. Diderot, *Salon of 1765.*
18. Diderot, *Salon of 1763.*
19. Hagedorn, *Réflexions sur la Peinture* (Leipzig, 1775).
20. Laugier, *Manière de bien juger les ouvrages de peinture* (Paris, 1771).
21. Taillasson, *Observations sur quelques grands peintres, dans lesquelles on cherche à fixer les caractères distinctifs de leur talent avec un précis de leur vie* (Paris, 1807).
22. Gault de Saint-Germain, *Les Trois Siècles de la Peinture en France, ou galerie des peintres français depuis Francois premier au règne de Napoléon, empereur et roi* (Paris, 1808).

CHAPTER EIGHT

1. *Lettres pittoresques à l'occasion des tableaux exposés au Salon de 1777.*
2. *Réflexions joyeuses d'un garcon de bonne humeur sur les tableaux exposés au Salon en 1781.*
3. *Lettres pittoresques à l'occasion des tableaux exposés au Salon de 1777.*
4. Quoted by E. Bricon, *Prudhon*, 1907.
5. Reproduced in *Gazette des Beaux-Arts* (Paris, 1918).
6. Lada Nikolenko, 'The Russian portraits of Mme Vigée-Lebrun', *Gazette des Beaux-Arts*, July 1967.

Index

175

1. *Self-portrait*

6. *La Lecture de la Bible*

7. Engraving after Teniers: *Le Bon Père*

8. Engraving after Teniers: *Les Joueurs de Cartes*

9. Un Écolier endormi sur son livre

10. *L'Aveugle Trompé*

11. *Portrait of Joseph*

13. *La Paresseuse Italienne*

12. *Piémontaise d'Asti*

14. *Le Geste Napolitain*

15. *Un Oiseleur accordant sa guitare*

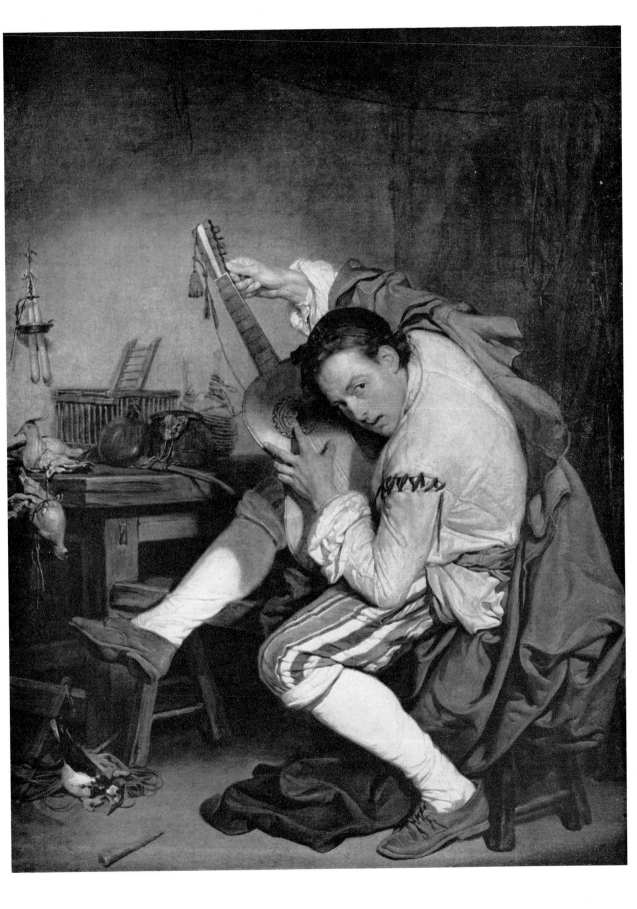

16. *Les Oeufs Cassés*

17. Engraving after Mieris: *L'Oeuf Cassé*

18. *La Fille Confuse*

19. *L'Enfant Gâté*
20. *Silence!*

21. *L'Ecureuse*

22. *La Dévideuse*

23. *Portrait of La Live de Jully*

24. *Portrait of the Marquise de Bezons*

25. *Portrait of Mlle de Amicis*

26. *Le Miroir Cassé*

27. *Portrait of Babuty*

28. *Portrait of Wille*

29. *L'Accordée de Village*

30. Study for *L'Accordée de Village*

31. *Portrait of the Comte d'Angivillers*
32. *Portrait of Monseigneur de Valras*

33. *Jeune fille vue de dos*

34. *Tête de jeune fille*

35. *Le Paralytique*

36. *La Charité Romaine*

37. *The Rest on the Flight into Egypt*

39. Study for *Le Fils Puni*

40. Study for *Sévère et Caracalla*

41. *Sévère et Caracalla*

42. Poussin: *Death of Germanicus*

43. *La Mère Bien-aimée*

44. Study for *La Mère Bien-aimée*

45. Study for *La Bénédiction Paternelle*

46. *Girl with dog*

47. *Jeune fille qui fait sa prière à l'Amour*

48. *La Poupée Dansante*

49. *La Cruche Cassée*

50. *La Vertu Chancelante*

51. *Boy with dog*

52. Girl with gauze scarf

53. *Portrait of Mme de Porcin*

54. *Portrait of Paul Stroganov*

55. *Portrait of Countess Schuvalov*
56. *Portrait of the Comte de Saint-Morys*

57. *Le Gâteau des Rois*

58. Study for *La Dame de Charité*

59. *La Dame de Charité*

60. David: *Antiochus and Stratonice*

61. *La Malédiction Paternelle*

291. Louvre - Le Fils puni (Greuze)

62. *Le Fils Puni*

63. Study for *Le Fils Puni*

64. *Le Donneur de Chapelets*

65. *Le Retour de l'Ivrogne*

66. David: *Belisarius*

67. La Belle-Mère

68. *Innocence, entraînée par les Amours et suivie du Repentir*

70. *La Prière du Matin*

69. *L'Admiration et le Désir*

71. *La Laitière*

72. *Le Petit Mathématicien*

73. *Portrait of Sophie Arnould*

74. *La Veuve et son Curé*

75. *Psyche*

76. *La Colombe Retrouvée*

77. *Innocence*

78. *Girl with Doves*

79. *Jeune fille qui pleure la mort de son oiseau*

80. *Portrait of Comtesse Mollien*

82. *L'Espagnole*

81. *The Letter Writer*

83. *Lamentation over the dead Christ*

84. *L'Amour parmi les jeunes filles*

85. *Psyche crowning Love*

86. David: *Paris and Helen*

87. *Portrait of Napoleon*

89. *Portrait of Cambacérès*

88. *Portrait of Gensonné*

90. Ingres: *Portrait of M. Rivière*

91. *Portrait of 'Talleyrand'*

92. *Portrait of Citizen Dubard*

93. *L'Effroi*

94. *Le Départ pour la Chasse*

95. *Le Premier Sillon*

96. *Self-portrait*
97. Lépicié: *L'Elève Curieux*

98. Lépicié: *Le Lever de Fanchon*

99. Lépicié: *La Réponse Désirée*

100. Aubry: *La Bergère des Alpes*

101. Aubry: *L'Amour Paternel*

102. Aubry: *Première Leçon d'Amitié Fraternelle*

104. Schenau: *Le Miroir Cassé*

103. Schenau: *L'Aventure Fréquente*

105. P. A. Wille: *La Double Récompense du Mérite*

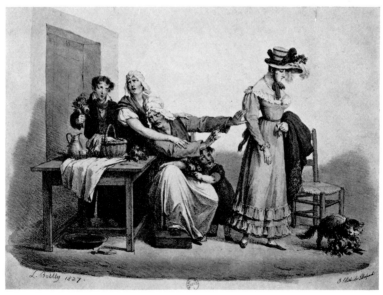

106. Boilly: *La Bienfaitrice*

107. Boilly: '*Je te donne ma malédiction*'

109. HOPPNER: *The Broken Pitcher*

108. RUSSELL: *Portrait of Anne Russell*

111. Romney: *Lady Hamilton at Prayer*

110. Geneviève Brossard de Beaulieu: *La Muse de la Poésie*

112. Wheatley: *John Howard relieving prisoners*

114. Morland: *Domestic Happiness*

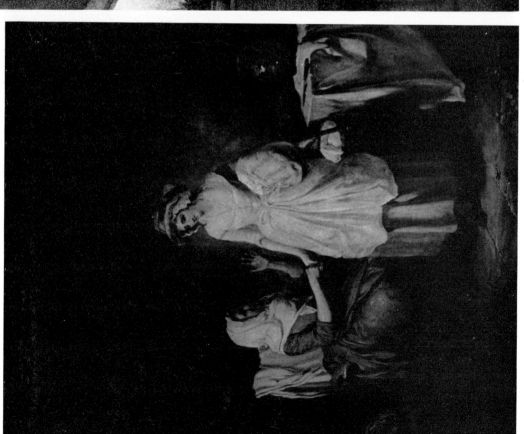

113. Wheatley: *Maidenhood*

115. Northcote: *Diligence and Dissipation*

116. Ibbetson: *The Married Sailor's Return*

117. Ibbetson: *The Unmarried Sailor's Return*